JUNIOR
LISTENING EXPERT

A Theme-Based List ng EFL Learners

Level **3**

JUNIOR
LISTENING EXPERT

Level 3

Series Editor	Dong-sook Kim
Project Editors	Yu-jin Lee, Hyun-joo Lee, Ji-hee Lee
Contributing Writers	Patrick Ferraro, Rebecca Cant, Susan Kim
Illustrators	Kyung-ho Jung, Eun-jung Shin
Design	Hoon-jung Ahn, Ji-young Ki, Hye-jung Yoon, Min-shin Ju
Editorial Designer	Jong-hee Kim
Sale	Ki-young Han, Kyung-koo Lee, In-gyu Park, Cheol-gyo Jeong, Nam-jun Kim, Woo-hyun Lee
Marketers	Hye-sun Park, Kyung-jin Nam, Ji-won Lee, Yeo-jin Kim
ISBN	979-11-253-4046-1
Photo Credits	www.fotolia.com
	www.dreamstime.com
	www.istockphoto.com

INTRODUCTION

Junior Listening Expert is a four-level listening series for EFL learners, particularly older elementary school students and junior high school students. Systematically designed to improve listening skills, its audio material is offered in a variety of formats, covering a wide-range of topics.

Features

Theme-Based Units

Every level contains twelve units, each covering a lively topic such as food, lifestyle, sports, IT, or social issues. A variety of listening formats expose students not only to everyday dialogues, but also to more advanced informative material.

Systematic Design

Each unit is composed of five closely related sections that allow students to develop their listening skills step-by-step. As students pass through each of the five sections, they have the opportunity to evaluate their progress and build confidence in their listening abilities.

A Variety of Question Types

A variety of question types are provided, including identifying the main idea, finding specific details, and making inferences. These serve to familiarize students with the standard types of listening test formats.

A Focus on Critical Thinking

Students are not only exposed to social issues through the listening material, but are also encouraged to think about these issues and form their own opinions.

Format

Getting Ready

This section utilizes a quiz to introduce the key vocabulary words and expressions that will appear in the unit. It is designed to facilitate easier understanding for students preparing to tackle challenging topics in English.

Listening Start

In this section, students have the chance to check their listening comprehension and master key expressions by answering questions and taking dictation. This prepares them for the Listening Practice and Listening Challenge sections.

Listening Practice

Students are given the opportunity to practice a variety of listening question types in this section. It enables them to develop the different listening skills required for each question type.

Listening Challenge

This section presents students with two long listening passages and a pair of checkup questions for each passage. This section challenges students to understand a higher level of English and upgrade their listening skills.

Critical Thinking

This section encourages students to think about a social issue related to the unit's topic. After listening to different opinions about an issue, students develop their own opinion, which they then express in a speaking activity.

Vocabulary List

This section provides easy access to key vocabulary. It contains the new vocabulary words from each unit.

Dictation

This section focuses on helping students improve the accuracy of their listening skills by requiring them to take dictation.

Table of **Contents**

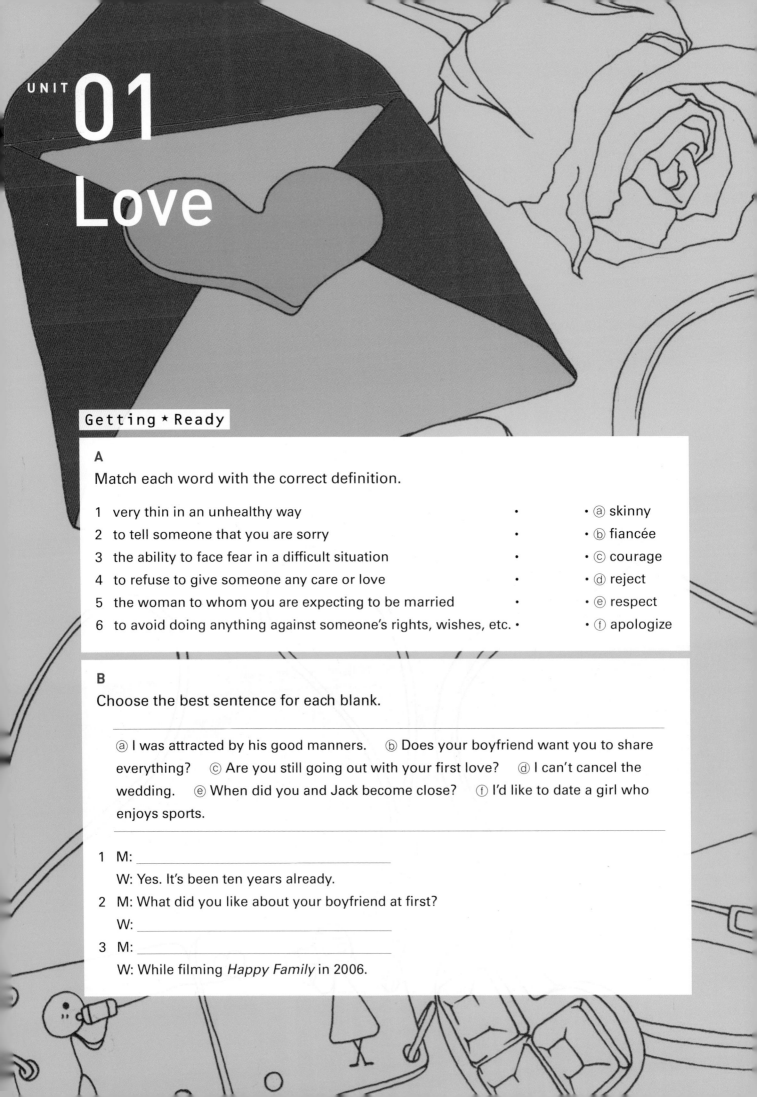

A

Match each word with the correct definition.

1 very thin in an unhealthy way   •   • ⓐ skinny
2 to tell someone that you are sorry   •   • ⓑ fiancée
3 the ability to face fear in a difficult situation   •   • ⓒ courage
4 to refuse to give someone any care or love   •   • ⓓ reject
5 the woman to whom you are expecting to be married   •   • ⓔ respect
6 to avoid doing anything against someone's rights, wishes, etc. •   • ⓕ apologize

B

Choose the best sentence for each blank.

___

ⓐ I was attracted by his good manners.   ⓑ Does your boyfriend want you to share everything?   ⓒ Are you still going out with your first love?   ⓓ I can't cancel the wedding.   ⓔ When did you and Jack become close?   ⓕ I'd like to date a girl who enjoys sports.

___

1 M: _____
   W: Yes. It's been ten years already.
2 M: What did you like about your boyfriend at first?
   W: _____
3 M: _____
   W: While filming *Happy Family* in 2006.

1 Where is the man going this weekend?

①  ② ③  ④

+ Listen again and fill in the blanks.

M: I'm going to _____ Jenny _____ on a date this weekend.
W: Really? Good for you. You finally found the courage.
M: But I can't decide _____ _____ _____ _____. Do you have any suggestions?
W: Hmm... how about an _____ _____? It would be fun and exciting.
M: Shouldn't I choose a more romantic place? An amusement park might be _____ _____.
W: In that case, how about taking her for a riverboat ride?
M: That is a good idea. I must go now to _____ _____ _____.
W: Don't forget to bring her some beautiful flowers.
M: Right. Thanks a lot.

2 What does each woman NOT like about her boyfriend?

(1) Emily: _____

(2) Michelle: _____

(3) Cindy: _____

ⓐ He doesn't earn much money.

ⓑ He is too friendly to other women.

ⓒ He doesn't have good fashion sense.

ⓓ He is too busy to see her often.

+ Listen again and fill in the blanks.

W: Yesterday, I met three of my friends, Emily, Michelle, and Cindy. They _____ _____ their boyfriends. As a famous fund manager, Emily's boyfriend earns _____ _____ _____ _____. But he is so busy that Emily can't see him often. Michelle's boyfriend is tall and handsome, but Michelle is worried that he is _____ _____ to other women. Cindy's boyfriend is a smart surgeon, but Cindy _____ _____ _____ his poor fashion style. Surprisingly, none of my friends wants to _____ _____ _____ her boyfriend!

1 What did the woman like the most about her husband?

① his voice

② his height

③ his appearance

④ his sense of humor

2 How did the girl's feeling change?

① nervous → satisfied

② interested → worried

③ depressed → pleased

④ excited → disappointed

3 What is the boy's problem?

① He likes his friend's girlfriend.

② He feels very shy in front of girls.

③ The girl he likes rejected his proposal.

④ He has to see his ex-girlfriend at school.

mini Quiz

mQ 1
Where did the woman meet her husband?

ⓐ at college
ⓑ at work
ⓒ at church

mQ 2
Which best describes the situation?

ⓐ Well begun is half done.
ⓑ Don't judge a book by its cover.

mQ 3
Where did the boy first meet Sandra?

ⓐ on a blind date
ⓑ in his drama club
ⓒ at a birthday party

4 What are they mainly talking about?

① their first loves

② their ideal types

③ their worst ever dates

④ the people whom they want to date

mini Quiz

mQ 4

Who was the woman's first love?

ⓐ her college senior

ⓑ her neighbor

ⓒ her classmate

5 What is the man's ideal type?

①

②

③

④

mQ 5

Why has the man NOT been dating anyone?

ⓐ He still misses his ex-girlfriend.

ⓑ He hasn't found anyone he likes.

6 Why did the woman break up with her boyfriend?

① He treated her badly.

② He was dating someone else.

③ She was in love with someone else.

④ They didn't have time to see each other.

mQ 6

Why does the man want to go to an amusement park with her?

ⓐ To make her feel better

ⓑ To introduce a man to her

A - 1 What is the relationship between the speakers?

① reporter – actor

② movie director – actor

③ reporter – movie director

④ talk show producer – talk show host

2 Which is NOT true about Silvia?

① She gets along well with strangers.

② She is good-looking.

③ She is positive.

④ She has a sense of humor.

B - 1 Why are the woman's parents against her marriage?

① She is too young to marry.

② Her fiancé doesn't make enough money.

③ Her fiancé strongly believes in superstition.

④ The fortune teller said the marriage would be unhappy.

2 What does the woman ask the man to do?

① Attend her wedding

② Give some good advice to her fiancé

③ Help her with her wedding preparations

④ Persuade her parents to approve of the marriage

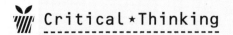 Critical ★ Thinking

Privacy between Lovers

1   What is the woman's problem?

① Her boyfriend often tells lies.

② Her boyfriend doesn't trust her.

③ Her boyfriend doesn't respect her privacy.

④ Her boyfriend used her personal information.

2   Who has the same opinion as Justin?

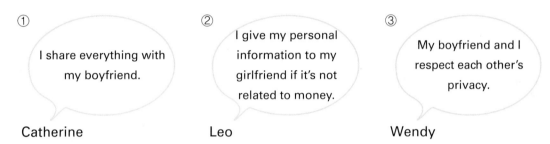

① I share everything with my boyfriend.

Catherine

② I give my personal information to my girlfriend if it's not related to money.

Leo

③ My boyfriend and I respect each other's privacy.

Wendy

What do you think?

1

Check [✓] if you have the same opinion. You can add your own opinion in the blank.

☐ Sharing personal information in a couple is a way to show that you trust each other.

☐ A couple shouldn't share personal information because they might break up someday.

☐ A couple should have no secrets, so it's okay to share personal information.

_____

2

Talk about the following questions with your partner.

• Have you ever shared your personal information with your boyfriend/girlfriend?

• What kind of personal information should you share with your boyfriend/girlfriend?

Shopping

Getting ★ Ready

A

Match each word with the correct definition.

1 money that is given back to someone   •   • ⓐ luxury

2 an opinion that you say or write about something   •   • ⓑ refund

3 to examine things to see how they are different   •   • ⓒ receipt

4 the food and other goods you buy in a supermarket   •   • ⓓ compare

5 a piece of paper which shows that money has been paid •   • ⓔ groceries

6 expensive and enjoyable but not necessary   •   • ⓕ comment

B

Choose the best sentence for each blank.

ⓐ May I see other skirts in a different style?   ⓑ You'll have to pay $2 for the delivery charge.   ⓒ It doesn't look good on me.   ⓓ Could it be delivered directly to my house?   ⓔ Please wrap it up nicely.   ⓕ Would you recommend one that goes with my pants?

---

1 M: Is there something wrong with the jacket?

  W: _____

2 M: _____

  W: Of course, but it will take a few days.

3 M: _____

  W: This blue shirt will look great with them.

1 When will the woman get the swimsuit?

   ① Monday   ② Tuesday

   ③ Thursday   ④ Friday

+ Listen again and fill in the blanks.

W: I like this swimsuit. Do you have a larger size?

M: The large ones are _____ _____. But I can order one for you.

W: _____ _____ _____ _____ _____?

M: About three days. Today is Monday, so it will arrive on Thursday.

W: Okay, I want to _____ _____. How much is it?

M: It's $46.

W: Here you go. I live far from here, so _____ _____ _____ _____ directly to my house?

M: Of course. But it's going to take one day longer.

W: That's fine.

M: Could you please _____ _____ _____ _____ and phone number?

W: Okay.

15

2 Match each person with the right shopping advice.

   (1) Lily   •   • ⓐ Make out a shopping list.

   (2) Jeff   •   • ⓑ You can buy good, cheap items at outlets.

   (3) Susan •   • ⓒ Buy one quality product instead of several cheap products.

+ Listen again and fill in the blanks.

W1: I'm Lily. I bought _____ _____ _____ cheap sandals to save money. But they broke after only a few days, so I had to buy another cheap pair. _____ _____ _____ after wearing them.

M: I'm Jeff. I shop at department stores. They have _____ _____ _____ quality items. The problem is the expensive prices. Is there any way to buy good products _____ _____ _____?

W2: I'm Susan. I go to discount stores to _____ _____ every week. There are so many cheap items that I buy things I don't need.

1 What are they doing now?

① Looking at a catalogue

② Shopping on the Internet

③ Shopping at a market

④ Watching a TV home shopping channel

mQ 1

What color bedcover did the boy choose?

ⓐ beige

ⓑ yellow

ⓒ green

2 Which skirt did the woman choose?

①

②

③

④

16

mQ 2

How much more is the woman going to pay?

ⓐ $5

ⓑ $15

ⓒ $45

3 Choose the wrong information.

Come to the Town Flea Market!

• What you can buy: ① clothes, accessories, instruments and books

• Where: ② 29th Street

• When: ③ Saturday from 10 a.m. to 6 p.m.

• Contact number: ④ 3142–0357

mQ 3

Choose all the information you can get from the online site.

ⓐ pictures of the market

ⓑ pictures of items on sale

ⓒ what visitors think about the market

4   Why could the woman NOT get a refund?

    ① She didn't have a receipt.

    ② The watch was scratched.

    ③ The watch was a sale item.

    ④ It was too long since she bought the watch.

mini Quiz

mQ 4
What did the woman NOT like about the watch?

ⓐ design
ⓑ color
ⓒ price

5   Choose the two things that the woman is going to sell.

    ① books

    ② clothes

    ③ sneakers

    ④ accessories

mQ 5
Why is the man going to have a garage sale?

ⓐ To buy an MP3 player
ⓑ To buy a present for his sister

6   Fill in the blank to explain the "Lipstick Effect."

> When the economy is bad, _____.

    ① women try to save money by not buying lipstick

    ② lipstick becomes more expensive, but sells more

    ③ women buy cheaper luxury goods to please themselves

    ④ cosmetic sales go up because women care about how

       they look

mQ 6
When did the "Lipstick Effect" happen first?

ⓐ in the 1930s
ⓑ after the 9/11 attacks

A - 1 Which is NOT mentioned as an advantage of Internet shopping?

① It's cheaper than shopping in malls.

② You don't have to visit stores in person.

③ It's easy to compare all the prices of items.

④ There are often sales on Internet sites.

2 Where will the woman buy an MP3 player?

① W Mall

② Mega Mall

③ King Market

④ Cherryville Mall

B - 1 Choose the wrong information.

> **Order Form #3**
>
> • **Type:** ① heart-shaped necklace
> • **Color:** ② pink
> • **Arrival Date:** ③ by the 16th
> • **Special request:** ④ wants it to be wrapped

2 How much will the man pay?

① $45

② $54

③ $58

④ $64

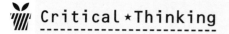

Designer Brand Products

1   **What are they mainly talking about?**

① Why are designer products popular?

② Are designer products worth buying?

③ Why are designer products expensive?

④ Are designer products high quality?

2   **Choose each person's opinion.**

(1) Leo: _____   (2) Judy: _____

ⓐ Designer products make people look nicer.

ⓑ It's a waste of money to buy designer products.

ⓒ Once you buy a designer product, you can keep it for a long time.

What do you think?

1

Check [✓] if you have the same opinion about designer brand products. You can add your own opinion in the blank.

☐ They are not worth the price.

☐ I don't get tired of them easily.

☐ I feel I'm special when I wear them.

_____

2

Talk about the following questions with your partner.

· Have you had a designer brand product? If so, were you satisfied with it?

· What do you think of people wearing designer brand products from head to toe?

Parties

Getting ★ Ready

A

Match each word with the correct definition.

1 a person who holds a party • • ⓐ host
2 a card inviting someone to an event • • ⓑ tease
3 an item for making something look better • • ⓒ costume
4 the set of clothes suitable for a particular event • • ⓓ invitation
5 to make jokes about someone for fun • • ⓔ suit
6 a set of clothes that are made of the same cloth • • ⓕ decoration

B

Choose the best sentence for each blank.

ⓐ I'm going to throw a party.　　ⓑ Would you like to come to my birthday party?
ⓒ I want something to dance to.　　ⓓ Everyone was wearing unique costumes.
ⓔ How did Wendy's wedding reception go?　　ⓕ Just dress as nicely as you can.

1 M: _____
　 W: You should've been there. It was so much fun.
2 M: Is there a dress code for the party?
　 W: No. _____
3 M: Do you want me to bring some music CDs to the party?
　 W: Yes. _____

1   Choose the correct food for each category.

(1)   (3)   (2)

Sandra   Tim

ⓐ spaghetti   ⓑ tuna salad

ⓒ fried chicken   ⓓ drinks

ⓔ fruit

+ Listen again
and fill
in the blanks.

W: Tim, I'm going to _____
_____ _____ _____
this Saturday. Would you like to
come?

M: Sure, Sandra. _____ _____
_____ _____ this time?

W: How about making spaghetti?
You make really tasty spaghetti.

M: I want to try a different dish.
Maybe I can _____ _____

_____ _____. What will
you cook?

W: I'm going to make some fried
chicken. I'll also buy _____
_____ _____ soda.

M: Don't you think we'll need more
drinks? I'll bring some more soda
_____ _____ _____.

W: Good. And I'll also buy some
fruit.

2   What will Mary probably do next?

① Call Nora

② Clean her room

③ Go on a date with Bob

④ Buy items for her party

+ Listen again
and fill
in the blanks.

(Telephone rings.)

W: Hello. _____ _____
_____ _____ Bob?

M: This is he.

W: Hey. This is Mary. What are you
doing?

M: I was just cleaning my room.
_____ _____?

W: I'm calling to invite you to my
birthday party. It's this Thursday
at my house.

M: _____ _____ _____.
Um… by the way, did you invite
Nora, too?

W: (laughs) Right. You told me you
want to date her. I think you
love her.

M: _____ _____ _____.
You know how much I like her.

W: Don't worry. I was about to call
her. So dress _____ _____
_____ _____ _____.

1 Check [✓] whether each person is a good guest or not. <u>mini Quiz</u>

(1) I arrived at the party twenty minutes early.

(□ Good / □ Not Good)

(2) I brought one of my friends to the party.

(□ Good / □ Not Good)

(3) I sent a thank-you note two days after the party.

(□ Good / □ Not Good)

mQ 1
What does the woman say about being almost ten minutes late?

ⓐ It's acceptable.
ⓑ It's rude.

2 What did Kate do on the weekend?

①  ②

③  ④

mQ 2
Choose the two items the woman bought for Mindy's baby.

ⓐ a pair of shoes
ⓑ clothes
ⓒ a hat

3 Choose the two things that Lisa will bring to the party.

① pajamas

② snacks

② a Beyonce CD

④ drinks

mQ 3
What kind of drink does Lisa prefer?

ⓐ Coke
ⓑ juice

22

4   Which is NOT part of Jenny's advice?

① Tell people that it's a surprise party.

② Have the guests arrive at the party before Sally does.

③ Prepare food the guests like.

④ Collect some money before the party.

mini Quiz

mQ 4

Why will the man hold a surprise party for Sally?

ⓐ To welcome her back

ⓑ To celebrate her birthday

5   Choose the right costume for each person.

(1) Nick: _____   (2) Tim: _____   (3) Ben: _____

ⓐ    ⓑ    ⓒ

mQ 5

Whose costume did the man like the most?

ⓐ Nick's

ⓑ Tim's

ⓒ Ben's

6   Check [✓] how the woman felt about the party.

	Good	So-so	Bad
(1) Interior			
(2) Food			
(3) Service			

mQ 6

Choose T for true or F for false.

(1) The couple prepared their dance for a week. (T / F)

(2) The woman doesn't have a boyfriend. (T / F)

A - 1   What kind of talk is this?

① a news report

② a job advertisement

③ a product advertisement

④ an office announcement

2   Which of the following is NOT mentioned in the talk?

① company information

② working hours

③ pay

④ requirements

B - 1   What is the purpose of the party?

① To sell food for Christmas

② To buy famous people's items

③ To collect money for poor children

④ To celebrate Christmas with famous people

2   Choose the two pieces of wrong information.

INVITATION CARD

You are invited to a special Christmas party!

① When: December 25th, 4:00 p.m.

② Where: At the Peace Convention Hall

③ Dress code: Casual clothes

④ Special guests: Will Smith, Britney Spears, etc.

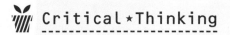 **Critical ★ Thinking**

Expensive Parties

1 Check [✓] if each person is for or against expensive birthday parties for children.

	For	Against
(1) Paul	☐	☐
(2) Ally	☐	☐
(3) Joe	☐	☐

2 Choose each person's opinion.

(1) Paul: _____   (2) Ally: _____   (3) Joe: _____

ⓐ Some parents show their love for their children by throwing expensive parties.

ⓑ You have to consider others who can't afford expensive parties.

ⓒ Expensive parties are only for showing off how much money you have.

What do you think?

1

Check [✓] if you have the same opinion. You can add your own opinion in the blank.

☐ Throwing an expensive party is unfair because only the rich can afford it.

☐ Spending a lot of money on one event is a total waste of money.

☐ Throwing an expensive party is a way of expressing your love for your children.

2

Talk about following questions with your partner.

· Have you ever had an expensive party or been invited to one? How was it?

· Do you want to throw an expensive party for your child in the future?

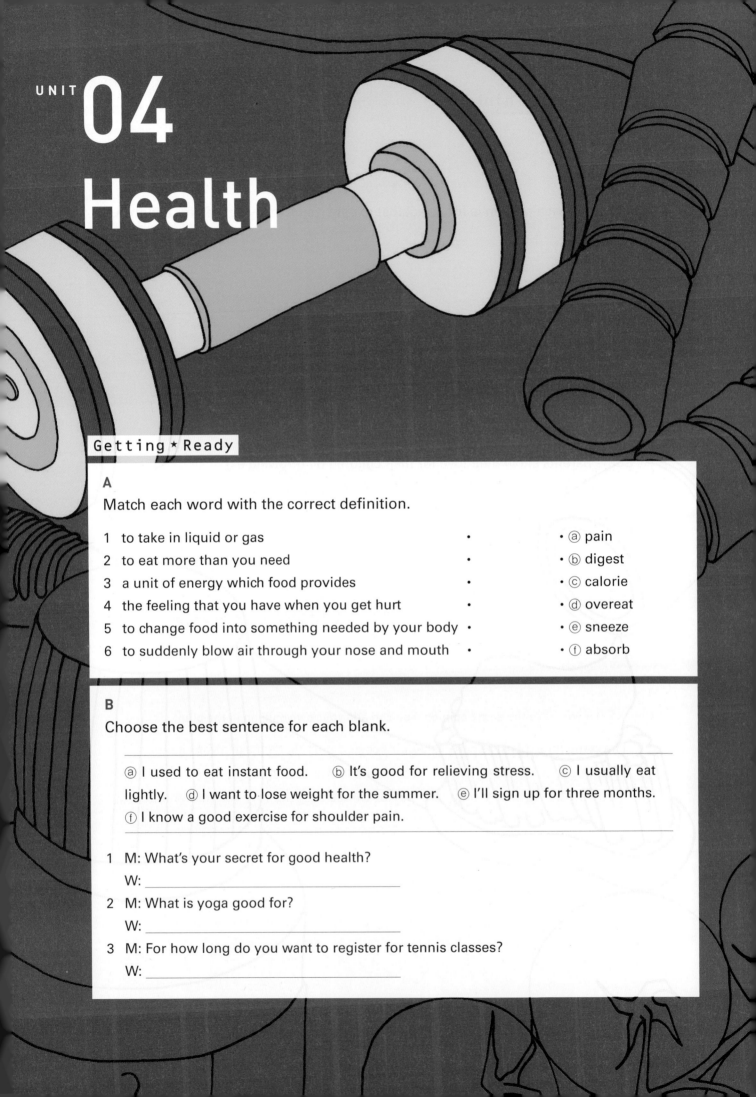

Getting ★ Ready

A

Match each word with the correct definition.

1　to take in liquid or gas · · ⓐ pain
2　to eat more than you need · · ⓑ digest
3　a unit of energy which food provides · · ⓒ calorie
4　the feeling that you have when you get hurt · · ⓓ overeat
5　to change food into something needed by your body · · ⓔ sneeze
6　to suddenly blow air through your nose and mouth · · ⓕ absorb

B

Choose the best sentence for each blank.

ⓐ I used to eat instant food.　ⓑ It's good for relieving stress.　ⓒ I usually eat lightly.　ⓓ I want to lose weight for the summer.　ⓔ I'll sign up for three months.　ⓕ I know a good exercise for shoulder pain.

1　M: What's your secret for good health?
　　W: _____

2　M: What is yoga good for?
　　W: _____

3　M: For how long do you want to register for tennis classes?
　　W: _____

<u>1</u> Choose two bad eating habits that the man has.

① He doesn't eat breakfast.

② He eats meals quickly.

③ He eats a lot of sweet snacks.

④ He eats too much fast food.

+ Listen again
and fill
in the blanks.

M: Doctor, I'm worried that I'm
_____ _____.

W: Let's see. Do you eat breakfast?

M: No, I'm never hungry in the morning.

W: It's not a good habit. If you
_____ _____, you may overeat during lunch and dinner.

M: I see.

W: How long does it take for you to
_____ _____ _____?

M: Usually ten minutes.

W: When you eat that fast, your body doesn't know _____
_____. So you may eat more than you need.

M: Wow, I didn't know that.

W: Do you often eat instant food?

M: I _____ _____ _____ instant food, but now I try not to.

W: Good for you. It is high
_____ _____.

27

<u>2</u> Choose the best food for each person.

(1) Joe: I caught a cold.   _____

(2) Amy: I forget things easily.   _____

(3) Sean: I don't want to get cancer.   _____

ⓐ broccoli

ⓑ garlic

ⓒ oranges

ⓓ blueberries

+ Listen again
and fill
in the blanks.

W: _____ _____ _____
_____ to some healthy foods. First, there's broccoli. You may have heard that broccoli is good for your body. Broccoli prevents cancer and has _____
_____ vitamin C. Secondly, there's garlic. Eat it if you want to have a strong heart or stomach. It's

also good when you're tired or
_____ _____ _____. It has a strong smell, though. And if you're looking for healthy food that _____ _____, blueberries are the answer. They're good for your eyes, and _____
_____ _____.

1   Which is NOT the woman's secret for good health?

① Look on the bright side.

② Get enough exercise.

③ Eat lightly.

④ Eat more fish than meat.

mQ 1
What is the relationship between the speakers?

ⓐ show host – singer
ⓑ composer – singer
ⓒ show host – producer

2   Choose two positions that the man tried.

①

②

③

④

mQ 2
Why does the man's shoulder hurt?

ⓐ He played computer games too long.
ⓑ He slept in a strange position.
ⓒ He hurt it during exercise.

3   What is the man mainly talking about?

① The causes of colds and the flu

② How a cold becomes the flu

③ The differences between colds and the flu

④ Things to do when having a cold or the flu

mQ 3
Which is NOT mentioned as a symptom of the flu?

ⓐ sneezing
ⓑ high fever
ⓒ muscle pain

4   What made the woman feel sick?

     ① a bad cold

     ② spoiled food

     ③ the low temperature of the office

     ④ taking too much medicine

mini Quiz

mQ 4
Which did the man NOT suggest?

ⓐ Do not use the air conditioner.
ⓑ Let fresh air into the office.
ⓒ Drink warm water.

5   Why does the woman want to do yoga?

     ① To lose weight

     ② To sleep well

     ③ To relieve stress

     ④ To make her skin clear

mQ 5
What time is the class the woman is going to join?

ⓐ 4 p.m.
ⓑ 6 p.m.
ⓒ 8 p.m.

6   Write T for true or F for false.

     (1) People who don't get enough potassium may

         get hot easily. _____

     (2) Bananas have more potassium than spinach. _____

     (3) It's good to take potassium with sugar. _____

mQ 6
What will they probably do next?

ⓐ Eat tomatoes
ⓑ Drop by a supermarket
ⓒ Prepare dinner

A - 1 What is the woman mainly talking about?

① Ways to treat our feet right

② Ways to keep our feet from drying up

③ The work that our feet do for our bodies

④ The importance of removing bacteria from our shoes

2 Who is doing something wrong?

① Jill: I try not to wear socks in summer.

② Tom: I dry my feet right after showering.

③ Betty: I always buy shoes with a cushion.

B - 1 Choose the wrong information.

NY Sports Club Membership

Membership No.	
0125	
Name	Program
① Cathy Brown	② Weight training
Class Type	Starting Date
③ Daily class	④ May 14th

2 How long will the woman attend the sports club?

① 1 month

② 3 months

③ 6 months

④ 10 months

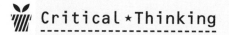 Critical ★ Thinking

Diet

1 What are they mainly talking about?

① The bad effects of dieting

② The fastest way to lose weight

③ Foods that are good for dieting

④ The best way to go on a diet

2 Choose each person's opinion.

(1) Steve: _____   (2) Jenny: _____

ⓐ Go see a doctor before going on a diet.

ⓑ Skipping meals is a fast way to lose weight.

ⓒ Eat proper meals and work out to lose weight.

What do you think?

1

Check [✓] if you have the same opinion. You can add your own opinion in the blank.

☐ Exercise is the best way to lose weight.

☐ Skipping dinner is helpful for losing weight.

☐ Losing a lot of weight in a short time can hurt our bodies.

_____

2

Talk about the following questions with your partner.

• Have you ever tried going on a diet? How was it?

• What do you think is a healthy way of maintaining a suitable body weight?

Transportation & Location

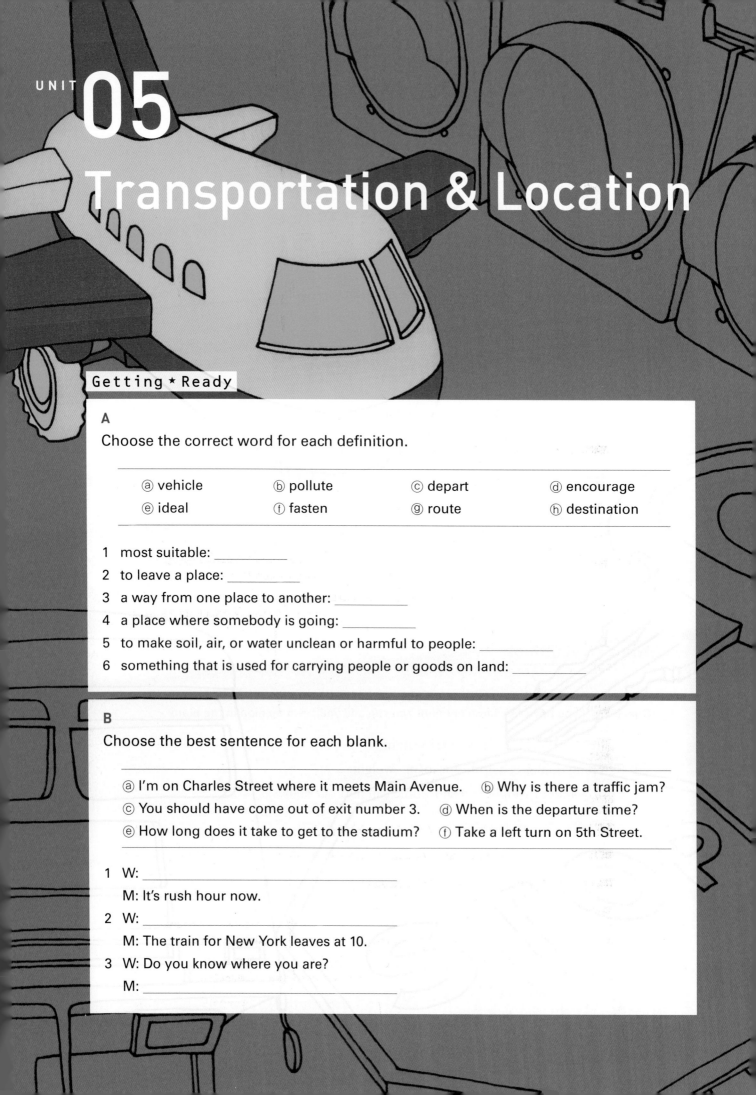

A

Choose the correct word for each definition.

| ⓐ vehicle | ⓑ pollute | ⓒ depart | ⓓ encourage |
| ⓔ ideal | ⓕ fasten | ⓖ route | ⓗ destination |

1 most suitable: _____

2 to leave a place: _____

3 a way from one place to another: _____

4 a place where somebody is going: _____

5 to make soil, air, or water unclean or harmful to people: _____

6 something that is used for carrying people or goods on land: _____

B

Choose the best sentence for each blank.

ⓐ I'm on Charles Street where it meets Main Avenue.   ⓑ Why is there a traffic jam?

ⓒ You should have come out of exit number 3.   ⓓ When is the departure time?

ⓔ How long does it take to get to the stadium?   ⓕ Take a left turn on 5th Street.

1 W: _____

M: It's rush hour now.

2 W: _____

M: The train for New York leaves at 10.

3 W: Do you know where you are?

M: _____

1   Why is there such a traffic jam?

① It's rush hour.

② There was a car accident.

③ There is roadwork going on.

④ It's raining heavily.

+ Listen again and fill in the blanks.

M: Good morning. _____ _____, ma'am?

W: To Harbor City, please. How long _____ _____ _____?

M: It usually takes about 15 minutes. But it might take longer _____ _____ heavy traffic.

W: It's not rush hour, so why is there a _____ _____?

Was there a car accident?

M: I don't think so. It's _____ _____ _____.

W: Oh, I see. I think I'm going to be late for the appointment with my friend.

M: _____ _____ _____ _____ your friend now?

W: I think I should.

33

2   What kind of transportation is the woman talking about?

①    ②    ③    ④

+ Listen again and fill in the blanks.

W: This kind of transportation is common in Thailand. _____ _____ _____ _____, it is powered by an engine and has handlebars. It has _____ _____, one in the front and two in the back. The driver sits in the front, and the passenger seat is in the back. _____ _____ _____ _____, it can hold two or three passengers. It has a roof but _____ _____. So when you use this kind of transportation, the pollution from _____ _____ may be unpleasant.

1 Which transportation will the woman use?

① bus

② taxi

③ subway

④ motorcycle

mQ 1

What is the advantage of taking a bus?

ⓐ It's cheaper.

ⓑ It takes less time.

ⓒ The bus stop is close to the stadium.

2 Choose the Farmer John's Restaurant on the map.

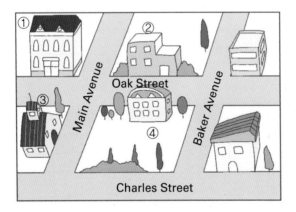

mQ 2

What time was the man's reservation changed to?

ⓐ 6

ⓑ 6:10

ⓒ 6:15

3 What is the woman's idea about future transportation?

 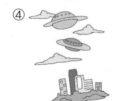

mQ 3

What does the man think is important about future transportation?

ⓐ beautiful design

ⓑ various functions

ⓒ environmental effects

34

4 When can you hear this announcement during flight?

① before taking off

② after taking off

③ before landing

④ after landing

mini Quiz

mQ 4

Write T for true or F for false.

(1) The local time in Vancouver is 10:06.

_____

(2) It is raining in Vancouver.

_____

5 Choose the wrong information.

> ꕔꕔ
> Ferry Ticket
>
> ① Destination: Bari ☑ / Brindisi ☐
>
> ② Departure time: 9:30 a.m. ☑ / 1:30 p.m. ☐
>
> ③ Seat type: Cabin ☑ / Deck ☐
>
> ④ Price: 75 euros ☐ / 150 euros ☑

35

mQ 5

What decides the price of a ferry?

ⓐ destination

ⓑ departure time

ⓒ type of seat

6 Choose the woman's opinion about each kind of transportation.

(1) airplane: _____

(2) train: _____

(3) bus: _____

ⓐ It is often delayed.

ⓑ The journey takes a long time.

ⓒ It runs a few times a day.

ⓓ The fare is too expensive.

mQ 6

When will the woman arrive in Edinburgh?

ⓐ 11 p.m.

ⓑ 7 a.m.

ⓒ 8 a.m.

A - 1   Choose the café that the man is going to.

2   What is the man going to buy?

① a birthday cake

② candles

③ a birthday card

④ flowers

B - 1   What is the man mainly talking about?

① Why some people feel hot on planes

② How the in-flight temperature is decided

③ What in-flight temperature people prefer

④ Why some airlines are colder than others

2   What is the usual temperature of the planes of African airlines?

① 21 degrees

② 22 degrees

③ 24 degrees

④ 25 degrees

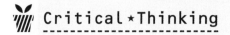 Critical ★ Thinking

Bicycle Lanes

1 Check [✓] if each person is for or against building bicycle lanes.

	For	Against
(1) Julia	☐	☐
(2) Daniel	☐	☐
(3) Sarah	☐	☐

2 Match each person with their opinion.

(1) Julia •   • ⓐ Riding a bicycle is good for the environment.

(2) Daniel •   • ⓑ Building more bicycle lanes will make traffic jams worse.

(3) Sarah •   • ⓒ Bicycle lanes are needed for bicycle riders' safety.

What do you think?

1

Check [✓] if you have the same opinion. You can add your own opinion in the blank.

☐ If more bicycle lanes are built, fewer bicycle accidents will happen.

☐ Roads will become more crowded if new bicycle lanes are built.

☐ A huge amount of money will be needed to build and repair bicycle lanes.

_____

2

Talk about the following questions with your partner.

• Do you often ride a bicycle? Why or why not?

• If bicycle lanes were built in your city, would you ride a bicycle more often?

06 Money

A

Choose the correct word for each definition.

ⓐ value　　ⓑ wage　　ⓒ purchase　　ⓓ separate
ⓔ manage　　ⓕ donate　　ⓖ organization　　ⓗ convenient

1　the act of buying something: _____
2　to give money to help others: _____
3　to use money or time without wasting it: _____
4　a group that works together for a particular purpose: _____
5　the amount of money that something can be sold for: _____
6　the amount of money that an employee gets per hour, week, or month: _____

B

Choose the best sentence for each blank.

ⓐ Could I ask how much you get paid?　　ⓑ What is her key to success?　　ⓒ What is the exchange rate?　　ⓓ You can figure out your spending habits.　　ⓔ What if he spends all his pocket money?　　ⓕ You should learn how to manage your money.

1　W: _____
　　M: One dollar equals about 1,200 won.
2　W: _____
　　M: Ten dollars per hour.
3　W: What is good about the money managing program?
　　M: _____

1   **What is the boy's problem?**

① He is jealous of his friend.

② His friend stole his money.

③ His friend never returns his money.

④ He spent all his pocket money on games.

+ Listen again and fill in the blanks.

M: I'm _____ _____ after school to earn my own pocket money. After I started working, my friend Gerry started asking to _____ _____ from me quite often. Each time, he asks for just _____ _____ _____ _____ _____, like 5 or 10 dollars. The problem is that he never pays me back. Gerry is from a rich family and _____ _____ _____ from his parents. But he spends all that money on stupid computer games. I'm very angry at him, but I don't know _____ _____ _____ _____.

2   **What are they mainly talking about?**

① How to give pocket money

② What teens spend their money on

③ How much pocket money is enough for teens

④ Why giving regular pocket money is important

+ Listen again and fill in the blanks.

M: Honey, I think it's time to give Paul _____ _____ _____. He's 10 years old now.

W: That's a good idea. He should learn _____ _____ _____ _____.

M: Then let's give him money every Monday.

W: Okay. And how about giving him separate money for _____ _____ _____ _____?

M: You mean we should give him one amount for snacks and another for clothes, like that?

W: That's right. _____ _____ _____, because he has never managed his own money before.

M: Great. But _____ _____ he spends all the money before Monday?

W: Then we'll make him work to get more money, by _____ _____ _____ _____.

1 Which country uses the euro?

mini Quiz

① Britain   ② France

③ Sweden   ④ Switzerland

mQ 1

How much is 600 dollars in pounds?

ⓐ about 360 pounds
ⓑ about 400 pounds
ⓒ about 600 pounds

2 What is the woman's advice?

① Plan your spending in advance.

② Keep a record of your spending.

③ Save some of your pocket money regularly.

④ Tell your parents that you need more money.

mQ 2

What will the woman probably do next?

ⓐ Visit the online site
ⓑ Tell the man a website address
ⓒ Download a computer program

3 Which person is using credit cards wisely?

①
I usually use credit cards when I travel abroad.

Sam

②
I study my credit card bill to check my spending habits.

Angela

③
I have three credit cards because each offers different benefits.

Brian

mQ 3

Which is mentioned as a disadvantage of using credit cards?

ⓐ They make you spend more money.
ⓑ Some stores don't accept credit cards.

40

4 What is the woman's problem?

① She is poorly paid.

② She had her money stolen.

③ She was fired for no reason.

④ She can't find a part-time job.

mini Quiz

mQ 4
How much does the woman get paid by the hour?

ⓐ $5.50
ⓑ $7
ⓒ $7.25

5 Which person is likely to earn the most money?

①

②

③

④

mQ 5
Circle what's true about Billy.

(1) Height: Tall / Short
(2) Weight: Heavy / Light

6 Which is NOT a condition that makes money valuable?

① Being old

② Being rare

③ Having a special design

④ Being in good condition

mQ 6
Why does the man collect money?

ⓐ To make money
ⓑ To exhibit his collection
ⓒ To learn about different cultures

A - 1 Which is the best title for the article that the man read?

① What Girls Want to Buy Most

② How to Start your Own Business

③ The Success Story of a School Girl

④ The Top 3 Online Shopping Malls for Teens

2 What is the woman going to sell online?

①  ②  ③  ④

B - 1 What are they mainly talking about?

① The life of a millionaire

② The role of the rich in society

③ The best way to spend money

④ The successful life of Bill Gates

2 Who has the same opinion as the woman?

① I don't know why I should donate my money to society.

Teddy

② The most important thing is making my family happy.

Stephanie

③ We should share what we have with others.

Nicole

 Critical ★ Thinking

Buying the Lottery

1   Check [✓] if each person is for or against buying lottery tickets.

	For	Against
(1) Matt	☐	☐
(2) Janet	☐	☐
(3) Tom	☐	☐

2   Match each person with their opinion.

(1) Matt ·   · ⓐ Playing the lottery is a waste of money.

(2) Janet ·   · ⓑ After buying a lottery ticket, I feel happy and hopeful.

(3) Tom ·   · ⓒ We can help people in need by buying lottery tickets.

What do you think?

1

Check [✓] if you have the same opinion. You can add your own opinion in the blank.

☐ I can help poor people by buying lottery tickets.
☐ If I keep playing the lottery, I may win it someday.
☐ You will be very disappointed each time you don't win the lottery.

_____

2

Talk about the following questions with your partner.

· Have you ever bought a lottery ticket?
· What would you do if you won the lottery?

UNIT

07 Travel

Getting ★ Ready

A

Match each word with the correct definition.

1 located on the land close to the sea   •   • ⓐ suburb

2 the outer area of a large town or city   •   • ⓑ arrange

3 to plan or prepare something in advance   •   • ⓒ coastal

4 a building or tower from which you can enjoy the view   •   • ⓓ souvenir

5 something you buy to remember a trip   •   • ⓔ construction

6 the work of building things such as buildings, roads, etc.   •   • ⓕ observatory

B

Choose the best sentence for each blank.

> ⓐ What if I get robbed?   ⓑ I'm thinking of staying at a hotel.   ⓒ It takes two hours by bus.   ⓓ Do you know how much to tip the taxi driver?   ⓔ It was a series of troubles.   ⓕ How long have you worked in this youth hostel?

1 M: How was your trip to Europe?
    W: _____

2 M: _____
    W: It's been almost five years.

3 M: _____
    W: I think it's 10% of the total fare.

1   Check [✓] what each person thinks about Hong Kong.

	Good	Bad
(1) Becky		
(2) Paul		
(3) Cathy		

+ Listen again
and fill
in the blanks.

W1: I'm Becky. I _____ _____ Hong Kong once. The streets were narrow and _____ _____. It's not a place I want to visit again.

M: I'm Paul. I love shopping and Hong Kong is _____ _____ _____ for it. There are many large and convenient shopping malls. _____

_____ _____ _____, I can purchase good products at low prices.

W2: I'm Cathy. In Hong Kong, I _____ _____ _____ _____ plenty of delicious Chinese food. I can't forget the mango dessert I had there. I didn't like mango before, but it was _____ _____.

2   How did the man's feeling change?

① angry → sad

② glad → confused

③ worried → relieved

④ excited → disappointed

+ Listen again
and fill
in the blanks.

M: Today was the 5th day of my trip. I was going to _____ _____ the 11 a.m. flight from Bristol Airport to Copenhagen. But I _____ _____ at 9 a.m. in the morning. I hurried to the train station to _____ _____ _____ _____.

On the train, I was so nervous that I couldn't _____ _____ _____ _____ my watch! I arrived ten minutes before the final check-in. I _____ _____ _____ and got on board. It was a miracle that I was on time.

1   What will the woman probably do next?

① Call the spa

② Fix the shower

③ Visit the room

④ Get a Thai massage

mini Quiz

mQ 1

What is the man's problem?

ⓐ The shower doesn't work at all.

ⓑ Hot water isn't running from the shower.

2   Why could they NOT visit the museum?

① It was under construction.

② The visiting hours were over.

③ There were too many visitors.

④ It had moved somewhere else.

mQ 2

What will they probably do next?

ⓐ Go to the tourist information center

ⓑ Find a place to have lunch

46

3   Choose the place that each person will visit.

ⓐ Mori Tower

ⓑ Tokyo Government Building

ⓒ Odaiba

(1)   I'd love to see a night view of the sea.   _____

(2)   I want to enjoy the city views in Shinjuku.   _____

(3)   I'd like to see Tokyo Tower shining at night.   _____

mQ 3

Write T for true or F for false.

(1) The Mori Tower has over 50 floors. _____

(2) Odaiba is located in the center of Tokyo. _____

4 Which is NOT a tip that the woman suggests?

① Take some toilet paper to the restroom.

② Only drink bottled water that you buy.

③ Eat at clean restaurants.

④ Agree on the price before getting in a rickshaw.

mini Quiz

mQ 4
Choose the two cities the man will visit.

ⓐ New Delhi
ⓑ Calcutta
ⓒ Agra

5 How much would you tip in each situation?

(1) When a bellboy carries two of your bags: $ _____

(2) When you leave a tip for a cleaning maid: $ _____

(3) When the taxi fare is $10: $ _____

mQ 5
According to the man, if you don't like the restaurant service, how much would you tip?

ⓐ 5%
ⓑ 10%
ⓒ 15%

6 Choose the two problems the woman had.

①  ②

③  ④

mQ 6
Why does the woman want to see the man?

ⓐ To give him a gift
ⓑ To tell him more about her trip

A - 1   What is the relationship between the speakers?

① tourist – tourist

② tourist – hostel worker

③ tourist – travel guide

④ tourist – local person

2   Which place will the man visit today?

① The Temple of Zeus

② The War Museum

③ Olympic Stadium

④ Cape Sounion

B - 1   Choose the two things that the man requested.

①   ②   ③   ④

2   What will the man probably do next?

① Go to the restroom

② Move his baggage

③ Take some medicine

④ Move to a different seat

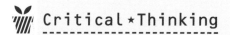 Critical★Thinking

Where to Stay during Travel

1 Where will the man stay in Spain?

① at a hotel

② at a youth hostel

③ at a guest house

④ at his friend's house

2 According to the woman, what are the two advantages of youth hostels?

① The price is cheap.

② They have cooking facilities.

③ You can learn about local culture.

④ You can get travel information from others.

What do you think?

1

Check [✓] if you have the same opinion. You can add your own opinion in the blank.

☐ I prefer hotels because they are safe and clean.

☐ I think it's better to save money by staying at a youth hostel.

☐ I'd like to meet people from different countries at a youth hostel.

_____

2

Talk about the following questions with your partner.

• If you get the chance to travel, what type of place would you prefer to sleep in?

• What would you consider when choosing a place to stay during your trip?

Advice

Getting ★ Ready

A

Choose the correct word for each definition.

ⓐ involve ⓑ field ⓒ anxiety ⓓ shoplift
ⓔ solution ⓕ reunion ⓖ sponsor ⓗ material

1 to include something: _____
2 a feeling of worry about something: _____
3 an event in which old friends gather together: _____
4 a particular area that someone is interested in or works in: _____
5 to steal something from a store without paying for it: _____
6 to give money to support a person or an organization: _____

B

Choose the best sentence for each blank.

ⓐ Those make students interested in the presentation. ⓑ I heard you were accepted by Harvard. ⓒ Make the students focus on your presentation. ⓓ I wish I were as talented as you. ⓔ I was so shocked that I couldn't say anything. ⓕ If I were you, I wouldn't miss the chance to study at Stanford.

1 W: What did you say when you saw him shoplifting?
   M: _____
2 W: What is most important when making a presentation?
   M: _____
3 W: Which university should I go to?
   M: _____

1   What does the girl's father want her to do?

① Go to bed earlier

② Stop seeing Mike

③ Come home by 8 o'clock

④ Be more careful with money

+ Listen again and fill in the blanks.

W: My father and I _____ _____ be very close. But things changed after I started _____ _____ _____ Mike. Now he tells me to come home by 8 o'clock. It's hard for me. I have _____ _____ _____ _____ after school besides meeting Mike. I often study in the library and go shopping with my friends. But he doesn't _____ _____ _____ and keeps making me return home by 8. He even tells me that he'll reduce my pocket money _____ _____ _____. I can't understand him anymore.

2   What made the man recommend that the woman enter Harvard?

① reputation   ② teaching staff

③ distance   ④ cost

+ Listen again and fill in the blanks.

M: Congratulations. I heard _____ _____ _____ _____ Harvard!

W: Thanks. But I also got accepted by Stanford. I can't decide which university I should go to.

M: What are you going to _____ _____?

W: English literature.

M: Hmm... isn't Stanford more famous _____ _____ _____?

W: Right. But Professor Cooper teaches at Harvard. She's a great scholar whom I really respect.

M: Really? Then, _____ _____ _____ _____ to enter that university.

W: The problem is, Harvard is much farther away from my family than Stanford.

M: If I were you, I wouldn't _____ _____ _____ to learn from a great scholar.

W: Thanks for your advice.

1   **What is the man going to wear?**

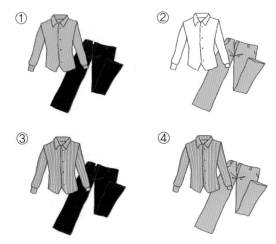

mQ 1

How does the man feel now?

ⓐ excited
ⓑ surprised
ⓒ disappointed

2   **What is the man's advice?**

① Change your major.

② Get experience as an intern.

③ Find a job in a small company first.

④ Apply to as many companies as possible.

mQ 2

What kind of company does
the woman want to join?

ⓐ advertising company
ⓑ trading company

3   **Why did the man fight with his girlfriend?**

① He didn't answer the phone.

② He was late for an appointment.

③ He is closer to his friend than to her.

④ He didn't tell her about his car accident.

mQ 3

What will the man probably
do next?

ⓐ Call his girlfriend
ⓑ Go to his girlfriend's
   university
ⓒ Attend a club meeting

4 What are they mainly talking about?

① Choosing a presentation topic

② Giving a successful presentation

③ Using materials in a presentation

④ Giving feedback on others' presentations

mini Quiz

mQ 4
What is the topic of the woman's presentation?

ⓐ Napoleon
ⓑ Rome
ⓒ World War II

5 Choose the wrong information about the center.

Teen Counseling Center

is waiting for you!

① Any teenagers in California are welcome.

② You can phone, email, or visit our center.

Opening times: ③ Weekdays 9 a.m. ~ 5 p.m.

④ Saturday 9 a.m. ~ 1 p.m.

mQ 5
Why is the counseling free?

ⓐ The center gets government support.
ⓑ The counselors are volunteers.

6 Which describes the woman's advice best?

① A good medicine tastes bitter.

② Actions speak louder than words.

③ The early bird catches the worm.

④ Success doesn't come overnight.

mQ 6
What is the relationship between the speakers?

ⓐ fan – singer
ⓑ actor – actress
ⓒ writer – director

A - 1   Why does the girl think Joel stole from a store?

① He is poor.

② He enjoyed doing it.

③ His friends forced him to do.

④ He wanted to get his parents' attention.

2   If the girl follows the man's advice, what is she likely to do?

① Talk to Joel's parents

② Go shopping with Joel

③ Lend some money to Joel

④ Tell Joel to stop his bad behavior

B - 1   Which is NOT mentioned about test anxiety?

① What it is

② How common it is

③ What symptoms it causes

④ How to avoid it

2   Which person is NOT likely to have test anxiety?

① I really want to get a perfect score on the test.

Carol

② I didn't spend a lot of time studying.

Neil

③ I don't worry too much about making mistakes.

Bobby

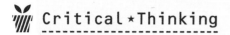 Critical ★ Thinking

Getting Advice

1   What are they mainly talking about?

① What they worry about most

② How they solve their problems

③ Why counselors are needed in schools

④ Who they talk to about their problems

2   Choose each person's opinion.

(1) Kelly: _____   (2) Simon: _____

ⓐ My parents suggest better solutions than my friends.

ⓑ I'm worried that my friends will tell my secrets to others.

ⓒ My friends can understand my problems better than others.

55

What do you think?

1

Check [✓] if you have the same opinion. You can add your own opinion in the blank.

☐ Parents and teachers are wiser than my friends, so I ask their advice.

☐ Friends can give me useful advice because their lives are similar to mine.

☐ I don't talk to anyone about my problems, and I try to solve them by myself.

_____

2

Talk about the following questions with your partner.

• Have you ever got helpful advice from others about your problems?

• Is there anything bothering you these days? Who do you want to talk to about it?

09 Entertainment

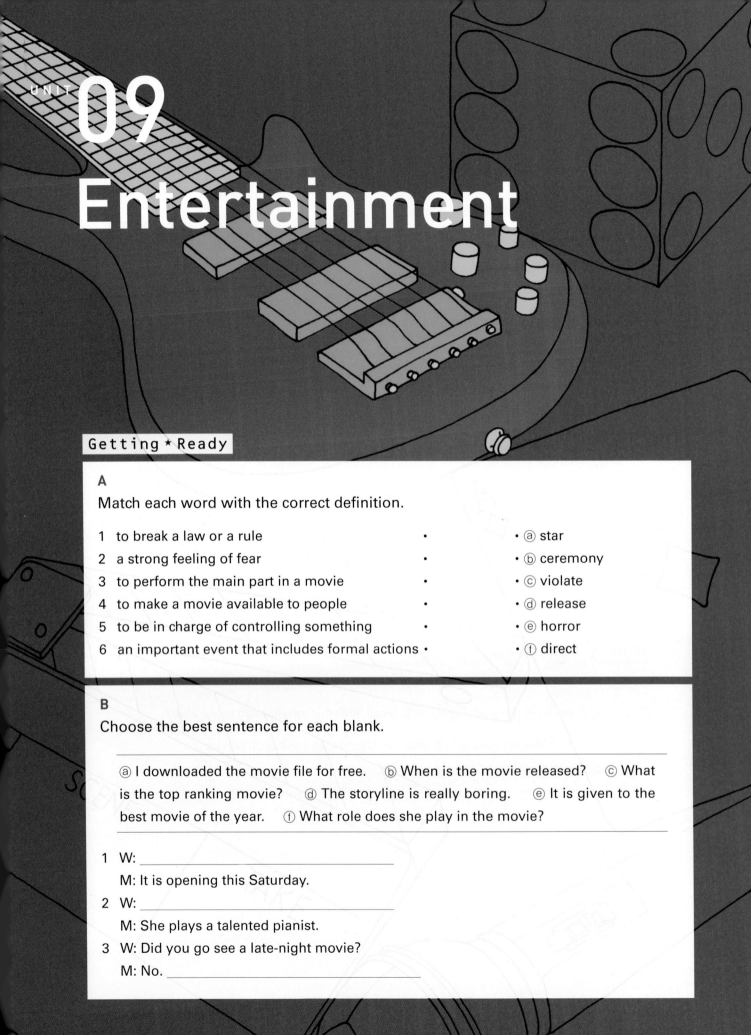

A

Match each word with the correct definition.

1 to break a law or a rule   • • ⓐ star
2 a strong feeling of fear   • • ⓑ ceremony
3 to perform the main part in a movie   • • ⓒ violate
4 to make a movie available to people   • • ⓓ release
5 to be in charge of controlling something   • • ⓔ horror
6 an important event that includes formal actions •   • ⓕ direct

B

Choose the best sentence for each blank.

ⓐ I downloaded the movie file for free.   ⓑ When is the movie released?   ⓒ What
is the top ranking movie?   ⓓ The storyline is really boring.   ⓔ It is given to the
best movie of the year.   ⓕ What role does she play in the movie?

1 W: _____
   M: It is opening this Saturday.
2 W: _____
   M: She plays a talented pianist.
3 W: Did you go see a late-night movie?
   M: No. _____

1   Choose each person's favorite movie genre.

(1) Peter: _____

(2) Jennifer: _____

(3) Henry: _____

> ⓐ action   ⓑ science fiction
>
> ⓒ horror   ⓓ comedy
>
> ⓔ romance

+ Listen again
and fill
in the blanks.

M1: I'm Peter. I like movies about _____ _____ _____. They allow me to see amazing scenes that I could never imagine. I hope I can _____ _____ _____, just like in those movies.

W: I'm Jennifer. I like to _____ _____ _____ when I'm depressed. They help me laugh and _____ _____. I rarely watch serious movies that make me sad.

M2: I'm Henry. I enjoy watching movies that are _____ _____ _____. When ghosts suddenly come out, I usually scream! But it's fun to try to guess _____ _____ _____ next.

2   How does the woman feel now?

① upset   ② excited

③ relieved   ④ pleased

+ Listen again
and fill
in the blanks.

M: Where are you going?

W: I'm _____ _____ _____ _____ to watch *Jump.*

M: Oh, I saw that movie yesterday. I was so sad when the _____ _____ died in the last scene.

W: No! How could you tell me the ending!

M: Didn't you know that? I thought you knew _____ _____ _____ _____.

W: No, I didn't. I was so excited about seeing that movie, but _____ _____ _____.

M: I didn't mean to. Don't be mad.

W: You know, I didn't read any movie reviews to _____ _____ _____. But it's useless now.

M: A movie spoiler?

W: It's information about the _____ _____ in a movie.

M: I'm sorry.

1 Which movie are they going to watch?

Star Trek	Screen 1	12:05	① 14:40
X-men	Screen 2	12:15	② 15:30
Taken	Screen 3	③ 14:20	16:30
	Screen 4	④ 14:40	16:50

mini Quiz

mQ 1
What will they probably do next?

ⓐ Buy some popcorn
ⓑ Purchase tickets
ⓒ Enter the theater

2 What is the man mainly talking about?

① The life of Audrey Hepburn

② Movies that Audrey Hepburn starred in

③ Audrey Hepburn's efforts to help children

④ The success of Audrey Hepburn's movies

mQ 2
Choose the movie that she won the Academy Award for.

ⓐ *Roman Holiday*
ⓑ *Ondine*
ⓒ *Breakfast at Tiffany's*

3 What number will each person press?

(1) I want to talk with a theater staff member. _____

(2) I want to buy a ticket for *Terminator*. _____

(3) I want to change the ticket time. _____

mQ 3
Where can you see *Transformers*?

ⓐ screen one
ⓑ screen two
ⓒ screen three

58

4 Choose the correct movie for each blank.

The Top 5 Movies at the Box Office

1   *Titanic*
2   (1) _____
3   (2) _____
4   *Shrek 2*
5   (3) _____

ⓐ *E.T.*

ⓑ *The Dark Knight*

ⓒ *Star Wars*

mQ 4
Choose the movie that the man has NOT seen.

ⓐ *Titanic*
ⓑ *Star Wars*

5 What are they doing now?

① Reading movie reviews

② Looking at movie posters

③ Writing reviews of new movies

④ Watching a movie award ceremony

mQ 5
Why does the woman refuse to watch *The Last Weekend*?

ⓐ She has already watched it.
ⓑ She doesn't like horror movies.

6 Which picture best describes the situation?

①

②

③

④

mQ 6
What is the man's job?

ⓐ actor
ⓑ movie director
ⓒ music director

A - 1 What role does Emma Winslet play in her new movie?

①  ②  ③ 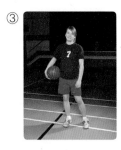 ④

2 When will the man go to see the movie?

① Thursday

② Friday

③ Saturday

④ Sunday

B - 1 Which is NOT true about the Golden Raspberry Awards?

① It chooses the worst movies and actors.

② It is held the night before the Academy Awards.

③ None of its winners have attended it.

④ It started in the early 1980s.

2 What will they probably do next?

① Vote for the Razzies

② Visit the Roosevelt Hotel

③ Find out the winners of the Razzies

④ Watch the Golden Raspberry Awards on TV

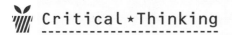 Critical ★ Thinking

Downloading Movies

1 **Choose the two reasons that the man downloads movies.**

① He can save money.

② He can watch movies late at night.

③ He can watch the same movie many times.

④ He can enjoy movies without going to the theater.

2 **Which is the woman's opinion about downloading movies?**

① Downloaders should go to jail.

② It can affect the price of movies.

③ It can discourage movie producers.

④ It can help movies gain popularity in a short time.

What do you think?

1

Check [✓] if you have the same opinion about downloading movies illegally. You can add your own opinion in the blank.

☐ If many people download movies for free, nobody will make movies.

☐ It is very convenient because I can enjoy movies anytime and anywhere.

☐ It's more fun to watch movies in a theater because of the large screen.

_____

2

Talk about the following questions with your partner.

• Have you ever downloaded a movie file illegally?

• Do you know what copyright law is? What will happen if you're caught violating it?

UNIT 10 Jobs

Getting ★ Ready

A

Match each word with the correct definition.

1 to finish doing something · · ⓐ weakness
2 having something to do with the law · · ⓑ legal
3 to speak for someone in a court of law · · ⓒ defend
4 a weak point in someone's character · · ⓓ complete
5 someone who has a degree from a university · · ⓔ graduate
6 a part of an organization that carries out particular work · · ⓕ department

B

Choose the best sentence for each blank.

ⓐ What made you quit the job?   ⓑ I want to do something active.   ⓒ I'm very satisfied with the work.   ⓓ I didn't major in marketing.   ⓔ Do you only work in film making?   ⓕ Have you considered your personality?

1 W: _____
   M: I had too much work to do.
2 W: What kind of job do you want to get?
   M: _____
3 W: How is your work in the amusement park?
   M: _____

1 Which is NOT mentioned about pet lawyers?

① What pet lawyers do

② How to become a pet lawyer

③ Why being a pet lawyer is so popular

④ How much money pet lawyers earn

+ Listen again and fill in the blanks.

M: Do you know what pet lawyers do? Pet lawyers _____ _____ legal problems to do with pets. For example, when a pet owner dies, they help decide who will _____ _____ _____. Also, when a dog bites someone, they defend the pet owner. Are you curious about their income? _____ _____, they earn $90,000 a year. It may _____ _____, but it's difficult to become a pet lawyer. They must _____ _____ law school and pass a special exam.

2 Choose each person's job.

(1) Maria: _____

(2) Eddy: _____

(3) Cindy: _____

ⓐ composer	ⓑ pro-gamer
ⓒ cameraperson	ⓓ conductor
ⓔ photographer	ⓕ game programmer

+ Listen again and fill in the blanks.

W1: I'm Maria. I _____ _____ an orchestra of over 40 people. I don't play a musical instrument, though. Instead, I _____ _____ _____ and lead the musicians so that they give a beautiful performance.

M: I'm Eddy. My job is filming videos for TV news. I can show people _____ _____ _____ through my camera. I sometimes _____ _____ in my shoulders because of the camera, but I'm happy with my job.

W2: I'm Cindy. As I play computer games, I try to _____ _____ what is good or bad about them. I also research _____ _____ _____ _____ people want to play. After that, I create new games.

1 What is the man's sister's job?

① cook

② food stylist

③ photographer

④ movie director

mini Quiz

mQ 1

Why does the man want to watch *First Kiss*?

ⓐ He loves the storyline.

ⓑ His sister recommended it.

ⓒ His sister worked for the movie.

2 Which part-time job is the woman interested in?

①

②

③

④

mQ 2

What will they probably do next?

ⓐ Call Bill

ⓑ Have lunch with Bill

ⓒ Go to the fitness center

3 What's the hard thing about the man's work?

① Standing all day long

② Repeating the same words

③ Smiling for such a long time

④ Working outside in hot weather

mQ 3

Why did the woman call the man?

ⓐ To get a cheap ticket

ⓑ To get a job at the amusement park

4 What did they NOT consider about the woman's future job?

① interest

② talent

③ salary

④ personality

mini Quiz

mQ 4
Which job would be good for the woman?

ⓐ math teacher
ⓑ fashion model
ⓒ travel writer

5 Choose the person that is right for the job.

	① Sandra	② May	③ Julie
Age	33	25	35
Major	fashion design	fashion design	French
Personality	friendly	active	humorous
Work Experience	O	X	O

65

mQ 5
Write T for true or F for false.

(1) People can apply online from July 21st. _____

(2) The result will be sent out by email. _____

6 What are they mainly talking about?

① Winning a video contest

② Creating a video resume

③ Preparing for a job interview

④ Making a good first impression

mQ 6
What kind of company is the man going to apply to?

ⓐ a game company
ⓑ an advertising company

A - 1   Why is the woman unhappy with her job?

① Her salary is too low.

② It doesn't suit her personality.

③ The future of the company isn't bright.

④ She is too busy to have time for herself.

2   What does the woman want to learn?

① cooking

② marketing

③ fashion design

④ Italian

B - 1   Why did the man quit his previous job?

① He had too much work to do.

② He wanted to work for a larger company.

③ He couldn't get along with his co-workers.

④ His job was not exactly what he wanted to do.

2   Which word does NOT describe the man's personality?

① creative

② positive

③ responsible

④ humorous

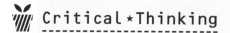

Critical ★ Thinking

Choosing a Job

1 What does the man want to be?

①  ②  ③  ④

2 What is important to each person when choosing a future job?

(1) Jack: _____   (2) Amy: _____

ⓐ Being able to do the job well   ⓑ Earning lots of money

ⓒ Having enough free time   ⓓ Being able to help others

What do you think?

1

Check [✓] if you have the same opinion. You can add your own opinion in the blank.

☐ I want a job that allows me to make a lot of money.

☐ It's important to consider my interests when choosing a job.

☐ I want to get a job that I think is important and worthwhile.

_____

2

Talk about the following questions with your partner.

· What would you like to be in the future? What's the reason?

· What are the good points and bad points of your future job?

11 Culture

Getting ★ Ready

A

Match each word with the correct definition.

1 a flat and round dish · · ⓐ slap

2 to hit someone with your palm · · ⓑ thumb

3 the short, thick finger on your hand · · ⓒ heritage

4 making someone feel bad by being rude · · ⓓ insulting

5 a piece of cloth for drying your tears or a runny nose · · ⓔ plate

6 traditions that pass from generation to generation · · ⓕ handkerchief

B

Choose the best sentence for each blank.

ⓐ Have you visited a sauna?   ⓑ I want to visit one of the World Cultural Heritage sites.   ⓒ It is related to important events in world history.   ⓓ Here's an interesting article about greetings.   ⓔ Does this gesture mean something bad?   ⓕ Are there any special table manners in your country?

1 M: _____
   W: Yes. It means that you are angry.

2 M: Why was the tower selected as a Cultural Heritage site?
   W: _____

3 M: _____
   W: Yes. We never eat before elder people start eating.

1   Which is NOT mentioned about afternoon tea?

① What it is

② When it started

③ What it includes

④ How it became popular

+ Listen again and fill in the blanks.

M: It's an _____ _____ to have "afternoon tea" at around 4 or 5 p.m. It was started by Anna Russell _____ _____ _____ _____. At that time, the English ate a heavy breakfast, light lunch, and late dinner. Anna was always _____ _____ _____, so she had afternoon tea with her friends. Her afternoon tea _____ _____ black milky tea with sandwiches, scones, cakes and biscuits. Now the English rarely have afternoon tea because of _____ _____ _____. But when they do, they simply have black milky tea with biscuits.

2   Why did the man get angry?

① Kate said bad words to him.

② He didn't like the way Kate talked.

③ Kate wouldn't go to the library with him.

④ He misunderstood Kate's body language.

+ Listen again and fill in the blanks.

M: Kate, _____ _____ _____ _____?

W: You asked me to go to the library after school, so I _____ _____. What's wrong?

M: That gesture doesn't mean okay.

W: What do you mean?

M: You made a ring with your thumb and _____ _____, right?

W: Yes. That's the sign for okay here. Didn't you know that?

M: Really? I had no idea.

W: Does it _____ _____ _____ in Brazil?

M: Yes. It has a very insulting meaning.

W: Oh, now I understand. _____ _____ that gestures have different meanings in different countries.

M: Yes, it is. I'm sorry that I _____ _____.

W: No problem.

1 Choose the wedding custom for each country.

(1) America: _____ (2) Sweden: _____ (3) Belgium: _____

ⓐ 　ⓑ 　ⓒ

mQ 1
What will the woman probably do next?

ⓐ Watch TV
ⓑ Go to a wedding
ⓒ Download the documentary

2 Which is NOT included in the tour program?

① Dancing with native performers

② Throwing boomerangs

③ Playing a traditional instrument

④ Watching Australian animals

mQ 2
Which is true?

ⓐ The tour departs every Tuesday.
ⓑ Adults should pay $3,000 for the tour.

3 What is the meaning of leaving food or rice on the plate?

(1) China: _____ (2) Japan: _____

ⓐ I'd like to eat more.

ⓑ The food was not tasty.

ⓒ I've had enough food.

ⓓ I'm ready to eat some dessert.

mQ 3
When invited, what is considered good table manners in Japan?

ⓐ Eating soup with a spoon
ⓑ Eating two bowls of rice

4   Choose the place each person will visit.

(1) Cindy: _____   (2) Tim: _____

ⓐ

The Taj Mahal

ⓑ

Ankor Wat

ⓒ

The Tower of London

ⓓ

The Great Wall

mQ 4

What is the Taj Mahal?

ⓐ a tomb
ⓑ a castle
ⓒ a church

5   What is the woman mainly talking about?

① What Mexicans do to avoid bad luck

② How Mexicans prepare for the New Year

③ What Mexicans buy for the New Year

④ What Mexicans wear to bring good luck

mQ 5

Which color underwear will Mexican women wear to get married?

ⓐ red
ⓑ yellow
ⓒ white

6   Circle whether it will bring good or bad luck.

(1)

(Good / Bad)

(2)

(Good / Bad)

(3)

(Good / Bad)

mQ 6

Write T for true or F for false.

(1) Thailand looks like an elephant's head on the map. _____

(2) There is still an elephant on the Thai national flag.

_____

A - 1 Who is greeting in the wrong way?

① Tibetans

② Maoris

③ Eskimos

2 Where is the conversation taking place?

① in a library

② at a bookstore

③ in a classroom

④ at an Internet café

B - 1 According to the woman, why are saunas so popular in Finland?

① They're good for sick people.

② They help people feel relaxed.

③ They're a great way to make friends.

④ They make people feel warm quickly.

2 Write T for true or F for false about Finnish saunas.

(1) Finns invite only close friends to a sauna. _____

(2) Steam is made by pouring hot water over cold stone. _____

(3) When feeling too hot in a sauna, Finns will bathe in a nearby lake. _____

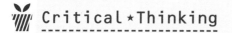 Critical ★ Thinking

Bullfighting

1 Check [✓] if each person is for or against bullfighting.

	For	Against
(1) Nick	☐	☐
(2) Kate	☐	☐
(3) Jason	☐	☐

2 Choose each person's opinion.

(1) Nick: _____   (2) Kate: _____   (3) Jason: _____

ⓐ We should make a law to stop bullfighting.

ⓑ Bullfighting plays a big role in the Spanish economy.

ⓒ Animal's rights are more important than people's enjoyment.

ⓓ Bullfighting is a great cultural heritage with a long history.

What do you think?

1

Check [✓] if you have the same opinion about bullfighting. You can add your own opinion in the blank.

☐ It should go on because it is a culturally important tradition.

☐ Bulls are living things. It's not right to kill animals for enjoyment.

☐ It should go on because many people will lose their jobs if it stops.

_____

2

Talk about the following questions with your partner.

• Have you seen bullfighting in person or on TV?

• Are there any traditions that cause arguments in your country?

12
IT

A

Choose the correct word for each definition.

ⓐ permission	ⓑ fixed	ⓒ intermediate	ⓓ edit
ⓔ report	ⓕ preview	ⓖ upload	ⓗ illegal

1 against the law: _____
2 located between high and low levels: _____
3 to watch something in advance: _____
4 to move data or programs to the Internet: _____
5 the act of allowing someone to do something: _____
6 to give information about an event: _____

B

Choose the best sentence for each blank.

ⓐ Did you open an unknown email?　ⓑ I'm uploading media files onto my blog.
ⓒ Should I go to the service center?　ⓓ People share photos and download them for free.　ⓔ All I'm considering is quality.　ⓕ What will you mainly use the computer for?

1 M: _____
   W: I'll use it for doing homework.
2 M: Are you surfing the Internet?
   W: No, _____
3 M: What is that website for?
   W: _____

1 Which computer is the man going to choose?

①

- foreign brand   • light
- free of noise   • $1,500

②

- local brand   • light
- a bit of noise   • $2,000

③

- local brand   • light
- free of noise   • $3,000

+ Listen again
and fill
in the blanks.

M: I'm going to buy a _____ _____ for the first time. What should I consider?

W: What will you mainly use the computer for?

M: I need it for _____ _____ during my business trips.

W: I see. How much are you willing to pay?

M: I don't _____ _____ _____ _____. All I'm considering is quality.

W: If you're traveling with it, it should be light.

M: You're right. Also, _____ _____ _____ _____.

W: Right. You should also consider whether you can get good _____ _____.

M: Oh, I hadn't thought about that.

W: For good after-sales service, _____ _____ _____ are better than foreign ones.

M: Okay. Thanks for the advice.

2 Which is NOT given as a tip by the man?

① Spend only a certain amount of time on the Internet.

② Buy software that blocks you from the Internet.

③ Set your computer up in the living room.

④ Have other interests besides using the Internet.

+ Listen again
and fill
in the blanks.

M: Lately, _____ _____ has become a serious social problem. It's especially serious _____ _____. Here are some tips to prevent Internet addiction. First, always set _____ _____ _____ _____ _____ for using the Internet. If you can't control yourself, you can get help from _____ _____ which sets a time limit on your Internet use. Also, _____ _____ _____ in the living room. If you spend time on the computer alone in your bedroom, it's harder to control yourself. Lastly, _____ _____ you can enjoy with family or friends.

75

1 Why did the woman call the man?

① To ask him his messenger ID

② To borrow some money from him

③ To ask him to chat on messenger

④ To check if he was using messenger

mini Quiz

mQ 1
What will the woman
probably do next?

ⓐ Save the message
ⓑ Change her password

2 What are they mainly talking about?

① The difficulties of learning Chinese

② The programs of an online Chinese class

③ The advantages of an online Chinese class

④ Well-known online Chinese learning sites

mQ 2
How much are online Chinese
classes for beginners?

ⓐ $50 per month
ⓑ $60 per month

3 Choose the screen that they are watching.

mQ 3
How did the woman learn to
use Photoshop?

ⓐ through a class
ⓑ from her friend
ⓒ through the Internet

4 Who is saying something wrong about Twitter?

① I can upload messages only by visiting the site.

② I can't write messages over 140 letters.

③ I can see Joe's updated messages without visiting his Twitter page.

mini Quiz

mQ 4

Why is Twitter called a mini blog?

ⓐ The size of the page is small.
ⓑ You can only write short messages.

5 Why did the man's computer slow down?

① It has a virus.

② It is out-of-date.

③ It doesn't have enough memory.

④ The Internet connection isn't working well.

mQ 5

What will they probably do next?

ⓐ Buy a vaccine program
ⓑ Go to a service center
ⓒ Buy a new computer

6 What do you have to do to use the photos from NEclick for business?

① Pay a small fee to the owner.

② Buy the copyrights to the photo.

③ Exchange photos with the owner.

④ Get permission from the owner.

mQ 6

Why is the woman trying to find a photo?

ⓐ for her blog
ⓑ for her homework

A - 1   Fill in the blanks according to the results of the older group.

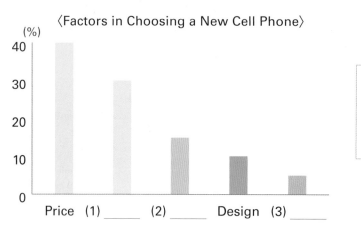

⟨Factors in Choosing a New Cell Phone⟩

ⓐ Brand
ⓑ Battery life
ⓒ Ease of use

Price (1) _____   (2) _____   Design (3) _____

2   Which was the least important thing according to the younger group?

① brand

② design

③ battery life

④ ease of use

B - 1   What are they mainly talking about?

① How to decorate a blog

② What kind of topics bloggers like

③ How to make a blog popular

④ How often to update a blog

2   Who is following the woman's advice?

① I cover various kinds of topics on my blog.

Ted

② I often update my blog and post video clips on it.

Billy

③ I exchange information with other bloggers offline.

John

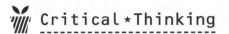 Critical ★ Thinking

ID Theft

1 **What happened to the man?**

① Someone changed his online password.

② Someone sold his personal information.

③ Someone used his ID to play online games.

④ Someone logged into messenger with his ID.

2 **According to the woman, what is the way to prevent ID theft?**

① Change your password often.

② Don't lend your ID to your friends.

③ Don't play online games on public computers.

④ Don't leave your information on public computers.

What do you think?

1

Check [✓] to see if you are careful enough about protecting yourself from ID theft. You can add your own method in the blank.

☐ I make my passwords very long.

☐ I often change my passwords.

☐ I know a site on which I can report illegal ID use.

☐ I always make sure to log out after I use public computers.

_____

2

Talk about the following questions with your partner.

• Have you ever had your ID stolen?

• How should we punish people who steal IDs?

Vocabulary ⋆ List

UNIT 01

ask ~ out (on a date)
finally
courage
suggestion
amusement park
romantic
crowded
in that case
riverboat
ride
arrangement
complain
fund manager
earn
huge
smart
surgeon
be ashamed of
surprisingly
break up with
college
boss
office romance
behind one's back
good-looking
most of all
be attracted by
a sense of humor
still
height
appearance
go out

pick
outfit
be supposed to-v
show up
apologize
with one's mouth full
satisfied
depressed
pleased
disappointed
judge
join
personality
fall in love with
reject
a couple of
introduce
shocked
forget
proposal
ex-girlfriend
blind date
guy
senior
next door
move
already
amazing
ideal type
neighbor
for some time
reason
fresh
instrument

prefer
skinny
miss
surprise
see
decision
maybe
treat
entertainment
announce
marriage
fiancée
viewer
film
leading character
besides
positive
director
producer
host
get along with
preparation
fiancé
custom
fortune teller
cancel
favor
trust
fully
believe in
superstition
attend
persuade
approve of

privacy
share
password
text message
respect
bank account
personal information
be related to

UNIT 02

swimsuit
be sold out
order
deliver
directly
a pair of
sandal
department store
a variety of
quality
item
product
discount store
groceries
make out
list
outlet
instead of
several
bedcover
comfortable
beige
either A or B

hostess	effect		snack
original	example		Coke
discount	attack	throw	prefer
catalogue	double	potluck party	study abroad
channel	goods	tasty	surprise party
exchange	please	dish	advice
look good on	cosmetic	tuna	invitation
section	mall	soda	explain
recommend	look for	just in case	prepare
go with	convenient	clean	collect
pocket	compare	invite	celebrate
perhaps	at one time	by the way	Halloween party
flea market	trust	tease	unique
various	discount	be about to-v	costume
accessory	in person	keep in mind	ugly
especially	necklace	on time	scary
used	pick up	show up	pirate
instrument	delivery	bother	sword
be located at	charge	host	bone
comment	wrap up	limit	suit
visitor	arrival	rude	powder
possible	request	thank-you note	wedding reception
design	designer brand	polite	laugh
refund	difference	within	wish
receipt	salary	express	lovely
scratch	waste	guest	so-so
sale	get tired of	acceptable	interior
garage sale	neat	baby shower	party planner
graduation	simple	be expecting a baby	assistant
sneakers	worth	gather	be located at
economy	would rather ~ than ...	tradition	following
lipstick	once	can't wait to-v	customer
scarf	keep	pajama party	discuss
luxury		pajamas	detail

81

decoration	heart	sneeze	bacteria
fluent	stomach	headache	bottom
friendly	cold	runny nose	pressure
résumé	blueberry	cough	knee
job advertisement	improve	digest	cushion
announcement	memory	air conditioner	treat
pay	receive	degree	remove
requirement	support	medicine	work out
purpose	energetic	turn up	weight training
raise	secret	temperature	purpose
be scheduled to-v	positive	air out	sign up for
participate	cheerful	regularly	daily
purchase	view	breathe	register
formal dress	lightly	spoil	discount
require	fat	yoga	membership
support	composer	lose weight	be[go] on a diet
dress code	shoulder	relieve	balanced
show off	hurt	stress	concern
afford	sleep the wrong way	clear	effect
offer	pain	available	proper
	circle	potassium	

82

UNIT 04	position	nutrient	UNIT 05
	ankle	vegetable	
gain weight	raise	spinach	due to
habit	upper body	amount	heavy traffic
skip	put down	alcohol	rush hour
overeat	flu	stop by	traffic jam
meal	get worse	on the way home	accident
instant food	totally	drop by	roadwork
calorie	virus	weight	appointment
healthy	go away	take good care of	transportation
broccoli	slight	toe	common
prevent	fever	prevent A from v-ing	similar to
cancer	cause	lotion	motorcycle
vitamin	muscle	absorb	power
garlic	sickness	sweat	engine

handlebar

wheel

passenger

along with

roof

pollution

vehicle

unpleasant

stadium

direct

quite

choice

advantage

on one's way to

get lost

go straight

take a left[right] turn

reservation

a bit

reschedule

ideal

someday

avoid

sensor

sense

possible

environment

function

imagine

energy

flight

international

fasten

seat belt

forward

window shade

land

local time

latest

weather report

temperature

degree

Celsius

take off

ferry

route

departure

depend on

cabin

euro

deck

destination

busy season

option

delay

long-distance

depart

journey

run

fare

exit

bakery

mention

corner

candle

airline

standard

maintain

blanket

complain

in-flight

seriously

pollute

breathe

harm

therefore

bicycle lane

encourage

law

protect

citizen

space

narrow

UNIT 06

part-time

earn

pocket money

borrow

pay back

stupid

jealous

steal

regular

manage

separate

item

garage

Britain

nearly

exchange

euro

pound

Sweden

Switzerland

exchange rate

equal

record

spending

figure out

cut down

download

in advance

keep a record of

regularly

credit card

convenient

tend to-v

cash

go over

bill

reduce

unnecessary

purchase

charge

payment

overseas

extra

fee

benefit

disadvantage

hourly

wage

employee

at least

quit

simply

poorly

fire

article

good-looking

helpful

similar

83

weigh

have nothing to do with

income

height

collect

coin

collection

culture

basic

valuable

value

particular

unique

condition

rare

exhibit

teenage

run

key

success

born

salesperson

successful

millionaire

mind

organization

donate

provide

education

health care

in need

role

society

share

waste

lottery

millions of

chance

false

impossible

excitement

for a while

hopeful

UNIT 07

crowded

convenient

purchase

be able to-v

plenty of

delicious

mango

dessert

flight

hurry

nervous

final

check-in

get on board

miracle

confused

relieved

disappointed

shower

repairman

fix

fully

book

offer

traditional

massage

spa

repair

reserve

museum

sign

construction

waste

tourist

location

recommend

observatory

floor

government

man-made

island

suburb

ocean

bridge

ferry

shine

India

capital

skip

toilet paper

restroom

instead of

bottled water

stomachache

free

rickshaw

pull

tip

and so on

normally

main

wage

total

bill

leave

bellboy

per

maid

a series of

trouble

wallet

steal

luckily

passport

souvenir

actually

youth hostel

traveler

fall in love with

stay

temple

Zeus

cape

coastal

sunset

local

cold

medicine

symptom

fever

sore throat

blanket

uncomfortable

neighbor

available

luggage

cabinet

illness

arrange

request

baggage

facility

exchange

stranger

get robbed

safe

environment

used to-v

go out with

besides

reduce

pocket money

accept

university

major in

literature

field

professor

scholar

respect

farther

reputation

teaching staff

distance

cost

reunion

beige

long-sleeved

gray

striped

pretty

apply

get hired

advertising

well-known

major

trade

career

experience

intern

have a fight with

accident

trust

answer one's phone

appointment

presentation

research

focus on

contact

material

video clip

successful

feedback

counseling

professional

counselor

email

in person

sponsor

government

for free

support

volunteer

honor

stage

act

talented

debut

performance

every single day

keep on v-ing

try one's best

bitter

loud

worm

overnight

shoplift

for fun

steal

shocked

behavior

keep silent

force

attention

natural

anxiety

involve

symptom

stomachache

headache

sweat

throw up

be likely to-v

avoid

be afraid of

make a mistake

have ~ in common

fully

notice

seriously

secret

care about

solution

space

allow A to-v

scene

imagine

alien

depressed

laugh

relieve

rarely

scary

thrilling

ghost

suddenly

scream

horror

cinema

main character

ending

blow it

mean to-v

review

spoiler

useless

upset

relieved

pleased

be sold out

show

view

loved

appear

star

receive
award
win
performance
continue
in need
cancer
effort
press
reserve
reservation
cancel
operator
staff
successful
box office
hit
rank
follow
episode
release
storyline
mention
disappointing
ceremony
refuse
direct
large-scale
talented
create
special effects
appreciate
role
cop
uniform
at least

event
appointment
miss
winner
embarrassed
show up
brave
search
vote
stay up late
download
late-night
bother
violate
copyright
big deal
pocket money
jail
affect
discourage
gain
popularity

UNIT 10

pet lawyer
deal with
legal
to do with
owner
raise
bite
defend
curious
income
on average

graduate from
law school
orchestra
musical instrument
lead
musician
film
pain
research
create
composer
cameraperson
conductor
delicious
tableware
plate
meal
strawberry
film making
review
be good at
fitness center
personal
trainer
in detail
amusement park
be satisfied with
indoors
customer
all day long
imagine
repeat
consider
be interested in
essay
well-organized

personality
be full of
talent
salary
personal shopper
include
proper
lifestyle
graduate
degree
apply
resume
result
require
unique
introduce
advertise
advertisement
hold
impression
employee
marketing
department
uncomfortable
suit
interior
co-worker
project
participate in
quit
creative
task
complete
weakness
previous
get along with

exactly

positive

responsible

pilot

surgeon

patient

honestly

reason

UNIT 11

tradition

century

consist of

black milky tea

scone

biscuit

rarely

gesture

thumb

index finger

insulting

get upset

misunderstand

body language

documentary

traditional

custom

rice

married

bride

coin

Belgium

handkerchief

ceremony

get married

tour package

experience

Aborigine

native

performer

boomerang

musical instrument

depart

adult

table manners

invite

plate

leave

at least

bowl

lightly

solid

chopstick

Taj Mahal

castle

tomb

heritage

site

UNESCO

select

related to

the Great Wall

Mexican

New Year's Day

sweep

dust

get rid of

make room

wealth

underwear

marriage

shape

Thailand

Thai

national flag

superstition

belly

come true

hold ~ in one's arms

unlucky

article

greeting

Tibetan

greet

pull

stick out

tongue

Maori

press

Eskimo

slap

cheek

borrow

contain

shelf

section

Finnish

suggest

sauna

Finn

Finland

steam

pour

lake

bathe

sausage

beer

take a break

relaxed

nearby

recently

movement

bullfighting

Spanish

consider

ban

pleasure

excuse

tourism industry

economic

growth

play a big role in

right

enjoyment

UNIT 12

laptop computer

for the first time

mainly

make a presentation

business trip

be willing to-v

quality

noisy

after-sales service

national

foreign

local

lately

addiction

serious

social problem

prevent

set

fixed

control

software

limit

place

certain

block

besides

messenger

ID

password

save

chat

lecture

be satisfied with

offline

attend

academy

over and over again

advanced

intermediate

beginner

link

preview

advantage

well-known

have one's picture taken

actually

edit

technology

skin

shiny

on my own

Twitter

blogging service

upload

as well as

letter

comment

board

follower

permission

update

suddenly

slow down

memory

space

unknown

run

virus

vaccine

address bar

out-of-date

connection

surf the Internet

share

copyright

for business

advertisement

contact

owner

fee

exchange

research

ease

factor

while

battery life

least

recipe

almost

big deal

post

review

similar

entertainment

media file

decorate

blogger

cover

video clip

game money

log in

in the world

public computer

report

illegal

common

nowadays

make sure

log out

personal information

theft

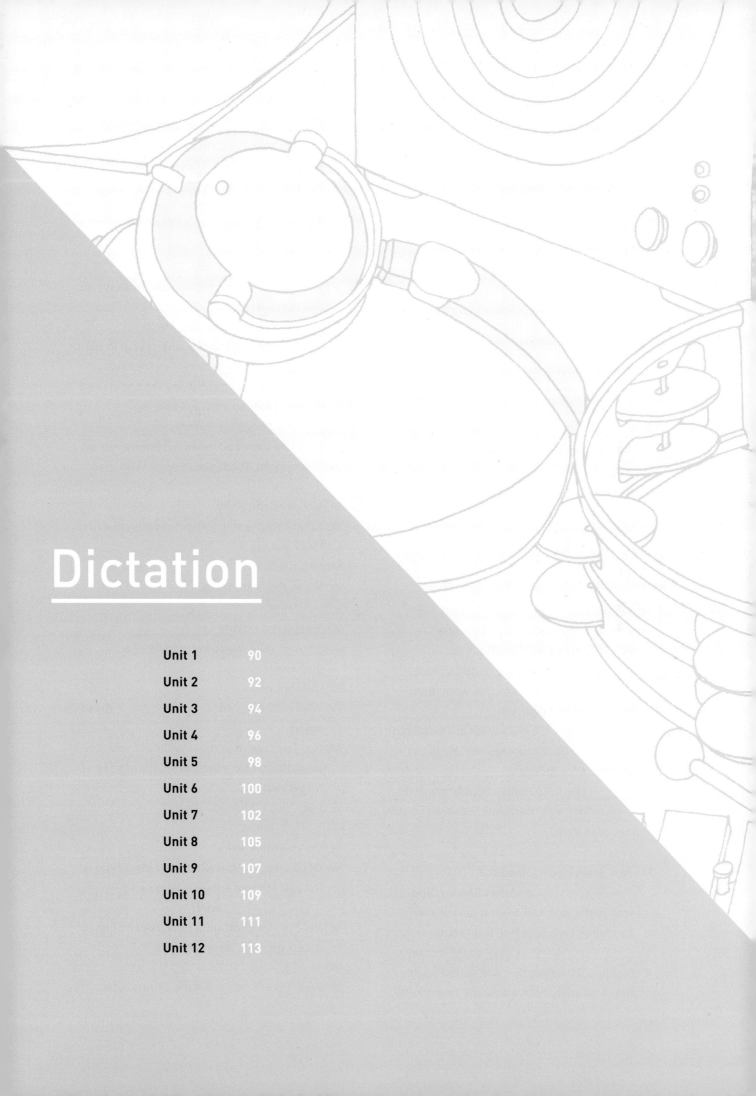

Dictation

UNIT 01 Love

1

M: Mom, how did you and Dad first meet?

W: Well, I got my first job at a company _____ _____, and your dad was my boss.

M: Wow, so was it an office romance?

W: Yes, it was.

M: _____ _____ _____ _____?

W: Well, it was difficult to find time to date behind everyone's back!

M: So what did you like about Dad?

W: _____ _____ _____, he was very tall and good-looking. But most of all, I was attracted by his great sense of humor.

M: Okay. But I don't know whether he was _____ _____.

W: Your father was and still is the most handsome man in my life.

M: Oh, Mom!

2

W: Yesterday, I _____ _____ with Mark, who is in my math class. I've never talked with him in class. But he's _____ _____, so I was happy to go out with him. It took me hours to pick what outfit to wear for our date. We _____ _____ _____ meet in a restaurant at 7 p.m., but he showed up 30 minutes late. He didn't apologize for it. And _____ _____ _____, he talked only about himself. He even talked with his mouth full. It was such a terrible date.

3

M: Two years ago, I joined the _____ _____ _____ and met Sandra. She was pretty and had a good personality, so I fell in love with her. But I've never _____ _____ _____ to tell her my feelings. I was worried she would reject me. A couple of days ago, my best friend

Leo _____ _____ to his new girlfriend. Surprisingly, his girlfriend was Sandra. I was really shocked. They said they met at a friend's birthday party _____ _____ _____ _____. I know that I should forget her, but it's really hard.

4

M: Susan, who is this guy _____ _____ _____? Is he the college senior that you like these days?

W: No. He was my first love. He _____ _____ _____ to me when I was in high school, but then his family moved away.

M: That's too bad. What did you like about him?

W: He was kind, and always told me _____ _____ about his friends.

M: I bet you were sad when his family moved.

W: You're right. What about you? Who was _____ _____ _____?

M: My girlfriend Kelly.

W: What? You're still going out with your first love?

M: Yes. It's been _____ _____ already.

W: Wow, that's amazing.

5

W: You haven't dated _____ _____ _____. Don't you want to have a girlfriend?

M: Um, not now.

W: Why not? Are you _____ _____ these days?

M: No. The reason is that I went out with my ex-girlfriend for a long time. It's hard to forget her.

W: I see. But I think you should _____ _____.

M: Do you think so?

W: Of course. Tell me what your ideal type is. Do you still like tall girls who can _____ _____ _____ well?

M: No. I prefer short girls now. And I'd like to date a girl who enjoys sports.

W: _____ _____?

M: Well, I don't really like the skinny type.

W: I see. I'll start looking!

6

W: I _____ _____ _____ my boyfriend last weekend.

M: What happened?

W: Well, I wanted to _____ _____, so I went to his company last Friday.

M: What a nice idea!

W: Yes. But he came out holding some other woman's hand. He was _____ ___ _____!

M: He's really a bad guy. You made the right decision to break up with him.

W: Maybe. But I _____ _____ now.

M: Cheer up! You don't have to feel depressed because of him.

W: But it's not easy.

M: _____ _____ going to an amusement park today? It'll cheer you up.

W: Well... I don't know.

M: Come on, I promise we'll _____ _____ _____ _____ there.

W: Okay. You're a really good friend.

Listening ★ Challenge Answers p. 2

A [1-2]

W: This is *TBN's Entertainment News*. Mickey Brown, _____ _____ the show.

M: Hello.

W: Everyone was surprised when you announced your marriage to Silvia yesterday. _____.

M: Thank you.

W: So when did you first meet your fiancée? The viewers are _____ _____ about it.

M: We first met in 2004 while working together on the movie *Rain*. We weren't close _____ _____ _____ because Silvia is very shy around new people.

W: So did you become close while filming *Happy Family* in 2006? You two _____ _____ _____ _____.

M: Yes. We started dating after that movie.

W: What do you like about Silvia, besides her beautiful appearance?

M: I _____ _____ _____ her positive personality and sense of humor.

W: Thank you for the interview. Our viewers and I wish you a happy life with her.

B [1-2]

M: How are your wedding preparations going?

W: Well... my parents are _____ _____ _____.

M: Your fiancé Jack has a great personality and a good job. What's the problem?

W: _____ _____ _____, there's a custom of asking a fortune teller about the future of the marriage.

M: That's interesting.

W: But the fortune teller said that we wouldn't be _____ _____. I don't believe him, but my parents do.

M: So your parents are against the marriage?

W: Yes. But I can't _____ _____ _____ just because of that.

M: Right.

W: Having said that, can I ask you a favor?

M: Sure, what is it?

W: My parents like you and _____ _____ _____. So please tell them that Jack is a great guy and that we will be happy together.

M: _____ _____. I really do think so.

Critical ★ Thinking Answers p. 2

W: Justin, I can't understand my boyfriend.

M: _____ _____?

W: Well, I believe each person's privacy is important, even in a couple. But he doesn't think so.

M: Does he want you to _____ _____?

W: Yes. He wants to know my email password. And he checks the text messages on my cell phone _____ _____ we meet.

M: Maybe he doesn't trust you.

91

W: But he says he does trust me.

M: Then _____ _____ _____?

W: He just thinks that if two people love each other, they should share everything. What do you think of that?

M: I think privacy should _____ _____ _____, even in a couple.

W: My boyfriend even wants to know my bank account password. I wish he would respect _____ _____.

UNIT 02 Shopping

Listening ★ Practice   Answers p. 2

1

W: David, look at this.

M: Is that a bedcover?

W: Yes. You _____ _____ a new bedcover. So what do you think?

M: It looks nice and comfortable.

W: It _____ _____ beige, yellow, and green. Which one do you like?

M: They all look good on the screen. Well... either _____ _____ _____.

W: Just pick one. The hostess said only a few of them are left.

M: Do we have to buy it today? I want to think about it.

W: _____ _____. The original price is $50, but there's a $10 discount for today only.

M: Really? Then I'll go with green.

W: Great! Let's call _____ _____.

2

M: _____ _____ _____ _____?

W: No, I'm not. I got this blue miniskirt as a present, but I want to exchange it.

M: Is there _____ _____ with it?

W: It doesn't look good on me. May I see other skirts in a different style?

M: Sure. The _____ _____ is over here.

W: Would you recommend one that goes with my blouse?

M: How about this gray one with pockets? Or perhaps _____ _____ _____?

W: I like this short one. Do you have it in a different color?

M: Yes. Here it is in green.

W: It's pretty. _____ _____ _____ _____?

M: It's $50. The blue skirt was $45, so you'll have to pay $5 more.

W: Okay. I'll take it.

3

W: Do you want to buy things _____ _____ _____? Come to the "Town Flea Market," the oldest and largest flea market in New York. There are _____ _____ and accessories, and we're especially famous for used instruments and books. _____ _____ _____ 39th Street and are open on Saturday from 10 a.m. to 6 p.m. Also, visit us online at www.townfm.com. You can see _____ _____ _____ _____ and comments from visitors. If you have things for sale, please call us at 3142–0357.

4

W: Hello. I bought this watch here. _____ _____ _____ _____?

M: Okay. When did you buy it?

W: A week ago. Is it possible to exchange it now?

M: Yes. But this watch _____ _____ _____ _____. Why do you want to exchange it?

W: It has a nice design, but I don't like the color. _____ _____ _____ get a white one.

M: I'm sorry, but the white ones are sold out.

W: Oh, no! Well, can I get a refund, then?

M: Okay. Did you _____ _____ _____?

W: Wait. Oh, no! I forgot to bring it. Can I get a refund without it?

M: I'm sorry. You can't.

W: Okay, then I'll _____ _____ tomorrow.

5

W: _____ _____ that MP3 player! Isn't it

nice?

M: It looks good. Are you going to buy it?

W: I'd like to, but I don't have _____

_____.

M: Jane, I know how you can get some money. How about selling things we don't need?

W: You mean _____ _____ _____?

M: Yes. Actually, I also need money for my sister's graduation gift.

W: Great! _____ _____ _____ _____?

M: I have some books and CDs that I can sell. How about you?

W: Maybe clothes and sneakers.

M: How about _____ _____? You don't wear many of them.

W: That's right. It would be better to sell accessories _____ _____ sneakers.

M: Okay.

6

M: When the _____ _____ _____, people don't shop as often. But products like lipstick and scarves sell more. This is because women buy _____ _____ _____ instead of expensive ones to cheer themselves up. This is called the "Lipstick Effect." _____ _____ _____ in America, when the economy was bad, lipstick sales went up while other sales _____ _____. That's when people started to call it the "Lipstick Effect." Another famous example was after the 9/11 attacks. At that time, lipstick sales _____ _____.

Listening ★ Challenge   Answers p. 3

A [1-2]

W: Do you want to go to the W Mall with me?

M: It's _____ _____ here. Why do you want to go there?

W: To buy an MP3 player. I heard they're _____ _____ _____ now.

M: Why don't you look for one on the

Internet? It's much cheaper.

W: _____ _____ _____ anything online.

M: It's convenient because you don't need to walk around to shop. And you can compare all the prices _____ _____ _____.

W: Do you know a good website?

M: You can trust sites like Mega Mall or King Market. I can give you a Mega Mall _____ _____.

W: But I want to look at the items myself.

M: Then, why don't you visit the Cherryville Mall to _____ _____ them, and buy one from Mega Mall?

W: Good idea.

B [1-2]

M: _____ _____ _____ a necklace for my sister. Could you recommend one?

W: How about this cat-shaped one or this heart-shaped one?

M: My sister _____ _____ the heart-shaped one. How much is it?

W: It's $54, after a 10% discount.

M: That's good. _____ _____ do you have?

W: There are two colors, silver and pink. But the silver ones are sold out.

M: Can I order a silver one?

W: Yes, but it'll take _____ _____ _____. Will that be okay?

M: That's fine.

W: Okay. Do you want to pick it up?

M: I don't think I have time. Could you _____ _____?

W: Yes, but you'll have to pay $4 for the delivery charge.

M: I see. That's fine.

W: _____ _____... today is the 14th. So it'll arrive by the 16th.

M: Thanks. Please wrap it up nicely.

Critical ★ Thinking   Answers p. 3

W: Leo, what do you think of this bag?

M: It looks okay. _____ _____ _____?

93

W: Yes. This is a famous designer brand product. Can't you see the difference?

M: Well... I don't know, Judy. You _____ _____ _____ a lot of money.

W: Let's just say that one month of my salary is gone.

M: That's crazy. Designer products are only expensive _____ _____ their names. I don't understand why people waste money on them.

W: But designer products are good quality. I can use them _____ _____ _____ _____.

M: Do you think so?

W: Sure. And I don't get tired of them easily because of their neat and simple design. Although they're expensive, _____ _____ _____!

M: Still, I would rather buy several cheaper items than one designer brand product.

UNIT 03 Parties

Listening * Practice   Answers p. 3

1

W: When you're invited to a party, there are some things you should _____ _____ _____. First, arrive at the party on time. If you show up early, it can bother the host. Being _____ _____ twenty minutes late is also bad. Second, when you bring new faces to a party, it should be limited to _____ _____ _____. Bringing too many new people can be rude. Finally, send a thank-you note to the host after the party. It's polite to send it _____ _____ _____. It's always nice to express your thanks.

2

M: What did you do _____ _____ _____, Kate?

W: I went to Mindy's baby shower.

M: A baby shower? What's that?

W: Oh, _____ _____ _____ for parents who are expecting a baby. People gather and give gifts to the parents. It's a _____ _____ in the U.S.

M: Interesting! So, what did you give as a present? _____ _____?

W: I was going to buy some baby clothes, but Mindy said she already had enough. So I bought _____ _____ _____ baby shoes and a hat.

M: Did Mindy like them?

W: Of course! She said they were cute. I _____ _____ _____ _____ Mindy's baby wear them.

3

W1: Hi, Lisa. _____ _____ _____ this Friday?

W2: Yes. What's up, Rachel?

W1: I'm planning to have a pajama party at my home. Would you like to come?

W2: _____ _____! What do I need to bring?

W1: Just bring your pajamas.

W2: Okay. And I'll _____ _____ _____ too.

W1: Great. Oh, and you have Beyonce's new CD, right?

W2: No. Why do you ask?

W1: I want something to _____ _____ at this party. I'll ask Sarah about it, then.

W2: What about drinks?

W1: I'll buy some. You like Coke, don't you?

W2: Actually, I _____ _____.

W1: Okay. Then I'll buy some juice, too.

4

M: Jenny, can I ask you a favor?

W: Sure. What is it, Paul?

M: Sally is _____ _____ from studying abroad. So, I'm planning a surprise party for her. Can you give me some advice?

W: Well, first, _____ _____ explaining that it's a surprise party.

M: Okay. And?

W: Tell the guests to arrive 30 minutes before Sally arrives. And prepare _____ _____ _____ and drinks.

M: What else should I do?

W: Why don't you collect some money from the guests before the party? You can use it to buy _____ _____ _____ for Sally. She'll be really happy.

M: Thanks. Jenny! That was a big help.

5

M: I went to a Halloween party yesterday. Everyone was wearing _____ _____. Nick was dressed like Hellboy. He wore a long brown coat with an ugly orange mask. It was _____ _____. Tim dressed like a pirate. He was wearing black pants with a sword _____ _____ _____. He also wore a big black hat with bones on the front. It was my favorite costume. Ben was _____ _____ Dracula. He was wearing a black suit. He even wore white powder and red lipstick. He _____ _____ _____.

6

M: How did Wendy's wedding reception go?

W: It was so much fun. I couldn't _____ _____.

M: What was so funny?

W: The couple did a funny dance together. They prepared it _____ _____ _____.

M: Wow, I wish I had seen it. And how did the wedding hall look?

W: I liked it. It was _____ _____, so it looked lovely.

M: Do you think it would be a good place for my wedding reception, too?

W: _____ _____. The food was a problem. It wasn't very fresh.

M: What about the service?

W: The service wasn't terrible, but it _____ _____ _____ either. If it were my wedding, I'd choose another place.

M: You should get a boyfriend first.

A [1-2]

W: Dream Party Planner is looking for an _____ _____ _____. We are one of the largest party planning companies in America. Our office _____ _____ _____ 40 Houston Street, Manhattan. Assistant party planners do the following: First, they meet customers to discuss the details of _____ _____. Then they order food and decorations. Finally, they send invitations. The _____ _____ are Monday to Friday, from 9 a.m. to 5 p.m. To be an assistant, you must speak fluent English and _____ _____ _____ MS Word, email, and web searching. And we're looking for a friendly person. Send your résumé to Jane@dpt.com _____ _____ _____.

B [1-2]

M: Hello, everyone. I'd like to invite all of you to a _____ _____ _____. The purpose of this party is to raise money for hungry children. A lot of famous actors and singers, _____ _____ Will Smith and Britney Spears, are scheduled to participate. They're going to sell some of their clothes and accessories. The _____ _____ will be used to purchase food for poor children. The party will be held on Christmas _____ _____ _____ at the Peace Convention Hall. Formal dress is required for the party. Anyone who wants to _____ _____ _____ is welcome. I hope you join this special event and spend a great Christmas with us.

M1: I'm Paul. I don't understand people who spend a lot of money on their _____ _____ _____. Throwing an expensive party is only to show off their money, not

95

to please their children.

W: I'm Ally. If you _____ _____ the money to throw an expensive party, why not? Parents want to offer the best things they can to their children. _____ _____ _____, throwing an expensive party can be one way to express their love.

M2: I'm Joe. I don't think that _____ _____ _____ for children is a good idea. Many children's parents can't afford expensive parties. When those children see others' luxury birthday parties, they'll _____ _____.

UNIT 04 Health

Listening ★ Practice   Answers p. 4

1

M: Welcome to *The Evening Show*, Sandra.

W: _____ _____ to be here again.

M: You received the Grammy for Album of the Year. That's amazing.

W: It's all _____ _____ the love and support of my fans.

M: You're in your 60s now, but you look so young and energetic. _____ _____ _____?

W: I try to be positive. I always try to have a cheerful view of life.

M: What else?

W: I usually _____ _____.

M: What kind of food do you enjoy?

W: I prefer fish to meat. Fish is low in fat, so it's _____ _____ meat.

M: I see. Now, we're excited to listen to some of your songs.

W: Okay. The first song I'm going to sing is *Yesterday*.

2

M: Ouch! My shoulder hurts.

W: Did you _____ _____ _____ for a long time again?

M: No. Maybe I slept the wrong way last night.

W: I know a good exercise for _____ _____.

M: Really? Please show me.

W: First, put both of your hands on your shoulders.

M: _____ _____?

W: Yes. And turn your arms in a large circle, ten times to the front and ten times _____ _____ _____.

M: Oh, it's not difficult.

W: There's another position. Lie on your stomach and _____ _____ _____ with your hands.

M: Okay.

W: Raise your upper body and legs, and then slowly put them down.

M: Wow, it's hard.

W: Your shoulder will _____ _____ if you do this several times a day.

M: Okay. Thanks.

3

M: Do you think the flu is a cold that has _____ _____? It's not. Colds and the flu are from totally different viruses. A cold will go away in 3 to 4 days, but if you _____ _____ _____, you could be sick for weeks. When you catch a cold, you might have a slight fever. But when you have the flu, you _____ _____ _____ _____. Also, flu viruses make you very tired and cause muscle pain. Finally, the flu can cause other sicknesses, but colds can't.

4

M: What brings you here?

W: I _____ _____ _____ and a runny nose.

M: Have you been coughing or sneezing?

W: No, but I have a problem digesting my food, too. I think it _____ _____ when I'm in the office.

M: Is the air conditioner in your office always on?

W: Yes. I usually feel cold _____ _____ _____ .

M: That could be the reason. If there's more than a five-degree difference between outside and inside, that can _____ _____ .

W: Will I get better by taking medicine?

M: You don't need medicine. Instead, _____ _____ the temperature at work. And air out the office regularly.

W: Okay.

M: Also, drink _____ _____ often. And try to exercise and breathe fresh air.

W: I see. Thank you, doctor.

5

W: Are you free this afternoon? Let's _____ _____ _____ _____ .

M: I can't. I should go to my yoga class.

W: Yoga? I thought yoga was something women did to _____ _____ . Why are you doing it?

M: You know I have problems sleeping. But after doing yoga, I sleep well.

W: That's good. What else is good about yoga?

M: It's good for _____ _____ . And it makes my skin clear.

W: Really? I'll have to try it for my skin. _____ _____ are you taking?

M: The 6 p.m. class. Let's go together.

W: Oh, I'm not available then. Is there _____ _____ ?

M: There are classes at 4 p.m. and 8 p.m., too.

W: Eight p.m. sounds good to me.

6

M: Why do you look so tired?

W: I'm just hot. I _____ _____ _____ .

M: Maybe it's because you don't get enough potassium.

W: Potassium? _____ _____ _____ ?

M: It's one of the nutrients needed for good health. It's in fruits like bananas and oranges, and _____ _____ spinach and tomatoes. So try to eat them a lot.

W: Which has the highest amount of potassium?

M: Tomatoes have _____ _____ , followed by spinach, bananas, and oranges.

W: Maybe I should eat tomatoes more often.

M: Also, coffee, alcohol, and sugar can push potassium _____ _____ _____ _____ . So don't have too much of those.

W: Okay. How about stopping by a supermarket for some tomatoes _____ _____ _____ _____ ?

M: All right.

Listening ∗ Challenge   Answers p. 4

A [1-2]

W: Although feet do the important work of _____ _____ _____ , people don't take good care of them. Let me tell you how you should care for your feet. First, it is important to dry in _____ _____ _____ after washing your feet. To prevent your feet from drying up, use foot cream or lotion. And it's good to _____ _____ to absorb sweat even in summer. Don't wear the same shoes every day. Bacteria could grow _____ _____ _____ . If the bottom of your shoes is too hard, it puts pressure on your ankles and knees, so wear shoes _____ _____ _____ .

B [1-2]

W: I want to _____ _____ . What kind of programs do you have?

M: Swimming, yoga, tennis, and weight training. What's the purpose of your exercise?

W: I want to _____ _____ for the summer.

M: Then, how about doing weight training and swimming?

W: I'll just _____ _____ _____ weight training.

M: Okay. Could you give us your name, please?

W: I'm Cathy Brown.

M: You can choose between a daily class and

a three-times-a-week class.

W: Three times a week will be fine for me.

M: Okay. When do you want to start?

W: From _____ _____.

M: How long do you want to register for? If you register for over six months, you can get a _____ _____.

W: Well, I'll just sign up for a month. How much will it be?

M: It's $90. Thank you for joining us.

Critical ★ Thinking   Answers p. 4

M: Jenny, let's have lunch together.

W: Sorry, Steve. I'm _____ _____ _____. So I'm just going to have a few tomatoes.

M: What? When did you _____ _____?

W: It's been a week. I eat tomatoes for lunch and don't eat dinner.

M: _____ _____ isn't a good way of losing weight.

W: Well... this is the only way to lose a lot of weight in a short time.

M: But you'll probably _____ _____ more weight after the diet. The best way to lose weight is through balanced eating and exercise.

W: But I gain weight easily _____ _____ I don't eat that much. So I have no other choice.

M: I'll lend you a book about eating _____ _____ _____. You'll change your mind after reading it.

W: All right. Thanks for your concern.

UNIT 05 Transportation & Location

Listening ★ Practice   Answers p. 4

1

W: Joe, do you know _____ _____ _____ _____ Dodger Stadium?

M: Oh, are you going to watch a baseball game?

W: Yes, there's a Dodgers game _____ _____. How can I get there?

M: The bus is quicker than the subway, because there is a _____ _____.

W: How long does it take?

M: About 20 minutes. The stadium is about a ten-minute walk _____ _____ _____ _____.

W: Ten minutes? That's quite far. I don't want to walk a lot.

M: _____ _____ _____ then. The subway station is just in front of the stadium.

W: That's good. How long does it take?

M: _____ _____ _____.

W: That sounds like my best choice.

2

(Telephone rings.)

W: Thank you for calling Farmer John's Restaurant.

M: Hello. I'm _____ _____ _____ _____ your restaurant, but I seem to have got lost.

W: Do you know where you are?

M: I'm on Baker Avenue _____ _____ _____ Charles Street.

W: I got it. Go straight one block along Baker Avenue and take a left turn on Oak Street.

M: Take a left turn on Oak Street?

W: Right. Then, you'll see the restaurant _____ _____ _____. It'll take about 15 minutes.

M: Fifteen minutes? I have a reservation at six, so I'm going to be _____ _____ _____.

W: Then I'll reschedule it to 6:10. Will that be okay?

M: Perfect. Thank you.

3

M: _____ _____ _____ your science report about the ideal transportation of the future?

W: I've almost finished.

M: What did you _____ _____?

W: I chose a car with wings. I hope that someday there's a car that can fly.

M: _____ _____ _____ _____. We could easily avoid traffic jams with those cars.

W: Also, they'd have a special sensor that could sense _____ _____.

M: Amazing!

W: What do you think the ideal transportation of the future is?

M: I think we should _____ _____ _____ the environment than design or functions.

W: I think you're right.

M: So I _____ _____ _____ which uses the energy from the sun. It's a small car for one person.

W: Great.

4

M: Ladies and gentlemen, have you _____ _____ _____? This is Captain Williams speaking. We'll be arriving at Vancouver International Airport _____ _____ _____ _____. All passengers must return to their seats and fasten their seat belts. Also, please put _____ _____ forward, and open the window shades for landing. The local time in Vancouver right now is _____ _____ _____ _____. According to the latest weather report, it is rainy in Vancouver, and the temperature is 19 degrees Celsius. Thank you.

5

M: How can I help you?

W: I'd like to _____ _____ _____ for a ferry to Italy.

M: You can choose from two routes. There is a ferry for Brindisi and one for Bari.

W: When are their _____ _____?

M: The ferry for Brindisi leaves at 9:30 a.m., and the one for Bari leaves at 1:30 p.m.

W: _____ _____ _____?

M: It depends on the type of seat. A cabin seat is 150 euros and a deck seat is 75 euros.

W: So it doesn't _____ _____ my destination, right?

M: Right.

W: I'll buy a ticket for tomorrow to Bari. And I'll _____ _____ _____ _____.

M: Okay.

W: Here it is.

6

W: This weekend, I'm going to _____ _____ _____ to Edinburgh. While planning the trip, I couldn't easily decide what transportation to take. _____ _____, I was going to take a plane. But it's the busy season, so the tickets are very expensive. I decided to _____ _____ _____. I don't like to take trains because they are often delayed. Finally, I decided to take a long-distance bus. It _____ _____ at 11 p.m., and arrives in Edinburgh at 7 a.m. It'll be a long journey, but I'm happy about _____ _____.

99

Listening * Challenge Answers p. 5

A [1-2]

(Telephone rings.)

W: Hello.

M: Hello, this is Alex.

W: Hey, _____ _____ _____? We've finished preparing for Sally's birthday party.

M: I came out of exit number 4, but I can't _____ _____ _____ you mentioned.

W: You should have come out of exit number 3, not number 4.

M: I guess I have to _____ _____ into the station, then.

W: Just tell me what you can see around you.

M: There is a church _____ _____ _____.

W: I got it. Go straight two blocks, and you'll see the bakery. Then turn left _____

M: Okay. And then?

W: Go straight one block and turn left at the corner. We are in the café that is _____ _____ _____.

M: I see.

W: Don't forget to buy candles for the cake on the way.

M: Okay. Did you buy a birthday card?

W: Yes. _____ _____.

B [1-2]

M: Do you know that each airline has _____ _____ for the temperature on their airplanes? The airlines usually set this standard temperature after _____ _____ _____. For example, the airlines of Africa and Southeast Asia keep the temperature around 25 degrees. American and European airlines _____ _____ _____ at around 22 degrees. But there is one interesting fact. The standard temperature is usually _____ _____ most passengers like. This is because if passengers feel cold, they can cover themselves with _____ _____. However, if it's too hot, they can only get angry and complain about it.

100

Critical ★ Thinking Answers p. 5

W1: I'm Julia. Cars seriously _____ _____ _____ we breathe. Bicycles, however, do not harm the environment. Therefore, we should build more _____ _____, and encourage people to use bikes instead of cars.

M: I'm Daniel. According to the law, a bicycle is a _____ _____ _____. That means we should ride our bikes on the road. However, doing so is very dangerous for bicycle riders. I think we should build bicycle lanes to _____ _____ _____.

W2: I'm Sarah. There's just not enough space to build new bicycle lanes in our city. If

we build bicycle lanes _____ _____ _____, the roads will become narrower. Imagine how bad the traffic jams will be.

UNIT 06 Money

Listening ★ Practice Answers p. 5

1

M: Hey, _____ _____ _____ _____ your trip to Britain?

W: Almost. I've nearly finished doing everything.

M: Did you exchange any money?

W: I don't _____ _____. After my mom went to France, she gave me 400 euro.

M: But the euro isn't used in Britain. British people still _____ _____ _____.

W: I thought all European countries used the euro.

M: Most of them do, but some countries like Sweden and Switzerland have _____ _____ money system.

W: I should go to a bank to exchange money, then.

M: How much are you going to exchange?

W: Well, _____ _____ _____ _____?

M: 10 US dollars equals about 6 pounds.

W: I think 600 dollars will be enough. That's about 360 pounds.

2

M: I've spent all my _____ _____.

W: Already? Didn't you receive it only a few days ago?

M: I did. I don't know where all the money has gone.

W: Why don't you _____ _____ _____? It's the best way to manage money.

M: How does that help?

W: Well, you can figure out your spending habits. So you can _____ _____ your spending and save some money every month.

M: That's what I need.

W: I use an online money managing program. It's very _____ _____ _____.

M: Can you send me the program?

W: You can download it from the Internet. I'll let you know the address.

M: Okay, thanks. I'll _____ _____ _____.

3

W: _____ _____ are very convenient. You can buy products with them even if you don't have money _____ _____ _____. However, it's easy to forget how much you've spent. That's why you tend to spend more with credit cards than _____ _____. To use your cards wisely, it's best to have only one card. Go over your credit card bill _____ _____ and reduce unnecessary purchases. Also, don't forget to pay your bill on time. _____ _____ _____ for late payments. And it's not good to use cards overseas because you will be charged extra fees.

4

M: Why are you so busy these days? I never see you!

W: I'm _____ _____ at a hamburger restaurant.

M: A hamburger restaurant? Could I ask how much you get paid?

W: Five dollars and fifty cents _____ _____.

M: It can't be! According to the law, hourly wages should be more than $7.

W: Really?

M: Yes. I heard employees should get _____ _____ $7.25 or something.

W: So should I quit the job? I'm worried because it's not easy to _____ _____ _____ _____.

M: Why don't you talk to your boss first? Maybe he simply doesn't know the law.

W: Okay. _____ _____ _____ _____.

5

W: Billy, what are you reading?

M: It's a very _____ _____. It says people who are good-looking earn about 12% more money than those who aren't.

W: Really? _____ _____ _____ _____ for that?

M: Good-looking people are believed to be more helpful.

W: That's interesting. Oh, I read a similar article before. It said _____ _____ earn more money.

M: What about people who weigh a lot like me? Do they earn more money _____ _____?

W: I'm sorry but weight has nothing to do with income.

M: That's too bad. What about people who are _____ _____ _____, like me?

W: Well... I don't know.

6

M: My hobby is _____ _____. Many people collect coins to earn money by selling their collections. But I started it to learn about _____ _____ through their money. The basic thing about collecting coins is to know which ones are valuable. People usually think all old money _____ _____ _____ _____, but if many people have a particular kind of coin, its value will be low. Also, if the money has a _____ _____ or special history, it goes up in value. Lastly, people will pay more for money which is _____ _____ _____.

Listening ⋆ **Challenge** Answers p. 5

A [1-2]

M: I read a newspaper article about a teenage girl yesterday. She runs an _____ _____ _____ and makes $40,000 a month.

W: That's amazing! What is her key to success?

M: She sells skirts to _____ _____. She understands what they want to wear.

W: She must be a born salesperson. I think _____ _____ _____ open a shopping mall for women in their 20s.

M: There are already too many malls like that, so you won't be successful.

W: You _____ _____ _____. So, would it be better to sell men's wear?

M: I think so. What about selling just one item, like jeans or T-shirts?

W: _____ _____. I think it would be good to sell jeans.

B [1-2]

W: If you were a millionaire, what would you like to do?

M: I'd like to spend my money _____ _____ _____ _____ with my family. I think that would be the best way to spend it.

W: I had the same idea, but I _____ _____ _____.

M: So what would you like to do?

W: I'd like to start an organization for poor people.

M: Oh, really? What made you _____ _____ that?

W: I heard about Bill Gates. He donated his money to provide education and health care to _____ _____ _____.

M: He's a great person, but I don't think I could do that. Making my family happy is _____ _____ to me.

W: I understand. But I believe we can make our world a better place by helping others.

Critical ★ Thinking Answers p. 5

M1: I'm Matt. I don't understand why people waste their money _____ _____ _____. Yes, it's true that I could win millions of dollars, but I have nearly zero chance of winning. It's better not to have _____ _____.

W: I'm Janet. I know it's almost impossible to win the lottery. However, I buy one ticket every week _____ _____ I can have hope and excitement for a while. I like to have such feelings.

M2: I'm Tom. I don't think it's _____ _____ _____ to buy lottery tickets. When we buy lottery tickets, some of the money is spent on helping the poor. So, it's okay even if I don't _____ _____ _____.

UNIT 07 Travel

Listening ★ Practice Answers p. 6

1

(Telephone rings.)

W: Front desk. How may I help you?

M: I'm _____ _____ _____. There's a problem with the shower again.

W: Is it the same problem as yesterday, when _____ _____ _____ at all?

M: No. It works, but no hot water is coming out.

W: I'm sorry. I'll _____ _____ _____ and send him to fix the problem.

M: But this is the second time. Can't I get another room?

W: I'm sorry, but all rooms are _____ _____.

M: I'm so disappointed in this hotel.

W: Why don't I offer you a free traditional Thai massage in our spa _____ _____ _____?

M: Well... that sounds nice.

W: I'll reserve the massage right away and then send a repairman to your room.

2

M: _____ _____ the map, the Coffee and Tea Museum should be here.

W: I know. This is Wood Street, right?

M: _____ _____ _____ on that street sign.

W: Could it be that building under construction?

M: It looks too small to be a museum.

W: Look! _____ _____ _____. It says
the Coffee and Tea Museum has been
moved to a different place.

M: What? I can't believe we wasted _____
_____ _____ trying to find it.

W: Hmm... what should we do now?

M: Why don't we go to the tourist information
center and ask about _____ _____
_____ the museum's new location?

W: That's a good idea.

M: Let's ask about _____ _____ _____
as well.

W: Okay. Let's hurry.

3

W: _____ _____ _____ to you some
places with beautiful night views in
Tokyo. The first place is the Mori Tower
observatory _____ _____ _____
_____ in the city center. You can see
Tokyo Tower from here. Secondly, if you
visit the Tokyo Government Building in
Shinjuku, _____ _____ _____ on
the 45th floor. It's in the center of the city,
so you can enjoy the city view. Finally,
there is Odaiba. Odaiba is a _____
_____ in the suburbs of Tokyo. The
view of the ocean, bridge and ferries looks
beautiful _____ _____.

4

M: _____ _____ a trip to India. But I can't
choose between New Delhi, Calcutta, and
Agra.

W: _____ _____ Agra. The Taj Mahal is
amazing.

M: Okay. And New Delhi is the capital, so I'll
skip Calcutta.

W: Do you want _____ _____ about India?

M: Sure.

W: Always take toilet paper to the restroom.
Indians use water _____ _____ toilet
paper.

M: Interesting.

W: And you must buy bottled water. I got
a stomachache after I _____ _____

_____ at a restaurant.

M: I'll be careful.

W: And you know what a rickshaw is, right?

M: Is it some kind of transportation pulled
_____ _____ _____?

W: Yes. Always set the price before you get
in. If not, the driver might ask for a lot of
money later.

5

M: When you travel to America, you should
know _____ _____ _____ _____
at restaurants, hotels, and so on. Normally,
waiters or waitresses give their best service
to get more tips, because the tips are
_____ _____ _____. If you have
good service in a restaurant, give 10~15%
of the total bill as a tip. But if the service
isn't good, _____ _____. In hotels,
when a bellboy carries your bag, give him
$1 per bag. Also, leave $1 _____
_____ _____ every morning for the
cleaning maid. Tipping 10% to a taxi
driver is enough.

6

(*Telephone rings.*)

M: Hello.

W: Hi, Ted. I'm back.

M: Hey, Marian. How was your _____
_____ _____?

W: Oh, it was a series of troubles.

M: What happened?

W: In Rome, I _____ _____ _____
_____ on the bus.

M: How terrible! Did you lose any money?

W: Yes. But luckily I'd left my passport at the
hotel.

M: Good for you.

W: _____ _____ _____. Once, I took the
wrong train and got off at Valencia instead
of Barcelona.

M: Oh, you really had _____ _____
_____ _____. By the way, did you buy
any souvenirs for me?

W: (*laughs*) Actually, that's why I called. Do

103

you have _____ _____ _____
tomorrow?

M: Yes. How about meeting at 6 p.m.?

W: Sounds great!

A [1-2]

M: Nice to meet you. I'm Tom.

W: It's good to meet someone _____
_____ _____. I'm Kelly.

M: How long have you worked in this youth hostel?

W: It's been ten years. I came here _____
_____ _____ and fell in love with Greece.

M: I'm going to stay in Athens for three days. Could you recommend _____ _____
_____?

W: Visit the Temple of Zeus. It is so big that you won't believe your eyes.

M: Oh, _____ _____ _____ _____.

W: Also, the War Museum and Olympic Stadium are famous. Do you know about Cape Sounion?

M: No, I don't.

W: It _____ _____ _____ from Athens by bus. There you can enjoy great coastal views and beautiful sunsets.

M: _____ _____ _____ _____. I'll go there today and visit the Temple of Zeus tomorrow.

B [1-2]

W: Did you call for help, sir?

M: Yes. Do you have _____ _____
_____ on the plane? I feel sick.

W: Yes, we do. What are your symptoms?

M: I have a fever and _____ _____
_____.

W: I see. I'll bring you some medicine and water.

M: I already have water. But could I get _____ _____ _____? I'm cold.

W: Sure. If you feel uncomfortable, let me

move you to a seat without neighbors.

M: Is there an _____ _____?

W: Yes. It's at the back of the plane.

M: I have some luggage in the cabinet above me. Should I bring it?

W: No, _____ _____ _____. Next time you travel, tell us you have an illness during check-in. Then we can arrange for you to have a more _____ _____.

M: Oh, really? That's nice.

W: Now, please follow me.

M: All right.

W: I heard you're going to Spain. Are you going to _____ _____ Susan's house?

M: No. She's also traveling now. So, I'm thinking of staying at a hotel.

W: _____ _____ _____ look for a youth hostel? They're much cheaper.

M: I'm not sure. Hotels are more expensive, but _____ _____ and they have convenient facilities.

W: But you will only sleep there.

M: If I stay at a youth hostel, I'll _____
_____ _____ things like soap and shampoo myself.

W: That's right. But at a youth hostel, you can _____ _____ _____ with other tourists.

M: But I don't want to sleep in a room with strangers. Plus, what if I get robbed?

W: That doesn't happen _____ _____.

M: Still, I'll choose a hotel for a clean and safe environment.

UNIT 08 Advice

Answers p. 6

Listening ⋆ Practice

1

M: I couldn't sleep at all _____ _____.

W: Why not?

M: I'm going to a high school reunion this evening. A girl I _____ _____ really like will come to the reunion.

W: I see. In that case, you should change your clothes.

M: Okay. _____ _____ _____ _____?

W: What colors of pants do you have?

M: I have black pants and beige pants.

W: What about _____ _____?

M: I have a white shirt and gray striped shirt.

W: I think beige pants with a white shirt would be _____ _____ _____.

M: But I forgot to wash those pants. They're pretty dirty.

W: Okay. Then I recommend the black pants with the _____ _____ _____.

M: Thanks. I hope she likes the way I look.

2

M: How are you doing?

W: I'm pretty busy looking for a job. I _____ _____ a couple of companies, but I didn't get hired.

M: What companies have you applied to?

W: I applied to ABC and NE Advertising.

M: Those are _____ _____ _____ advertising companies. It must be hard to get a job in such famous companies.

W: I know. Besides, _____ _____ is trade.

M: Right. Since you didn't major in advertising, it's even harder.

W: _____ _____ _____.

M: Why don't you apply to a smaller company and try to build your career first? After that, you can move to _____ _____ _____.

W: Thanks for your advice.

3

M: I had a fight with my girlfriend Amy.

W: Were you _____ _____ a date again?

M: No. I had a car accident yesterday, but I didn't tell Amy about it.

W: Why not?

M: I didn't want to _____ _____ _____. But she heard about it from another friend.

W: Now I got it. Women want their boyfriends to _____ _____ with them, but you didn't.

M: Is that a big problem?

W: Of course. Amy might think you don't _____ _____.

M: Really? Then I should talk to her right now. But she's not answering her phone.

W: She must still be _____ _____ _____ because of a club meeting. Go meet her instead.

M: Okay, thanks.

4

M: What is your presentation topic for history class?

W: I _____ _____ _____ on Napoleon. But I'm really worried about it.

M: About what? About giving a presentation?

W: Exactly. _____ _____, my last presentation was really bad.

M: Do you mean the presentation about Rome? I liked it. It was _____ _____ _____, though.

W: So how can I make this presentation more interesting?

M: _____ _____ _____ _____ is to make the students focus on your presentation.

W: How?

M: Make eye contact and ask questions. _____ _____ _____ to just stand there and speak.

W: I see.

M: And I often use materials such as video clips or pictures. Those _____ _____ _____ in the presentation too.

105

5

W: Do you have any problems with your family or friends? Do you _____ _____ your future? If so, why don't you get counseling at the Teen Counseling Center? You can _____ _____ about your problems from our professional counselors. This center is for teenagers _____ _____ _____. You can call, email, or visit our center in person. It is sponsored by the government, so all of our services are offered _____ _____. We're open from 9 a.m. to 6 p.m. on weekdays. _____ _____, we open at 9 a.m. and close at 1 p.m.

6

M: Ms. Taylor, it was _____ _____ _____ _____ to be with you on stage.

W: Thank you. It was a nice experience for me, too.

M: How can you act, sing, and _____ _____ _____? I wish I were as talented as you.

W: Wasn't it your debut musical performance? You'll get better.

M: But people always tell me I'm not good enough.

W: I heard _____ _____ _____ when I debuted.

M: I can't believe that!

W: It's true. But I've been practicing _____ _____ _____ for 15 years. That's why I'm here now.

M: I see. I'll keep on trying my best.

Answers p. 6

Listening ★ Challenge

A [1-2]

W: Mr. Jackson, can I talk to you _____ _____ _____?

M: Sure. Do you have a problem?

W: It's about my friend, Joel. I _____ _____ _____ from a store.

M: Oh, boy. Do you know why he would do such a thing?

W: I think he did it _____ _____. His family isn't poor, so I don't know why else he would steal.

M: Did you _____ _____ to him at that time?

W: No. I was so shocked that I couldn't say anything.

M: He might think you accept that behavior because you _____ _____.

W: Then should I tell him that he shouldn't do it again? But what if he hates me?

M: Just think about _____ _____ _____ _____, if you are really worried about him.

W: Okay.

B [1-2]

M: It's natural that you feel nervous just before _____ _____ _____. However, if you become too nervous to focus on your test, you may be experiencing _____ _____. Test anxiety involves symptoms such as stomachaches, headaches, or sweating. Some students even throw up because of strong test anxiety. So, who experiences test anxiety? If you're not _____ _____ tests, you may experience it. Students who worry about their scores a lot are also likely to get test anxiety. _____ _____ this nervous feeling, you need to be well-prepared for the test. It's also important not to _____ _____ _____ making mistakes.

Answers p. 7

Critical ★ Thinking

W: I'm Kelly. When I'm worried about something, I ask my friends _____ _____ _____. My friends and I have a lot in common. We are the same age, _____ _____, and go to the same school. So they can fully understand my problems and give me helpful advice. _____ _____ _____ my parents and teachers before, but I noticed they didn't take my problems seriously.

M: I'm Simon. I _____ _____ talk to my friends when I needed advice. We felt closer after sharing our secrets. But I couldn't get _____ _____ _____ about my problems. Now I ask my parents for advice. They care about me _____ _____ _____ _____. So they try to find the best solution to my problems.

UNIT 09 Entertainment

Listening * Practice   Answers p. 7

1

W: _____ _____ do you want to see?

M: I want to see *Star Trek*.

W: But the tickets for 2:40 p.m. are all _____ _____. We have to wait for hours to see the next show.

M: Then how about watching *X-men*? There are _____ _____ _____ for the 3:30 show.

W: Sorry, but I've already watched that movie.

M: Never mind. Have you seen *Taken* too?

W: No, _____ _____. Let's watch it.

M: Great. It's showing on two screens, screen 3 and screen 4.

W: I _____ _____ _____. It's a bigger screen with a better view.

M: Okay. The movie starts at 2:40. Let's go buy the tickets.

W: Sure. How about _____ _____ _____ before entering the theater?

M: Good idea.

2

M: Audrey Hepburn was one of _____ _____ _____ _____ in the world. She first appeared in an European movie in 1948. After she starred in *Roman Holiday*, she _____ _____ _____. For this movie, she received the Academy Award

for Best Actress. She also won a Tony Award for her performance _____ _____ _____ called *Ondine*. Audrey continued to appear in many movies, including *Breakfast at Tiffany's*, and *My Fair Lady*. _____ _____ _____ _____, she spent much of her time helping children in need. She died of cancer in 1993.

3

W: _____ _____ _____ Movie House. We are now showing *Terminator* on screen one, *Transformers* _____ _____ _____, and *Night at the Museum* on screen three. If you want to know the movie schedule, _____ _____ _____. If you would like to reserve a ticket, press two. If you want to make a change to _____ _____, press three. If you want to cancel your reservation, press four. Please press zero to _____ _____ _____ _____. Thank you.

4

M: Do you know what movie was the most successful _____ _____ _____ _____?

W: Let me guess. It was *E.T.*, wasn't it? I remember it was a big hit.

M: No. That's _____ _____.

W: Really? What is the top ranking movie, then?

M: It's *Titanic*. I haven't seen it, but I should _____ _____ to watch it.

W: So what movie is ranked in second place?

M: *The Dark Knight*. And *Star Wars* _____ _____ after *The Dark Knight*.

W: Which episode of *Star Wars*?

M: The one released in 1977, _____ _____ _____. It's an old movie, but I've seen it on DVD.

W: Me too. What about fourth place?

M: *Shrek 2*.

5

W: Look at this. *In Spain* doesn't seem very

interesting. It only gets one star.

M: Yes. Someone said the storyline is really boring.

W: _____ _____ what other people think about *The Man* starring Jim Smith.

M: Okay. Somebody mentioned that the ending is _____ _____ _____.

W: Umm... what else is on the list?

M: Look. This movie gets four stars. Many people are _____ _____.

W: *The Last Weekend*? Do you know what this movie is about?

M: It's a horror movie starring Sally Taylor.

W: Sorry. You know I can't _____ _____

_____.

M: Then why don't we just watch *The Man* tonight? You like Jim Smith.

W: All right.

6

M: (*excited*) Thank you! I _____ _____ I'm dreaming right now. Umm... just after reading the storyline, I knew it would be _____ _____ _____. But it wasn't an easy job, because I've never directed such a large-scale movie. I'd like to thank _____ _____ _____ _____, who helped me so much. Hey, Joe! You are the most talented music director _____ _____ _____! And thank you, Sam. You created such fantastic special effects. Well, all my actors and actresses, I really _____ _____ _____ _____. Oh, today is the best day of my life!

Listening ⋆ Challenge Answers p. 7

A [1-2]

W: Last night, *Hollywood Report* _____ _____ _____ with Emma Winslet.

M: I didn't watch the show. What was the interview about?

W: About her _____ _____, *Drummer*.

M: What role does she play in it?

W: She plays a smart cop.

M: I can't wait to see it. When she _____ _____, _____ _____ in her last movie, she looked beautiful even in a uniform.

W: Oh, please stop! You've told me that _____ _____ 100 times.

M: Have I? Anyway, when is the movie released?

W: Next Friday. But there will be a red carpet event on Saturday at Mega Theater.

M: No! I _____ _____ _____ that day. I'll have to watch it on Sunday instead.

W: Sorry to hear that.

M: But... I can't _____ _____ _____ to see Emma. I'll cancel the appointment!

B [1-2]

W: Can I use your computer _____ _____ _____ _____? I want to know who won the Razzies.

M: What are the Razzies?

W: _____ _____ the Golden Raspberry Awards. You know the Academy Awards, right?

M: Of course. They're given to _____ _____ _____ and actors of the year.

W: Well, the Golden Raspberry Awards are given to the worst ones.

M: _____ _____!

W: Right. And the Razzies are held at the Roosevelt Hotel _____ _____ _____ the Academy Awards.

M: But the winners must be embarrassed. Do they _____ _____ to the ceremony?

W: Only a few people have ever showed up to the ceremony since the Razzies started in 1981.

M: They were _____ _____. Now I want to know the winners of this year.

W: Okay. Let's search the Internet.

Critical ⋆ Thinking Answers p. 7

M: I _____ _____ _____ at night watching the movie *Ice Age 3*. I'm so tired.

W: Did you go see a late-night movie?

M: No. I _____ _____ _____ _____
   for free.

W: What? You shouldn't do that!

M: Why not? I don't want to be bothered with
   going to the theater.

W: Don't you know you're _____ _____?
   It's like stealing someone else's things.

M: But everybody does it.

W: That's not important.

M: Come on. It's not _____ _____
   _____. I can't watch several movies a
   month with my pocket money.

W: But you should know that it costs a lot of
   money to _____ _____ _____.

M: Haven't you ever downloaded a movie file
   for free?

W: No. If we keep downloading, nobody will
   want to make movies. I don't want to

   _____ _____ _____.

UNIT 10 Jobs

Listening * **Practice**   Answers p. 8

1

M: Let's go see the movie, *First Kiss*.

W: I heard that movie is _____ _____.

M: But I have to watch it. My sister prepared
   all the food that appears in the movie.

W: Is your sister a cook?

M: Not really. Her job is making food _____
   _____ in pictures and movies.

W: How does she do that?

M: The easiest way is to choose the right
   tableware, _____ _____ plates and
   spoons.

W: I see. I guess even a plate could make a
   meal look different.

M: And sometimes she _____ _____ to
   make a strawberry look redder.

W: That's funny. Does she only work in film
   making?

M: No. She _____ _____ TV shows and

writes books as well.

2

W: I'd like to work part-time, but I don't know

   _____ _____ _____.

M: What about working at a summer camp?

W: I've done it before, so I'd like to do

   _____ _____.

M: Then, you could write reviews after playing
   new video games. That would be fun.

W: Well... _____ _____ _____ _____
   games.

M: That's too bad. How about working at a
   fitness center?

W: As a personal trainer?

M: Right. I heard that job isn't _____

   _____.

W: That sounds interesting. I'll think about it.

M: Why don't you ask Bill about the job
   _____ _____? He already does that.

W: Really? I should call Bill, then.

M: Wait! I'm going to meet him for lunch
   now. _____ _____.

W: Thanks!

3

(Telephone rings.)

M: Hello.

W: Hello, Stanley. It's Jennifer.

M: Hey, _____ _____?

W: I heard you work at an amusement park
   these days. How's your work?

M: I'm very _____ _____ the work. It
   pays well, and I'm having a lot of fun.

W: Isn't it hard because of _____ _____
   _____?

M: Actually, it doesn't matter because I work
   indoors. But I do find it difficult to smile to
   customers _____ _____ _____.

W: Oh, I can imagine.

M: Anyway, why don't you visit me at work?

W: Actually, _____ _____ I'm calling. Can
   you give me a discount? I'm planning to
   go there next weekend.

M: Sure. I can give you _____ _____.

W: Thanks!

4

W: What do you want to be, Tim?

M: I want to be a _____ _____. What about you?

W: Well, I have no idea, so I'm very worried.

M: You should _____ _____ _____ when deciding your future job. First, think about what you're interested in.

W: Well, I like to travel and _____ _____.

M: And then consider what you're good at.

W: I'm good at writing. People say my essays are _____ _____ _____ and well-organized.

M: I agree. Finally, you must consider your personality.

W: I'm _____ _____ _____, so I want to do something active.

M: Then how about becoming a travel writer? You can write _____ _____ around the world.

W: Great!

5

M: Bella Department Store _____ _____ _____ personal shoppers. The job includes recommending proper clothes to our customers _____ _____ their job, age, and lifestyle. We only want graduates with a degree in fashion design. We also prefer _____ _____. If you are friendly, active and humorous, you'll be welcomed. _____ _____ aged 26 to 35 can apply. Please send your resume to our website www.bellastore.com _____ _____ _____. We'll let you know the result by email a week later.

6

W: You look busy, Michael.

M: I need to make a video resume to _____ _____ _____ _____ at Tiger Advertising Company.

W: I heard many companies require video resumes these days.

M: Right. But I don't know how to _____ _____ _____ _____. I don't want to just stand and introduce myself.

W: Yes, that would be boring. I think you must _____ _____ in a new, interesting way.

M: Do you have any idea?

W: What about making a resume _____ _____ _____ _____ for yourself?

M: That's a good idea!

W: Last month, there was a video resume contest held by Next Game Company. You could _____ _____ _____ from it.

M: Thanks a lot.

Listening ∗ Challenge   Answers p. 8

A [1-2]

W: When I _____ _____ at this company, I was really happy. This company is very famous and pays employees well. But soon I found it's not _____ _____ _____. I work in a marketing department and meet new people every single day. But I'm a shy person, so I _____ _____ doing my job. I'm sure it would be best for me to change jobs. Now I'm thinking of _____ _____ _____ in Italy. It was my old dream. But I'm worried it's too late to start a new life. Also, I don't _____ _____. I really can't decide what to do.

B [1-2]

W: Mr. Archer, you didn't _____ _____ interior design, did you?

M: No. My major is fashion design, but I worked for Sam's Interiors _____ _____ _____.

W: How was your job at Sam's?

M: I was often very busy, but I _____ _____ with good co-workers.

W: What projects did you participate in?

M: I designed the interiors of the W Mall and Best Stores.

W: What made you _____ _____ _____?

M: My dream is to be a hotel interior designer. But Sam's usually does mall interiors.

W: I see. Could you tell me about _____
_____?

M: I'm a creative person and I always try to
look on the bright side. And when a task
is given to me, I _____ _____ _____
to complete it.

W: What are your weaknesses?

M: Well, I'm not really humorous enough to
_____ _____ _____.

Critical ★ Thinking   Answers p. 8

W: What do you want to be in the future, Jack?

M: I wanted to be a pilot _____ _____,
but now I want to be a surgeon.

W: Oh, you want to help patients, right?

M: Honestly, that's _____ _____ _____.
I just want to earn huge amount of money.

W: What? Have you considered your _____
_____ _____?

M: Not really. I believe that having a lot of
money will _____ _____ _____.

W: Perhaps, but I don't think it's the most
important thing.

M: Then, what do you think is the most
important thing when _____ _____
_____, Amy?

W: I think people should choose a job they
can do well. So I want to be a teacher.

M: _____ _____ _____ the perfect job
for you.

UNIT 11 Culture

Listening ★ Practice   Answers p. 8

1

M: I saw a great documentary yesterday.

W: _____ _____ _____ _____?

M: It showed traditional wedding customs in
different countries.

W: Like what?

M: In America, for example, guests _____

_____ at the married couple. It's to wish
them to have many children and be rich.

W: Interesting.

M: And _____ _____, a bride's parents
put gold and silver coins in the bride's
shoes.

W: I see.

M: There's more. In Belgium, the bride _____
_____ _____ during the ceremony.
After, she hangs the handkerchief on the
wall of her house until someone in her
family _____ _____.

W: Sounds interesting. I'd like to watch that
documentary now. Which channel was it
on?

M: K-channel.

W: Great. I'll _____ _____ _____ from
the website.

2

M: Happy Travel would like to introduce a
_____ _____ _____. This special
package allows you to experience the
traditional culture of the Aborigines, the
_____ _____ of Australia. First, there's
a traditional dance show. You can join the
performers and dance on the stage. Next,
native people will teach you _____
_____ throw boomerangs and play a
traditional musical instrument called the
didgeridoo. It _____ _____ things
from nature, such as animals or wind. This
tour departs on Thursdays and returns on
Tuesdays. The price is $3,000 for adults
and _____ _____ _____.

3

W: Are there any special table manners in
your country?

M: Yes. In China, _____ _____ to dinner,
you should not eat all of the food on your
plate.

W: Why is that?

M: Leaving some food means you were given
_____ _____ _____.

W: In Japan, leaving rice on the plate means

you want to eat more.

M: Interesting. Are there any other special
_____ _____ in Japan?

W: When invited to dinner, you should eat at
least two bowls of rice.

M: How about someone who _____
_____?

W: The bowl is small enough that anyone can
eat two.

M: I understand.

W: And when we have soup, we drink it
_____ _____ _____ _____. We eat
solid food from the soup with chopsticks.

4

W: Tim, I'm going to _____ _____ to see
the Taj Mahal.

M: Do you mean the beautiful white castle,
Cindy?

W: It's not a castle. _____ _____ _____
built by a king for his dead wife.

M: I didn't know that.

W: It was _____ _____ one of the World
Cultural Heritage sites by UNESCO.

M: World Cultural Heritage sites? How are
they selected?

W: They are sites which are old, unique or
_____ _____ _____ _____ in
world history. Like Angkor Wat or the
Tower of London.

M: I want to visit one of the World Cultural
Heritage sites.

W: Your aunt _____ _____ _____. Why
don't you visit the Great Wall? It's also a
World Cultural Heritage site.

M: Maybe I should go there _____ _____.

5

W: I'm going to tell you how Mexicans _____
_____ _____ New Year. The day
before New Year's Day, people sweep all
the dust out of their houses. They do this
to _____ _____ _____ bad luck from
the old year and make room for good luck
in the coming year. Also, they _____
_____ in their shoes to wish for wealth.

For women, wearing red underwear on
New Year's Day will _____ _____.
Yellow will bring money and white will
bring marriage.

6

M: Do you know that the shape of Thailand
_____ _____ an elephant's head? That
might be one of the reasons why elephants
are Thai people's _____ _____. Up
until 1917, the elephant was on the
national flag. Because of the great love
for elephants, there are _____ _____
about them in Thailand. Thai people
believe that passing under the belly of an
elephant makes wishes _____ _____.
To dream of holding an elephant in one's
arms means that good things will happen.
But _____ _____ getting an elephant
as a present means something unlucky
will happen.

Listening ★ Challenge   Answers p. 9

A [1-2]

W: Jack, here's an interesting article _____
_____ in various countries.

M: What's so interesting?

W: Well, Tibetans greet by pulling their ears
and _____ _____ their tongues.

M: That sounds funny.

W: Yes! And the Maoris of New Zealand greet
by _____ _____ _____ together.

M: Wow, that's friendly.

W: But the most interesting one is the Eskimo
greeting. They slap the other _____
_____.

M: If that happened to me without knowing
why, I would be really angry.

W: So would I!

M: So are you going to _____ _____
_____ today?

W: Yes, I am. Why?

M: I want to read it, too. It _____ _____
contain very interesting articles.

W: Oh, there are more on the shelf. So you can borrow one, too.

M: Really? Do you know _____ _____ it's in?

W: Yes. It's right there in the culture section.

M: Thanks.

B [1-2]

M: My Finnish friend suggested that we _____ _____ _____ _____ together. Isn't that strange?

W: Not really. Finns often invite others to the sauna to get to know them better.

M: Really?

W: Oh, yes. Finns _____ _____. They visit them at least once a week.

M: Why are saunas so popular here?

W: Well, Finland is _____ _____ _____. I guess saunas are the best way to feel warm in a short time.

M: Have you visited a sauna here in Finland?

W: Yes. Steam _____ _____ _____ pouring cold water over hot stones.

M: Interesting.

W: Also, saunas are usually near a cold lake. So, when Finns _____ _____ _____ in the sauna, they go and bathe in the lake.

M: I see.

W: And one more thing – don't miss out on sausages with beer while _____ _____ _____ at the sauna.

Critical ★ Thinking   Answers p. 9

M1: I'm Nick. Recently, a movement has begun to _____ _____. But bullfighting was started in the 17th century. Many Spanish people consider it a kind of art, _____ _____ _____ a national cultural heritage. As it's a long Spanish tradition, it should not be banned.

W: I'm Kate. _____ _____ _____ are killed every year because of bullfighting. Killing animals for people's pleasure isn't the _____ _____ to do. Keeping a

country's tradition and cultural heritage cannot be an excuse for _____ _____.

M2: I'm Jason. Many tourists expect to watch bullfighting in Spain. Bullfighting is a big part of the Spanish _____ _____. It really helps our country's economic growth.

UNIT 12 IT

Listening ★ Practice   Answers p. 9

1

(*Telephone rings.*)

M: Hello?

W: Daniel, this is Sandy. Are you _____ _____?

M: No, I'm watching TV right now.

W: So you're not talking with me on messenger, right?

M: No. My computer _____ _____ _____.

W: Someone just asked me for money using your ID.

M: What? So did you send the money?

W: _____ _____ _____. The way he talked was a little different from you. So I called to check.

M: I heard that people have been _____ _____ _____ on messenger services using other people's ID and password these days.

W: So what should I do?

M: Save that message and call the police.

W: Okay. Don't forget to change your messenger password quickly.

2

M: What are you watching?

W: I'm watching an _____ _____ _____.

M: Is it good? I'm interested in taking online Chinese classes.

W: I'm quite satisfied with it. I think online classes are _____ _____ offline classes.

M: What makes you think so?

113

W: You can only attend a lecture once at an academy. But online, you can watch it

_____ _____ _____ _____ .

M: That's good. What else?

W: It's so much cheaper.

M: _____ _____ _____ _____ for a month?

W: Advanced and intermediate classes are $60. And beginner's classes are $50.

M: Wow, they're _____ _____ .

W: I'll send you a link to the site. You can preview a class for free.

M: That's great.

3

M: Is this your _____ _____ ? Can I look at it?

W: Sure.

M: Wow, you had your picture taken with Johnny Depp. Where did you meet him?

W: Actually, _____ _____ _____

_____ .

M: What are you talking about?

W: I edited the photo using the Photoshop program.

M: I can't believe it! And you look _____

_____ _____ in the photo.

W: It's also the power of technology. I cleaned up my skin and made my hair shiny.

M: No wonder! Did you learn _____

_____ _____ the program in school?

W: No, I studied on my own.

M: How?

W: There are many _____ _____ _____ teaching how to use Photoshop.

M: Great. Maybe I should learn how to use it.

4

W: Twitter is a kind of a blogging service. It allows users to _____ _____ from cell phones or messenger services as well as by visiting the site. On Twitter, the message must be _____ _____ 140 letters. You just simply write short comments on the board whenever you want. That's why Twitter is called _____ _____ _____ .

If you want to check out another person's messages, you should become his or her "follower." You _____ _____ a person's permission to be their follower. If you become someone's follower, messages that person writes are updated _____

_____ _____ _____ , too.

5

M: My computer suddenly _____ _____ . Maybe it's because it's too old.

W: Are you sure it isn't because there's not _____ _____ ?

M: I've checked it. It has enough space.

W: Did you open an unknown email?

M: No. Oh, I think it slowed down after I _____ _____ _____ from a friend.

W: That CD must've had a computer virus.

M: Should I go to the service center?

W: I'll teach you _____ _____ _____ . Buy a vaccine program online and run it on your computer.

M: Do you know any good sites that sell _____ _____ ? Let's find one now.

W: Okay. Type in www.vaccine11.com in the address bar. _____ _____ _____

_____ which vaccine program to buy.

M: Thanks.

6

M: What are you doing?

W: I'm _____ _____ _____ .

M: Are you updating your blog again?

W: No. I'm looking for photos for my science report. But they're _____ _____

_____ .

M: Why don't you try the NEclick site?

W: I've never heard about it. Is it a site that _____ _____ ?

M: No. It's where people upload pictures they took. They share photos and download them _____ _____ .

W: What about copyrights?

M: If you don't use it for business, it's okay.

W: For business?

M: Yes. _____ _____ , you can't use the

photos for books or advertisements.

W: Is there any way to use them for business?

M: Yes. You need to _____ _____ _____ of the picture and get their permission.

W: I see.

Listening ★ Challenge   Answers p. 9

A [1-2]

M: Recently, an American company researched _____ _____ _____ _____ to people when choosing a new cell phone. This research focused on two groups, people aged _____ _____ _____ and those aged 25 to 44. Both groups chose price as the most important thing and brand as the next. The older group chose _____ _____ _____ as the third most important factor, while the younger group chose battery life. Design was chosen _____ _____ _____ most important thing by the older group, while ease of use was chosen by the younger group. _____ _____ _____ chose battery life as least important, while the younger group chose design.

B [1-2]

M: What are you doing?

W: I'm uploading pictures and _____ _____ _____ I made onto my blog.

M: Wow, almost 1,000 people visited your blog today.

W: It's _____ _____ _____. It happens everyday.

M: Wow, I also have a blog, but not many people visit it. How can I make my blog _____ _____ ?

W: What's your blog about?

M: I post movie reviews.

W: Visit other blogs _____ _____ _____ and exchange information. For example, visit blogs about movie stars or entertainment.

M: Why should I do that?

W: Then they'll _____ _____ _____, too.

M: Oh, that's a good idea.

W: Also, you need to update your information often and _____ _____ _____ or media files.

M: But I'm not good at editing them.

W: It's easy. I'll _____ _____ _____.

M: Thanks a lot.

Critical ★ Thinking   Answers p. 9

M: Look! My game money is all gone. I haven't _____ _____ recently.

W: Someone might be playing online games with your ID. Did you lend it to someone?

M: Never. How _____ _____ _____ could someone find out my ID and password?

W: Have you saved them on a public computer before?

M: I think I have _____ _____ _____ _____. What should I do?

W: Change your ID and password right away.

M: Okay.

W: And _____ _____ _____ where you can report illegal ID use. Illegal use of another person's ID is common nowadays.

M: I didn't know it could happen to me.

W: To prevent it, make sure to log out so that your personal information _____ _____ _____ on public computers.

M: I wish I had known about this sooner. Then I wouldn't have lost my _____ _____.

115

JUNIOR
LISTENING EXPERT

A Theme-Based Listening Course for Young EFL Learners

Level 3

Answer Key

NE_ Neungyule

JUNIOR
LISTENING EXPERT

A Theme-Based Listening Course for Young EFL Learners

Answer Key

Level 3

UNIT 01 Love

Getting ★ Ready p. 8
A 1 ⓐ 2 ⓕ 3 ⓒ 4 ⓓ 5 ⓑ 6 ⓔ
B 1 ⓒ 2 ⓐ 3 ⓔ

Listening ★ Start p. 9
1 ③ / ask, out, where to take her, amusement park, too crowded, make the arrangements
2 (1) ⓓ (2) ⓑ (3) ⓒ / complained about, huge amounts of money, too nice, is ashamed of, break up with

Listening ★ Practice p. 10
1 ④　mQ1 ⓑ　2 ④　mQ2 ⓑ　3 ①　mQ3 ⓑ
4 ①　mQ4 ⓑ　5 ④　mQ5 ⓐ　6 ②　mQ6 ⓐ

Listening ★ Challenge p. 12
A 1 ①　2 ①　B 1 ④　2 ④

Critical ★ Thinking p. 13
1 ③　2 ③

Dictation
Listening ★ Practice p. 90
1 after college, What was that like, As you know, very good-looking
2 went out, very handsome, were supposed to, during the meal
3 school drama club, had the courage, introduced me, a few weeks before
4 in the picture, lived next door, funny stories, your first love, ten years
5 for some time, too busy, start fresh, play an instrument, Anything else
6 broke up with, surprise him, seeing someone else, feel sad, How about, have a great time

Listening ★ Challenge p. 91
A welcome to, Congratulations, very curious, at that time, played the leading characters, was attracted by
B against our marriage, In my country, happy together, cancel the wedding, trust you fully, No problem

Critical ★ Thinking p. 91
What's wrong, share everything, every time, what's his problem, always be respected, my privacy

UNIT 02 Shopping

Getting ★ Ready p. 14
A 1 ⓑ 2 ⓕ 3 ⓓ 4 ⓔ 5 ⓒ 6 ⓐ
B 1 ⓒ 2 ⓓ 3 ⓕ

Listening ★ Start p. 15
1 ④ / sold out, How long does it take, order one, could it be delivered, write down your address
2 (1) ⓒ (2) ⓑ (3) ⓐ / a pair of, My feet hurt, a variety of, at low prices, buy groceries

Listening ★ Practice p. 16
1 ④　mQ1 ⓒ　2 ④　mQ2 ⓐ　3 ②　mQ3 ⓐ, ⓒ
4 ①　mQ4 ⓑ　5 ②, ④　mQ5 ⓑ　6 ③　mQ6 ⓐ

Listening ★ Challenge p. 18
A 1 ④　2 ②　B 1 ②　2 ③

Critical ★ Thinking p. 19
1 ②　2 (1) ⓑ (2) ⓒ

Dictation
Listening ★ Practice p. 92
1 asked for, comes in, beige or green, Hurry up, right now
2 Are you being helped, something wrong, skirt section, this yellow one, How much is it

2

3 at low prices, various clothes, We're located at, pictures of the market

4 Can I exchange it, looks good on you, I'd like to, bring the receipt, come back

5 Look at, enough money, a garage sale, What should we sell, your accessories, instead of

6 economy is bad, cheaper luxury items, In the 1930s, went down, almost doubled

Listening ★ Challenge p. 93

A far from, having a sale, I've never bought, at one time, discount coupon, look at

B I'm looking for, would like, What colors, about two days, deliver it, Let's see

Critical ★ Thinking p. 93

Is it new, must have spent, because of, for a long time, they're worth it

UNIT 03 Parties

Getting ★ Ready p. 20
A 1 ⓐ **2** ⓓ **3** ⓕ **4** ⓒ **5** ⓑ **6** ⓔ
B 1 ⓔ **2** ⓕ **3** ⓒ

Listening ★ Start p. 21
1 (1) ⓒ, ⓔ (2) ⓑ (3) ⓓ / throw a potluck party, What should I cook, make a tuna salad, six bottles of, just in case
2 ① / Can I speak to, What's up, I'll be there, Stop teasing me, as nicely as you can

Listening ★ Practice p. 22
1 (1) Not Good (2) Good (3) Not Good
mQ1 ⓐ **2** ③ mQ2 ⓐ, ⓒ **3** ①, ② mQ3 ⓑ
4 ③ mQ4 ⓐ **5** (1) ⓒ (2) ⓑ (3) ⓐ mQ5 ⓑ
6 (1) Good (2) Bad (3) So-so mQ6 (1) F
(2) T

Listening ★ Challenge p. 24
A 1 ② **2** ③ **B 1** ③ **2** ①, ③

Critical ★ Thinking p. 25
1 (1) Against (2) For (3) Against
2 (1) ⓒ (2) ⓐ (3) ⓑ

Dictation

Listening ★ Practice p. 94

1 keep in mind, more than, one or two, within 24 hours

2 on the weekend, it's a party, popular tradition, Baby clothes, a pair of, can't wait to see

3 Are you free, Of course, bring some snacks, dance to, prefer juice

4 coming back, send invitations, her favorite food, a little present

5 unique costumes, so scary, by his side, dressed like, looked very funny

6 stop laughing, for two weeks, painted pink, Not really, wasn't that great

Listening ★ Challenge p. 95

A assistant party planner, is located at, each party, job's hours, be good at, by May 4th

B special Christmas party, such as, collected money, at 5 p.m., support poor children

Critical ★ Thinking p. 95

children's birthday parties, can afford, To some parents, throwing expensive parties, feel unhappy

UNIT 04 Health

Getting ★ Ready p. 26
A 1 ⓕ **2** ⓓ **3** ⓒ **4** ⓐ **5** ⓑ **6** ⓔ
B 1 ⓒ **2** ⓑ **3** ⓔ

3

★　★

Listening ★ Start p. 27

1 ①, ② / gaining weight, skip breakfast, finish a meal, you're full, used to eat, in calories

2 (1) ⓑ (2) ⓓ (3) ⓐ / Let me introduce you, lots of, have a cold, tastes good, improve your memory

Listening ★ Practice p. 28

1 ② mQ1 ⓐ 2 ①, ③ mQ2 ⓑ 3 ③ mQ3 ⓐ
4 ③ mQ4 ⓐ 5 ④ mQ5 ⓒ 6 (1) T (2) F
(3) F mQ6 ⓑ

Listening ★ Challenge p. 30

A 1 ① 2 ① B 1 ③ 2 ①

Critical ★ Thinking p. 31

1 ④ 2 (1) ⓒ (2) ⓑ

Dictation

Listening ★ Practice p. 96

1 I'm glad, thanks to, What's your secret, eat lightly, healthier than

2 play computer games, shoulder pain, Like this, to the back, hold your ankles, get better

3 got worse, catch the flu, get a high fever

4 have a headache, gets worse, in the office, cause problems, turn up, warm water

5 go to the movies, lose weight, relieving stress, Which class, another time

6 get hot easily, What is that, vegetables like, the most, out of your body, on the way home

Listening ★ Challenge p. 97

A supporting our weight, between the toes, wear socks, in the shoes, with a cushion

B work out, lose weight, sign up for, May 14th, 10% discount

Critical ★ Thinking p. 98

on a diet, start dieting, Skipping meals, gain back, even though, a healthy diet

UNIT 05 Transportation & Location

Getting ★ Ready p. 32

A 1 ⓔ 2 ⓒ 3 ⓖ 4 ⓗ 5 ⓑ 6 ⓐ
B 1 ⓑ 2 ⓓ 3 ⓐ

Listening ★ Start p. 33

1 ③ / Where to, will it take, due to, traffic jam, because of roadwork, Why don't you call

2 ③ / Similar to a motorcycle, three wheels, Along with a driver, no doors, other vehicles

Listening ★ Practice p. 34

1 ③ mQ1 ⓑ 2 ② mQ2 ⓑ 3 ② mQ3 ⓒ
4 ③ mQ4 (1) F (2) T 5 ② mQ5 ⓒ 6 (1) ⓓ
(2) ⓐ (3) ⓑ mQ6 ⓑ

Listening ★ Challenge p. 36

A 1 ② 2 ② B 1 ② 2 ④

Critical ★ Thinking p. 37

1 (1) For (2) For (3) Against
2 (1) ⓐ (2) ⓒ (3) ⓑ

Dictation

Listening ★ Practice p. 98

1 how to get to, this evening, direct bus, from the bus stop, Take a subway, About 40 minutes

2 on my way to, where it meets, on your right, a bit late

3 Have you finished, write about, That would be great, possible danger, worry more about, imagined a car

4 enjoyed your flight, in about 15 minutes, your seats, ten minutes past six

5 buy a ticket, departure times, What's the price, depend on, take a cabin seat

6 take a trip, At first, find another option, departs London, saving money

4

Listening ★ Challenge **p. 99**

A where are you, find the bakery, go back, on my left, at the corner, on your right, Hurry up

B different standards, studying their passengers, maintain the temperature, colder than, more blankets

Critical ★ Thinking **p. 100**

pollute the air, bicycle lanes, kind of vehicle, protect our citizens, along the roads

UNIT **06** Money

Getting ★ Ready p. 38
A 1 ⓒ **2** ⨍ **3** ⓔ **4** ⑨ **5** ⓐ **6** ⓑ
B 1 ⓒ **2** ⓐ **3** ⓓ

Listening ★ Start p. 39
1 ③ / working part-time, borrow money, a small amount of money, gets pocket money, how to tell him
2 ① / regular pocket money, how to manage money, different kinds of items, It'll help him, what if, cleaning out the garage

Listening ★ Practice p. 40
1 ② mQ1 ⓐ **2** ② mQ2 ⓑ **3** ② mQ3 ⓐ
4 ① mQ4 ⓐ **5** ④ mQ5 (1) Short (2) Heavy
6 ① mQ6 ⓒ

Listening ★ Challenge p. 42
A 1 ③ **2** ② **B 1** ③ **2** ③

Critical ★ Thinking p. 43
1 (1) Against (2) For (3) For
2 (1) ⓐ (2) ⓑ (3) ⓒ

Dictation

Listening ★ Practice **p. 100**

1 are you ready for, need to, use the pound, their own, what's the exchange rate
2 pocket money, record your spending, cut down, easy to use, check it out
3 Credit cards, at the time, with cash, every month, There's a charge
4 working part-time, per hour, at least, get a new job, I think I should
5 interesting article, Is there any reason, taller people, as well, short but handsome
6 collecting coins, other cultures, has a high value, unique design, in good condition

Listening ★ Challenge **p. 101**

A online shopping mall, teenage girls, I'd like to, have a point, I agree

B traveling around the world, changed my mind, think of, people in need, more important

Critical ★ Thinking **p. 102**

playing the lottery, false hope, so that, wasting my money, win the lottery

UNIT **07** Travel

Getting ★ Ready p. 44
A 1 ⓒ **2** ⓐ **3** ⓑ **4** ⓕ **5** ⓓ **6** ⓔ
B 1 ⓔ **2** ⓕ **3** ⓓ

Listening ★ Start p. 45
1 (1) Bad (2) Good (3) Good / went to, really crowded, the best place, During the discount season, was able to enjoy, really delicious
2 ③ / get on, woke up, get to the airport, take my eyes off, quickly checked in

5

★　★

Listening ★ Practice p. 46
1 ① mQ1 ⓑ 2 ④ mQ2 ⓐ 3 (1) ⓒ (2) ⓑ
(3) ⓐ mQ3 (1) T (2) F 4 ③ mQ4 ⓐ, ⓒ
5 (1) 2 (2) 1 (3) 1 mQ5 ⓐ 6 ①, ③ mQ6 ⓐ

Listening ★ Challenge p. 48
A 1 ② 2 ④ B 1 ①, ③ 2 ④

Critical ★ Thinking p. 49
1 ① 2 ①, ④

Dictation

Listening ★ Practice p. 102
1 in room 706, it wasn't working, call the
  repairman, fully booked, during the repair
2 According to, It says so, Read that sign,
  half an hour, how to find, where to eat
3 Let me recommend, on the 52nd floor,
  there's an observatory, man-made island,
  at night
4 I'm planning, Don't miss, some tips,
  instead of, drank free water, by a bicycle
5 how much to tip, their main wage, leave
  5%, on the bed
6 trip to Europe, had my wallet stolen, That's
  not all, a lot of troubles, any free time

Listening ★ Challenge p. 104
A from my country, as a traveler, some
  good places, I've heard about it, takes two
  hours, Thanks for the information
B any cold medicine, a sore throat, one
  more blanket, available seat, just leave it,
  comfortable seat

Critical ★ Thinking p. 104
stay at, Why don't you, they're cleaner, have
to carry, exchange travel information, very
often

UNIT 08 Advice

Getting ★ Ready p. 50
A 1 ⓐ 2 ⓒ 3 ⓕ 4 ⓑ 5 ⓓ 6 ⓖ
B 1 ⓔ 2 ⓒ 3 ⓕ

Listening ★ Start p. 51
1 ③ / used to, going out with, many things to
  do, listen to me, if I'm late
2 ② / you were accepted by, major in, in that
  field, it would be better, miss the chance

Listening ★ Practice p. 52
1 ③ mQ1 ⓐ 2 ③ mQ2 ⓐ 3 ④ mQ3 ⓑ
4 ② mQ4 ⓐ 5 ③ mQ5 ⓐ 6 ④ mQ6 ⓑ

Listening ★ Challenge p. 54
A 1 ② 2 ④ B 1 ② 2 ③

Critical ★ Thinking p. 55
1 ④ 2 (1) ⓒ (2) ⓐ

Dictation

Listening ★ Practice p. 105
1 last night, used to, What should I wear,
  long-sleeved shirts, the best choice, gray
  striped shirt
2 applied to, the most well-known, my major,
  I guess so, a bigger company
3 late for, make her worried, share
  everything, trust her, at the university
4 did some research, You know, a bit boring,
  The most important thing, It's not good,
  make students interested
5 worry about, get advice, living in
  California, for free, On Saturdays
6 such a great honor, dance so well, the
  same thing, every single day

Listening ★ Challenge p. 106
A for a second, saw him shoplifting, for fun,
  say anything, kept silent, what's best for

him

B taking a test, test anxiety, prepared for, To avoid, be afraid of

Critical ★ Thinking **p. 106**
what to do, study together, I've talked with, used to, any useful advice, more than anyone else

Getting ★ Ready p. 56
A 1 ⓒ **2** ⓔ **3** ⓐ **4** ⓓ **5** ⓕ **6** ⓑ
B 1 ⓑ **2** ⓕ **3** ⓐ

Listening ★ Start p. 57
1 (1) ⓑ (2) ⓓ (3) ⓒ / robots or space, meet aliens someday, watch funny movies, relieve stress, scary and thrilling, what will happen
2 ① / going to the cinema, main character, how the movie ends, you blew it, avoid movie spoilers, important events

Listening ★ Practice p. 58
1 ④ mQ1 ⓑ **2** ① mQ2 ⓐ **3** (1) 0 (2) 2 (3) 3 mQ3 ⓑ **4** (1) ⓑ (2) ⓒ (3) ⓐ mQ4 ⓐ
5 ① mQ5 ⓑ **6** ② mQ6 ⓑ

Listening ★ Challenge p. 60
A 1 ② **2** ③ **B 1** ③ **2** ③

Critical ★ Thinking p. 61
1 ①, ④ **2** ③

Dictation
Listening ★ Practice **p. 107**
1 What movie, sold out, several tickets left, not yet, prefer screen 4, buying some popcorn

2 the most loved actresses, became very popular, in a play, During her later life
3 Thanks for calling, on screen two, please press one, your reservation, speak to an operator
4 at the box office, ranked fifth, take time, follows along, the first one
5 Let's see, a bit disappointing, recommending it, watch scary scenes
6 feel like, a great movie, all of my staff, in the world, appreciate your hard work

Listening ★ Challenge **p. 108**
A showed an interview, new movie, played a basketball player, at least, have an appointment, miss a chance
B for a short while, It means, the best movies, That's interesting, the night before, show up, very brave

Critical ★ Thinking **p. 108**
stayed up late, downloaded the movie file, violating copyright, a big deal, make a movie, let that happen

Getting ★ Ready p. 62
A 1 ⓓ **2** ⓑ **3** ⓒ **4** ⓐ **5** ⓔ **6** ⓕ
B 1 ⓐ **2** ⓑ **3** ⓒ

Listening ★ Start p. 63
1 ③ / deal with, raise the pet, On average, sound great, graduate from
2 (1) ⓓ (2) ⓒ (3) ⓕ / work with, study music carefully, what's going on, get pain, find out, what kinds of games

Listening ★ Practice p. 64
1 ② mQ1 ⓒ **2** ④ mQ2 ⓑ **3** ③ mQ3 ⓐ

4 ③ mQ4 ⓒ **5** ① mQ5 (1) F (2) T **6** ②
mQ6 ⓑ

Listening ★ Challenge p. 66
A 1 ② **2** ① **B 1** ④ **2** ④

Critical ★ Thinking p. 67
1 ② **2** (1) ⓑ (2) ⓐ

Dictation
Listening ★ Practice p. 109
1 really boring, look delicious, such as, uses
lipstick, works for
2 what to do, something new, I'm not good
at, so difficult, in detail, Join us
3 what's up, satisfied with, the hot weather,
all day long, that's why, 50% off
4 math teacher, consider several things, take
pictures, easy to read, full of energy, while
traveling
5 is looking for, according to, experienced
workers, Any women, by July 21st
6 apply for a job, make my video unique,
advertise yourself, like a TV advertisement,
get some ideas

Listening ★ Challenge p. 110
A started working, what I wanted, feel
uncomfortable, learning to cook, speak
Italian
B major in, for three years, enjoyed working,
quit the job, your personality, do my best,
make people laugh

Critical ★ Thinking p. 111
at first, not the reason, interest or personality,
make me happy, choosing a job, That sounds
like

UNIT **11** Culture

Getting ★ Ready p. 68
A 1 ⓔ **2** ⓐ **3** ⓑ **4** ⓓ **5** ⓕ **6** ⓒ
B 1 ⓔ **2** ⓒ **3** ⓕ

Listening ★ Start p. 69
1 ④ / English tradition, in the 19th century,
hungry after lunch, consisted of, their busy
schedules
2 ④ / what's wrong with you, gestured okay,
index finger, mean something bad, It's
interesting, got upset

Listening ★ Practice p. 70
1 (1) ⓒ (2) ⓐ (3) ⓑ mQ1 ⓒ **2** ④ mQ2 ⓑ
3 (1) ⓒ (2) ⓐ mQ3 ⓑ **4** (1) ⓐ (2) ⓓ
mQ4 ⓐ **5** ② mQ5 ⓒ **6** (1) Good (2) Good
(3) Bad mQ6 (1) T (2) F

Listening ★ Challenge p. 72
A 1 ② **2** ① **B 1** ④ **2** (1) F (2) F (3) T

Critical ★ Thinking p. 73
1 (1) For (2) Against (3) For
2 (1) ⓓ (2) ⓒ (3) ⓑ

Dictation
Listening ★ Practice p. 111
1 What was it about, throw rice, in Sweden,
holds a handkerchief, gets married,
download the show
2 new tour package, native people, how to,
sounds like, $2,000 for children
3 when invited, enough to eat, table
manners, eats lightly, out of the bowl
4 travel India, It's a tomb, chosen as, related
to important events, lives in Beijing, this
summer
5 get ready for, get rid of, put coins, bring
love
6 looks like, favorite animals, many

superstitions, come true, dreaming of

Listening ★ Challenge p. 112
A about greetings, sticking out, pressing
  their noses, person's cheek, borrow that
  magazine, seems to, which section
B go to the sauna, love saunas, a cold country,
  is made by, get too hot, taking a break

Critical ★ Thinking p. 113
stop bullfighting, as well as, Thousands of
bulls, right thing, killing animals, tourism
industry

UNIT 12 IT

Getting ★ Ready p. 74
A 1 ⓗ 2 ⓒ 3 ⓕ 4 ⓖ 5 ⓐ 6 ⓔ
B 1 ⓕ 2 ⓑ 3 ⓓ

Listening ★ Start p. 75
1 ③ / laptop computer, making presentations,
  care about the price, it shouldn't be
  noisy, after-sales service, national brand
  computers
2 ② / Internet addiction, among teenagers,
  a fixed amount of time, special software,
  place your computer, find hobbies

Listening ★ Practice p. 76
1 ④ mQ1 ⓐ 2 ③ mQ2 ⓐ 3 ① mQ3 ⓒ
4 ① mQ4 ⓑ 5 ① mQ5 ⓐ 6 ④ mQ6 ⓑ

Listening ★ Challenge p. 78
A 1 (1) ⓐ (2) ⓒ (3) ⓑ 2 ② B 1 ③ 2 ②

Critical ★ Thinking p. 79
1 ③ 2 ④

Dictation
Listening ★ Practice p. 113
1 on messenger, isn't even on, Of course
  not, asking for money
2 online Chinese lecture, better than, over
  and over again, How much is it, really
  cheap
3 photo album, I've never met him, so much
  prettier, how to use, free Internet sites
4 upload messages, less than, a mini blog,
  don't need, on your Twitter page
5 slowed down, enough memory, ran a CD,
  what to do, vaccine programs, I'll let you
  know
6 surfing the Internet, hard to find, sells
  photos, for free, For example, contact the
  owner

Listening ★ Challenge p. 115
A what is most important, 18 to 24, ease of
  use, as the fourth, The older group
B recipes of food, no big deal, more popular,
  with similar topics, visit your blog, upload
  some photographs, teach you how

Critical ★ Thinking p. 115
logged in, in the world, in a school library,
visit a site, won't be saved, game money

9

UNIT 01 Love

Getting ★ Ready p. 8

A 1 ⓐ 2 ⓕ 3 ⓒ 4 ⓓ 5 ⓑ 6 ⓔ
B 1 ⓒ 2 ⓐ 3 ⓔ

B 1 남: 너 아직 첫사랑과 사귀고 있니?
　　여: 응. 벌써 10년이 되었어.

　2 남: 처음에 남자 친구의 어떤 점이 좋았던 거야?
　　여: 그 애의 좋은 매너에 끌렸어.

　3 남: 너는 Jack과 언제 가까워지게 된 거야?
　　여: 2006년에 'Happy Family'를 찍는 동안에.

Listening ★ Start p. 9

1 ③ / ask, out, where to take her, amusement park, too crowded, make the arrangements
2 (1) ⓓ (2) ⓑ (3) ⓒ / complained about, huge amounts of money, too nice, is ashamed of, break up with

1

M: I'm going to ask Jenny out on a date this weekend.
W: Really? Good for you. You finally found the courage.
M: But I can't decide where to take her. Do you have any suggestions?
W: Hmm... how about an amusement park? It would be fun and exciting.
M: Shouldn't I choose a more romantic place? An amusement park might be too crowded.
W: In that case, how about taking her for a riverboat ride?
M: That is a good idea. I must go now to make the arrangements.
W: Don't forget to bring her some beautiful flowers.
M: Right. Thanks a lot.

남: 이번 주말에 Jenny에게 데이트 신청을 할 거야.
여: 정말? 잘되었네. 마침내 용기를 냈구나.
남: 하지만 그 애를 어디로 데리고 갈지 결정하지 못했어. 제안할만한 거 있니?
여: 음… 놀이 공원은 어때? 재밌고 신날 거야.
남: 좀 더 로맨틱한 장소를 골라야 하지 않을까? 놀이 공원은 너

무 북적거릴 거야.
여: 그렇다면 강에서 유람선을 타는 것이 어때?
남: 좋은 생각이다. 그럼 가서 준비를 해야겠어.
여: 예쁜 꽃을 주는 것도 잊지 마.
남: 알았어. 정말 고마워.

어휘
ask ~ out (on a date) ~에게 데이트 신청하다　finally [fáinəli] ⊕ 마침내　courage[kɔ́ːridʒ] ⑲ 용기
suggestion[səgdʒéstʃən] ⑲ 제안　amusement park 놀이 공원　romantic[roumǽntik] ⑲ 낭만적인　crowded [kráudid] ⑲ 붐비는　in that case 그런 경우라면
riverboat[rívərbòut] ⑲ 유람선, 강에서 타는 배　ride[raid] ⑲ 탐, 타고 감　arrangement[əréindʒmənt] ⑲ 준비

문제 해설
Q: 남자가 이번 주말에 갈 곳은?
　　남자는 로맨틱한 데이트를 위해 유람선을 타기로 결정했다.

2

W: Yesterday, I met three of my friends, Emily, Michelle, and Cindy. They complained about their boyfriends. As a famous fund manager, Emily's boyfriend earns huge amounts of money. But he is so busy that Emily can't see him often. Michelle's boyfriend is tall and handsome, but Michelle is worried that he is too nice to other women. Cindy's boyfriend is a smart surgeon, but Cindy is ashamed of his poor fashion style. Surprisingly, none of my friends wants to break up with her boyfriend!

여: 전 어제 세 명의 친구들 Emily와 Michelle, Cindy를 만났어요. 그 애들은 본인들의 남자 친구에 대해서 불평했어요. 유명한 펀드매니저인 Emily의 남자 친구는 아주 많은 돈을 벌어요. 하지만 그가 너무 바빠서 Emily는 그를 자주 만날 수가 없어요. Michelle의 남자 친구는 키가 크고 잘생겼지만 Michelle은 그가 다른 여자들에게 너무 친절해서 걱정이에요. Cindy의 남자 친구는 유능한 외과 의사인데 Cindy는 그의 패션 감각이 떨어지는 것이 부끄럽대요. 놀랍게도 제 친구들 중 아무도 남자 친구와 헤어지길 원하진 않아요!

어휘
complain[kəmpléin] ⑧ 불평하다　fund manager 펀드 매니저　earn[əːrn] ⑧ (돈을) 벌다　huge[hjuːdʒ] ⑲ 거대한; *막대한　smart[smɑːrt] ⑲ 유능한, 똑똑한　surgeon [sə́ːrdʒən] ⑲ 외과 의사　be ashamed of ~을 부끄러워하다　surprisingly[sərpráiziŋli] ⊕ 놀랍게도　break up with ~와 헤어지다

10

문제 해설

Q: 각 여자가 자신의 남자 친구에 대해서 좋아하지 <u>않는</u> 점은?

(1) Emily는 남자 친구가 바빠서 자주 만날 수 없다고 했다.

(2) Michelle은 남자 친구가 다른 여자들에게 친절한 것이 걱정스럽다고 했다.

(3) Cindy는 남자 친구의 패션 감각이 좋지 못하다는 점을 말했다.

Listening ★ Practice   p. 10

1 ④   mQ1 ⓑ   2 ④   mQ2 ⓑ   3 ①   mQ3 ⓑ
4 ①   mQ4 ⓑ   5 ④   mQ5 ⓐ   6 ②   mQ6 ⓐ

1

M: Mom, how did you and Dad first meet?

W: Well, I got my first job at a company after college, and your dad was my boss.

M: Wow, so was it an office romance?

W: Yes, it was.

M: What was that like?

W: Well, it was difficult to find time to date behind everyone's back!

M: So what did you like about Dad?

W: As you know, he was very tall and good-looking. But most of all, I was attracted by his great sense of humor.

M: Okay. But I don't know whether he was very good-looking.

W: Your father was and still is the most handsome man in my life.

M: Oh, Mom!

남: 엄마, 엄마랑 아빠는 처음에 어떻게 만났어요?

여: 음, 대학 졸업하고 첫 직장으로 회사에 들어갔는데 네 아빠가 상사였단다.

남: 와, 그럼 사내 연애였어요?

여: 응, 그랬지.

남: 어땠어요?

여: 음, 아무도 모르게 데이트를 할 시간을 내기가 힘들었지!

남: 아빠의 어떤 점이 좋았는데요?

여: 알다시피 아빠는 키가 크고 잘생겼었지. 하지만 무엇보다도 아빠의 유머 감각이 뛰어난 것에 끌렸지.

남: 그렇군요. 그런데 아빠가 아주 잘생겼는지는 모르겠는데요.

여: 네 아빠는 예전에도 그랬고 아직도 내 인생에서 최고로 잘생긴 사람이란다.

남: 아, 엄마!

어휘

college[kɑ́lidʒ] 몡 대학 boss[bɔːs] 몡 상사 office romance 사내 연애 behind one's back ~가 모르게

good-looking[gúdlúkiŋ] 혱 잘생긴 most of all 무엇보다도 be attracted by ~에 끌리다 a sense of humor 유머 감각 still[stil] 뷔 아직도 [문제] height[hait] 몡 키 appearance[əpí(ː)ərəns] 몡 외모

문제 해설

Q: 여자는 남편의 어떤 점이 가장 좋았나?

외모도 좋았지만 유머 감각 때문에 가장 끌렸다고 했다.

mQ1: 여자가 남편을 만난 곳은?

여자는 첫 직장에서 상사였던 남편을 만났다고 했다.

2

W: Yesterday, I went out with Mark, who is in my math class. I've never talked with him in class. But he's very handsome, so I was happy to go out with him. It took me hours to pick what outfit to wear for our date. We were supposed to meet in a restaurant at 7 p.m., but he showed up 30 minutes late. He didn't apologize for it. And during the meal, he talked only about himself. He even talked with his mouth full. It was such a terrible date.

여: 난 어제 수학 수업을 같이 받는 Mark와 데이트했어. 수업에서는 그 애랑 얘기해 본 적이 없었어. 그런데 그 애가 아주 잘생겨서 데이트를 하게 되어 기뻤지. 데이트에 입을 옷을 고르는 데 몇 시간이 걸렸어. 저녁 7시에 음식점에서 만나기로 했는데 그 애가 30분 늦게 나타났어. 그 애는 사과도 안 했어. 그리고 식사 중에는 자기 얘기만 했어. 심지어 입에 음식이 가득한 채로 얘기하는 거야. 정말 끔찍한 데이트였어.

어휘

go out (이성과) 사귀다; *데이트하다 pick[pik] 동 고르다 outfit[ɑ́utfit] 몡 옷, 의복 be supposed to-v ~하기로 되어 있다 show up 나타나다 apologize[əpɑ́lədʒàiz] 동 사과하다 with one's mouth full 입에 음식이 가득찬 채로 [문제] satisfied[sǽtisfàid] 혱 만족스러운 depressed[diprést] 혱 우울한 pleased[pliːzd] 혱 기쁜 disappointed[dìsəpɔ́intid] 혱 실망한 judge[dʒʌdʒ] 동 판단하다

문제 해설

Q: 소녀의 감정은 어떻게 바뀌었나?

소녀는 처음에는 잘생긴 친구와의 데이트에 흥분되는 마음이었다가 실제로 만나보고 실망했다.

mQ2: 상황을 가장 잘 묘사한 것은?

ⓐ 시작이 반이다.

ⓑ 책의 표지로 그 책을 판단하지 마라.

남자의 잘생긴 외모만으로 좋아했다가 실망한 내용이므로 겉모습만 보고 판단하지 말라는 말이 가장 적절하다.

3

M: Two years ago, I joined the school drama club and met Sandra. She was pretty and had a good personality, so I fell in love with her. But I've never had the courage to tell her my feelings. I was worried she would reject me. A couple of days ago, my best friend Leo introduced me to his new girlfriend. Surprisingly, his girlfriend was Sandra. I was really shocked. They said they met at a friend's birthday party a few weeks before. I know that I should forget her, but it's really hard.

남: 2년 전에 저는 교내 연극부에 들었고 Sandra를 만났습니다. 그녀는 예쁘고 성격이 좋아서 전 그녀를 사랑하게 되었죠. 그런데 그녀에게 제 감정을 말할 용기가 없었어요. 그 애가 절 거절할까 봐 걱정스러웠죠. 며칠 전에 제 가장 친한 친구인 Leo가 자신의 새 여자 친구를 제게 소개해 주었습니다. 놀랍게도 그의 여자 친구는 Sandra였습니다. 전 정말 충격을 받았어요. 그들은 몇 주 전에 친구 생일 파티에서 만났대요. 그녀를 잊어야 한다는 걸 알지만 정말 힘들어요.

어휘
join[dʒɔin] 동 가입하다 personality[pə̀rsənǽləti] 명 성격 fall in love with ~를 사랑하게 되다 reject[ridʒékt] 동 거절하다 a couple of 두 서넛의, 몇 개의 introduce[ìntrədjúːs] 동 소개하다 shocked[ʃɑkt] 형 충격을 받은 forget[fərɡét] 동 잊다 [문제] proposal[prəpóuzəl] 명 프로포즈 ex-girlfriend[éksɡə́ːrlfrènd] 명 전 여자 친구 blind date 소개팅

문제 해설
Q: 소년의 문제는?
① 그는 친구의 여자 친구를 좋아한다.
② 그는 여자들 앞에서 아주 수줍어한다.
③ 그가 좋아하는 여자가 그의 프로포즈를 거절했다.
④ 그는 학교에서 전 여자 친구를 봐야만 한다.
소년이 좋아하는 여자가 친구의 여자 친구가 된 것을 알고 힘들어하고 있다.

mQ3: 소년이 Sandra를 처음 만난 곳은?
소년이 들어간 연극부에서 Sandra를 처음으로 만났다고 했다.

4

M: Susan, who is this guy in the picture? Is he the college senior that you like these days?
W: No. He was my first love. He lived next door to me when I was in high school, but then his family moved away.
M: That's too bad. What did you like about him?
W: He was kind, and always told me funny stories about his friends.
M: I bet you were sad when his family moved.
W: You're right. What about you? Who was your first love?
M: My girlfriend Kelly.
W: What? You're still going out with your first love?
M: Yes. It's been ten years already.
W: Wow, that's amazing.

남: Susan, 사진 속의 이 사람은 누구야? 요즘 네가 좋아하는 대학 선배야?
여: 아니. 그 애는 내 첫사랑이었어. 내가 고등학교 다닐 때 이웃집에 살았는데, 그 후에 그의 가족이 이사를 가버렸어.
남: 안됐네. 그 애의 어떤 점이 좋았는데?
여: 그는 친절했고, 항상 친구들에 관한 재미있는 얘기를 해 줬어.
남: 그의 가족이 이사를 가서 너 참 슬펐겠다.
여: 맞아. 넌 어때? 네 첫사랑은 누구야?
남: 내 여자 친구 Kelly.
여: 뭐? 넌 아직도 첫사랑하고 사귀고 있단 말이야?
남: 응. 벌써 10년째야.
여: 와, 대단하다.

어휘
guy[gai] 명 녀석, 사람 senior[síːnjər] 명 선배 next door 이웃집에 move[muːv] 동 위치를 옮기다; *이사하다 already[ɔːlrédi] 부 벌써, 이미 amazing[əméiziŋ] 형 놀라운 [문제] ideal type 이상형 neighbor[néibər] 명 이웃

문제 해설
Q: 그들이 주로 이야기하고 있는 것은?
첫사랑을 어디에서 만났고 어떤 점을 좋아했는지 등 자신의 첫사랑에 대해 이야기하고 있다.

mQ4: 여자의 첫사랑은 누구였나?
여자의 첫사랑은 이웃집에 살고 있던 남자이다.

5

W: You haven't dated for some time. Don't you want to have a girlfriend?
M: Um, not now.
W: Why not? Are you too busy these days?
M: No. The reason is that I went out with my ex-girlfriend for a long time. It's hard to forget her.
W: I see. But I think you should start fresh.
M: Do you think so?
W: Of course. Tell me what your ideal type is. Do you still like tall girls who can play an instrument well?
M: No. I prefer short girls now. And I'd like to date a girl who enjoys sports.

12

W: Anything else?

M: Well, I don't really like the skinny type.

W: I see. I'll start looking!

여: 너 한동안 데이트를 안 했잖아. 여자 친구를 사귀고 싶지 않니?

남: 음, 지금은 아니야.

여: 왜 아냐? 요즘 너무 바쁘니?

남: 아니. 전 여자 친구와 오랜 시간 사귀어서 그래. 그녀를 잊기가 힘들어.

여: 그렇구나. 하지만 새롭게 시작해야 할 것 같은데.

남: 그렇게 생각하니?

여: 물론이지. 네 이상형이 뭔지 말해 봐. 아직도 악기를 잘 연주하는 키가 큰 여자를 좋아하니?

남: 아니. 이젠 작은 여자가 더 좋아. 그리고 스포츠를 즐기는 여자와 데이트하고 싶어.

여: 또 다른 것은?

남: 음, 아주 마른 타입은 정말 좋아하지 않아.

여: 알았어. 찾아보기 시작할게!

어휘

for some time 한동안   reason[ríːzən] 명 이유
fresh[freʃ] 부 새롭게   instrument[ínstrəmənt] 명 악기
prefer[prifə́ːr] 동 선호하다   skinny[skíni] 형 비쩍 마른,
앙상한   [문제] miss[mis] 동 놓치다; *그리워하다

문제 해설

Q: 남자의 이상형은?

남자는 키가 작고 너무 마르지 않으며 스포츠를 좋아하는 여자가 이상형이라고 했다.

mQ5: 남자가 아무와도 사귀고 있지 않았던 이유는?

ⓐ 아직도 전 여자 친구를 그리워한다.

ⓑ 자신이 좋아하는 사람을 찾지 못했다.

남자는 전 여자 친구와 오랜 시간을 사귀었기 때문에 잊기가 힘들다고 말했다.

6

W: I broke up with my boyfriend last weekend.

M: What happened?

W: Well, I wanted to surprise him, so I went to his company last Friday.

M: What a nice idea!

W: Yes. But he came out holding some other woman's hand. He was seeing someone else!

M: He's really a bad guy. You made the right decision to break up with him.

W: Maybe. But I feel sad now.

M: Cheer up! You don't have to feel depressed because of him.

W: But it's not easy.

M: How about going to an amusement park today? It'll cheer you up.

W: Well... I don't know.

M: Come on, I promise we'll have a great time there.

W: Okay. You're a really good friend.

여: 지난 주말에 남자 친구와 헤어졌어.

남: 무슨 일이 있었어?

여: 음, 그를 놀라게 해 주려고 지난주 금요일에 그의 회사에 갔었어.

남: 멋진 생각인걸!

여: 그래. 그런데 그가 어떤 다른 여자의 손을 잡고 나오는 거야. 다른 사람을 만나고 있었던 거야!

남: 아주 나쁜 사람이구나. 헤어지기로 한 건 잘 결정한 거야.

여: 아마도. 하지만 지금은 슬퍼.

남: 기운 내! 그 사람 때문에 네가 우울해할 필요가 없어.

여: 하지만 그게 쉽지 않아.

남: 오늘 놀이 공원에 가는 게 어때? 기분이 좋아질 거야.

여: 음… 모르겠어.

남: 가자, 즐거운 시간이 될 거라는 걸 약속해.

여: 좋아. 넌 참 좋은 친구야.

어휘

surprise[sərpráiz] 동 놀라게 하다   see[siː] 동 데이트하다
decision[disíʒən] 명 결정   maybe[méibi] 부 아마도
[문제] treat[triːt] 동 *대우하다; 다루다

문제 해설

Q: 여자가 남자 친구와 헤어진 이유는?

① 그가 그녀를 막 대했다.

② 그가 다른 사람과 사귀고 있었다.

③ 그녀가 다른 사람을 사랑하게 되었다.

④ 그들은 서로 만날 시간이 없었다.

남자 친구가 다른 사람을 사귀고 있다는 사실을 알고 여자가 헤어지기로 결심했다.

mQ6: 남자가 여자와 함께 놀이 공원에 가고자 하는 이유는?

ⓐ 그녀의 기분을 나아지게 하려고

ⓑ 그녀에게 남자를 소개해 주려고

남자 친구와 헤어진 후에 슬퍼하고 있는 여자의 기분이 나아질 수 있게 놀이 공원에 가자고 했다.

Listening ★ Challenge   p. 12

A 1 ① 2 ①   B 1 ④ 2 ④

A [1-2]

W: This is *TBN's Entertainment News*. Mickey Brown, welcome to the show.

M: Hello.

W: Everyone was surprised when you announced your marriage to Silvia

13

yesterday. Congratulations.

M: Thank you.

W: So when did you first meet your fiancée? The viewers are very curious about it.

M: We first met in 2004 while working together on the movie *Rain*. We weren't close at that time because Silvia is very shy around new people.

W: So did you become close while filming *Happy Family* in 2006? You two played the leading characters.

M: Yes. We started dating after that movie.

W: What do you like about Silvia, besides her beautiful appearance?

M: I was attracted by her positive personality and sense of humor.

W: Thank you for the interview. Our viewers and I wish you a happy life with her.

여: 'TBN 연예 뉴스'입니다. Mickey Brown 씨, 프로그램에 나와주셔서 감사합니다.

남: 안녕하세요.

여: 어제 Silvia 씨와의 결혼을 발표하셔서 모두가 놀랐는데요. 축하합니다.

남: 고맙습니다.

여: 그럼 약혼녀를 언제 처음 만났나요? 시청자 분들이 아주 궁금해하세요.

남: 2004년에 함께 'Rain'이란 영화를 작업하면서 처음 만났어요. Silvia가 낯을 많이 가려서 그때는 친하지가 않았어요.

여: 그럼 2006년에 'Happy Family'를 찍으면서 가까워진 건가요? 두 분이 주연을 맡았었죠.

남: 네. 그 영화 후에 데이트를 하기 시작했어요.

여: Silvia 씨의 아름다운 외모 이외에 어떤 점이 좋으세요?

남: 그녀의 긍정적인 성격과 유머 감각에 끌렸어요.

여: 인터뷰를 해 주셔서 감사합니다. 시청자 분들과 저는 두 분이 행복하시길 빌겠습니다.

어휘

entertainment[èntərtéinmənt] 몡 연예　announce [ənáuns] 통 발표하다　marriage[mǽridʒ] 몡 결혼　Congratulations. 축하합니다.　fiancée[fi:ɑːnséi] 몡 약혼녀　viewer[vjúːər] 몡 시청자　film[film] 통 영화를 찍다　leading character 주연　besides[bisáidz] 전 ~외에　positive[pázitiv] 혱 긍정적인　[문제] director[diréktər] 몡 감독　producer[prədjúːsər] 몡 프로듀서, 연출가　host [houst] 몡 주인; *진행자　get along with ~와 잘 지내다

문제 해설

Q1: 화자 간의 관계는?

　연예 뉴스에 출연한 배우와 뉴스 기자와의 대화 내용이다.

Q2: Silvia에 대해 사실이 아닌 것은?

　낯을 많이 가린다고 했다.

B [1-2]

M: How are your wedding preparations going?

W: Well... my parents are against our marriage.

M: Your fiancé Jack has a great personality and a good job. What's the problem?

W: In my country, there's a custom of asking a fortune teller about the future of the marriage.

M: That's interesting.

W: But the fortune teller said that we wouldn't be happy together. I don't believe him, but my parents do.

M: So your parents are against the marriage?

W: Yes. But I can't cancel the wedding just because of that.

M: Right.

W: Having said that, can I ask you a favor?

M: Sure, what is it?

W: My parents like you and trust you fully. So please tell them that Jack is a great guy and that we will be happy together.

M: No problem. I really do think so.

남: 결혼 준비는 어떻게 되어 가?

여: 음… 우리 부모님이 결혼을 반대하셔.

남: 네 약혼자 Jack은 성격이 좋고 직업도 좋잖아. 뭐가 문제야?

여: 우리나라에서는 결혼의 미래에 대해서 점쟁이에게 물어보는 관습이 있어.

남: 그거 흥미로운걸.

여: 그런데 점쟁이가 우리가 행복하지 않을 거라고 말했어. 난 그를 믿지 않지만 우리 부모님은 믿으셔.

남: 그래서 부모님이 결혼에 반대하셔?

여: 응. 그런데 난 단지 그것 때문에 결혼을 취소할 수는 없어.

남: 맞아.

여: 얘기가 나와서 말인데 부탁 좀 들어줄래?

남: 물론이지, 뭔데?

여: 우리 부모님은 널 좋아하고 전적으로 믿잖아. 그러니 Jack이 좋은 사람이고 우리가 함께 행복할 거라고 말씀 좀 드려줘.

남: 문제 없어. 난 정말 그렇게 생각하거든.

어휘

preparation[prèpəréiʃən] 몡 준비　fiancé[fi:ɑːnséi] 몡 약혼자 《남자》　custom[kʌ́stəm] 몡 관습　fortune teller 점쟁이　cancel[kǽnsəl] 통 취소하다　favor[féivər] 몡 부탁　trust[trʌst] 통 신뢰하다　fully[fúli] 부 완전히　[문제] believe in ~을 믿다　superstition[sùːpərstíʃən] 몡 미신　attend[əténd] 통 참석하다　persuade[pərswéid] 통 설득하다　approve of ~을 승인하다, 찬성하다

문제 해설

Q1: 여자의 부모가 결혼을 반대하는 이유는?

① 그녀는 결혼하기엔 너무 어리다.

② 그녀의 약혼자가 돈을 충분히 벌지 못한다.

③ 그녀의 약혼자가 미신을 맹신한다.

④ 점쟁이가 그들의 결혼이 불행할 것이라고 말했다.

점쟁이가 결혼이 불행할 것이라고 했기 때문에 반대를 한다고 했다.

Q2: 여자가 남자에게 해 달라고 부탁한 것은?

① 결혼식에 참석해 주어라.

② 약혼자에게 좋은 조언을 해 주어라.

③ 결혼 준비를 도와주어라.

④ 결혼에 찬성하도록 부모를 설득해 주어라.

부모님이 자신의 결혼을 인정하도록 설득해 달라고 남자에게 부탁했다.

Critical ★ Thinking p. 13

1 ③ 2 ③

> W: Justin, I can't understand my boyfriend.
> M: What's wrong?
> W: Well, I believe each person's privacy is important, even in a couple. But he doesn't think so.
> M: Does he want you to share everything?
> W: Yes. He wants to know my email password. And he checks the text messages on my cell phone every time we meet.
> M: Maybe he doesn't trust you.
> W: But he says he does trust me.
> M: Then what's his problem?
> W: He just thinks that if two people love each other, they should share everything. What do you think of that?
> M: I think privacy should always be respected, even in a couple.
> W: My boyfriend even wants to know my bank account password. I wish he would respect my privacy.

여: Justin, 난 내 남자 친구를 이해할 수가 없어.

남: 무슨 문제인데?

여: 음, 난 커플이라고 해도 각자의 사생활이 중요하다고 믿어. 하지만 그는 그렇게 생각하지 않아.

남: 그는 너와 모든 걸 공유하길 바라니?

여: 응. 내 이메일 비밀번호를 알고 싶어해. 그리고 만날 때마다 내 휴대전화의 문자 메시지를 확인해.

남: 아마 널 못 믿나 보구나.

여: 하지만 그는 날 정말 믿는다고 말해.

남: 그럼 그의 문제는 뭐야?

여: 그는 두 사람이 서로 사랑하면 모든 걸 공유해야 한다고 생각하는 거야. 넌 어떻게 생각하니?

남: 난 커플이라고 해도 사생활은 언제나 존중되어야 한다고 생각해.

여: 내 남자 친구는 내 은행 계좌의 비밀번호까지 알고 싶어해. 그가 내 사생활을 존중해줬으면 좋겠어.

어휘

privacy[práivəsi] 몡 사생활   share[ʃɛər] 동 공유하다
password[pǽswə̀rd] 몡 비밀번호   text message 문자 메시지   respect[rispékt] 동 존중하다   bank account 은행 계좌   [문제] personal information 개인 신상 정보
be related to ~에 연관되어 있다

문제 해설

Q1: 여자의 문제는?

남자 친구가 자신의 사생활을 존중해주지 않아서 고민하고 있다.

Q2: Justin과 같은 의견을 가진 사람은?

① Catherine: 난 남자 친구와 모든 걸 공유해.

② Leo: 난 돈과 관련된 것이 아니라면 개인 정보를 여자 친구에게 알려줘.

③ Wendy: 내 남자 친구와 나는 서로의 사생활을 존중해.

Justin의 생각은 커플이라고 해도 사생활을 존중해야 한다는 것이므로 Wendy와 같은 의견이다.

15

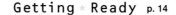

UNIT 02 Shopping

Getting ★ Ready p. 14

A 1 ⓑ 2 ⓕ 3 ⓓ 4 ⓔ 5 ⓒ 6 ⓐ
B 1 ⓒ 2 ⓓ 3 ⓕ

B 1 남: 재킷에 뭐가 문제가 있나요?
   여: 저한테 안 어울려요.

  2 남: 저희 집으로 직접 배달되나요?
    여: 물론이죠. 하지만 며칠 걸릴 거예요.

  3 남: 제 바지랑 어울리는 걸로 추천해 주시겠어요?
    여: 이 파란색 셔츠가 그것과 잘 어울릴 거예요.

Listening ★ Start p. 15

1 ④ / sold out, How long does it take, order one, could it be delivered, write down your address
2 (1) ⓒ (2) ⓑ (3) ⓐ / a pair of, My feet hurt, a variety of, at low prices, buy groceries

1

W: I like this swimsuit. Do you have a larger size?

M: The large ones are sold out. But I can order one for you.

W: How long does it take?

M: About three days. Today is Monday, so it will arrive on Thursday.

W: Okay, I want to order one. How much is it?

M: It's $46.

W: Here you go. I live far from here, so could it be delivered directly to my house?

M: Of course. But it's going to take one day longer.

W: That's fine.

M: Could you please write down your address and phone number?

W: Okay.

여: 이 수영복이 마음에 드네요. 더 큰 치수 있나요?

남: 큰 사이즈는 다 팔렸어요. 하지만 손님을 위해서 주문할 수 있어요.

여: 얼마나 걸려요?

남: 대략 3일 정도요. 오늘이 월요일이니까 목요일에 도착할 거예요.

여: 알겠어요, 하나 주문하고 싶어요. 얼마예요?

남: 46달러예요.

여: 여기요. 제가 여기서 멀리 떨어진 데 살아서요. 저희 집으로 직접 배달되나요?

남: 물론이죠. 하지만 하루 더 걸릴 거예요.

여: 괜찮아요.

남: 손님 집 주소랑 전화번호 좀 써 주시겠어요?

여: 네.

어휘

swimsuit[swímsùːt] 몡 수영복 be sold out 매진되다
order[ɔ́ːrdər] 동 주문하다 deliver[dilívər] 동 배달하다
directly[diréktli] 뿐 직접, 곧장

문제 해설

Q: 여자는 수영복을 언제 받을 것인가?

수영복이 매장에 목요일에 도착할 것이라고 했고, 집으로 배송을 받으려면 하루가 더 걸린다고 했으므로 금요일에 받을 수 있을 것이다.

2

W1: I'm Lily. I bought a pair of cheap sandals to save money. But they broke after only a few days, so I had to buy another cheap pair. My feet hurt after wearing them.

M: I'm Jeff. I shop at department stores. They have a variety of quality items. The problem is the expensive prices. Is there any way to buy good products at low prices?

W2: I'm Susan. I go to discount stores to buy groceries every week. There are so many cheap items that I buy things I don't need.

여1: 난 Lily야. 나는 돈을 아끼려고 값이 싼 샌들을 한 켤레 샀어. 하지만 며칠 만에 망가져서 싼 걸 또 하나 사야 했어. 그걸 신고 나면 발이 아파.

남: 난 Jeff야. 난 백화점에서 쇼핑을 해. 거기엔 좋은 품질의 다양한 물건들이 있거든. 문제는 비싼 가격이지. 저렴한 가격에 좋은 물건을 살 방법이 있을까?

여2: 난 Susan이야. 난 매주 식료품을 사러 할인 매장에 가. 싼 물건들이 너무 많아서 내가 필요하지 않은 것들을 사게 돼.

어휘

a pair of 한 켤레[쌍]의 sandal[sǽndəl] 몡 샌들
department store 백화점 a variety of 다양한
quality[kwáləti] 몡 질; *혱 양질의 item[áitem] 몡 상품, 품목 product[prɑ́dəkt] 몡 상품 discount store 할인 매장 groceries[gróusəriz] 몡 식료품, 잡화 [문제] make out 작성하다 list[list] 몡 목록 outlet[áutlet] 몡 직판점 instead of ~대신에 several[sévərəl] 혱 몇 개의

문제 해설

Q: 각 인물과 그에 적절한 쇼핑에 관한 충고를 연결하시오.

ⓐ 쇼핑 목록을 작성해라.

ⓑ 직판점에서 질이 좋고 값싼 물건을 살 수 있다.

ⓒ 값싼 물건을 여러 개 사느니 질 좋은 제품을 하나 사라.

(1) Lily는 싼 샌들을 여러 개 사지만 제품의 질에 만족하지 못하고 있으므로 질 좋은 제품을 하나 사는 게 나을 것이다.

(2) Jeff는 저렴한 가격에 좋은 물건을 살 방법에 대해 고민하고 있으므로 직판점에서 쇼핑하는 것을 추천해줄 수 있을 것이다.

(3) Susan은 할인 매장에 가서 필요하지 않은 물건들까지 산다고 했으므로 쇼핑 목록을 작성할 필요가 있을 것이다.

Listening ★ Practice p. 16

1 ④ mQ1 ⓒ 2 ④ mQ2 ⓐ 3 ② mQ3 ⓐ, ⓒ
4 ① mQ4 ⓑ 5 ②, ④ mQ5 ⓑ 6 ③ mQ6 ⓐ

1

W: David, look at this.

M: Is that a bedcover?

W: Yes. You asked for a new bedcover. So what do you think?

M: It looks nice and comfortable.

W: It comes in beige, yellow, and green. Which one do you like?

M: They all look good on the screen. Well...

16

either beige or green.

W: Just pick one. The hostess said only a few of them are left.

M: Do we have to buy it today? I want to think about it.

W: Hurry up. The original price is $50, but there's a $10 discount for today only.

M: Really? Then I'll go with green.

W: Great! Let's call right now.

perhaps this yellow one?

W: I like this short one. Do you have it in a different color?

M: Yes. Here it is in green.

W: It's pretty. How much is it?

M: It's $50. The blue skirt was $45, so you'll have to pay $5 more.

W: Okay. I'll take it.

여: David, 이것 좀 보렴.

남: 그거 침대 커버예요?

여: 응. 네가 새 침대 커버 사달라고 했잖니. 어떻게 생각하니?

남: 예쁘고 아늑해 보이네요.

여: 베이지색, 노란색, 녹색이 있어. 어느 게 좋니?

남: 화면상으로는 다 좋아 보여요. 음… 베이지색이나 녹색 중에 하나요.

여: 하나만 골라 봐. 진행자가 몇 개밖에 안 남았다고 말했어.

남: 오늘 사야 해요? 전 생각 좀 해보고 싶은데요.

여: 서둘러야 해. 원래 가격은 50달러인데 오늘만 10달러 할인해 주거든.

남: 정말요? 그럼 녹색으로 할게요.

여: 좋아! 지금 바로 전화하자.

남: 도와드릴까요?

여: 네. 이 청색 미니스커트를 선물로 받았는데 교환하고 싶어서요.

남: 뭔가 문제가 있나요?

여: 저한테 안 어울려요. 다른 스타일의 치마 좀 볼 수 있을까요?

남: 그럼요. 치마 섹션은 이쪽이에요.

여: 제 블라우스랑 어울리는 것 좀 추천해 주시겠어요?

남: 주머니가 달린 이 회색 치마는 어때요? 아니면 혹시 이 노란색 치마는요?

여: 전 이 짧은 게 마음에 들어요. 다른 색 있어요?

남: 네. 여기 녹색이요.

여: 예쁘네요. 얼마예요?

남: 50달러예요. 청색 치마가 45달러였으니까 5달러 더 내셔야겠네요.

여: 알았어요. 그걸로 할게요.

어휘

bedcover[bédkÀvər] 명 침대 커버 comfortable [kÁmfərtəbl] 형 편안한, 아늑한 beige[beiʒ] 명 베이지색 either A or B A나 B 둘 중 하나 hostess[hóustis] 명 여주인; *여성 사회자 original[ərídʒənəl] 형 원래의 discount[dískaunt] 명 할인 [문제] catalogue [kǽtəlɔ̀(:)g] 명 상품 목록, 카탈로그 channel[tʃǽnəl] 명 채널

문제 해설

Q: 그들이 지금 하고 있는 일은?

진행자가 상품을 소개하고 있고 두 사람은 화면상으로 상품을 보고 있으며 여자가 마지막에 주문 전화를 하려고 하는 것으로 보아 TV 홈쇼핑을 보고 있음을 알 수 있다.

mQ1: 소년이 선택한 침대 커버 색깔은?

소년은 베이지색과 녹색 중에 고민하다가 녹색을 선택했다.

어휘

Are you being helped? 도와드릴까요? exchange [ikstʃéindʒ] 통 교환하다 look good on ~에게 어울리다 section[sékʃən] 명 구역 recommend[rèkəménd] 통 추천하다 go with ~와 어울리다 pocket[pákit] 명 주머니 perhaps[pərhǽps] 부 아마도, 혹시

문제 해설

Q: 여자는 어느 치마를 골랐는가?

여자는 녹색의 짧은 치마를 골랐다.

mQ2: 여자가 더 지불해야 하는 금액은?

여자가 선물 받은 치마는 45달러이고 교환하기로 한 치마는 50달러이므로 5달러를 추가로 지불해야 한다.

2

M: Are you being helped?

W: No, I'm not. I got this blue miniskirt as a present, but I want to exchange it.

M: Is there something wrong with it?

W: It doesn't look good on me. May I see other skirts in a different style?

M: Sure. The skirt section is over here.

W: Would you recommend one that goes with my blouse?

M: How about this gray one with pockets? Or

3

W: Do you want to buy things at low prices? Come to the "Town Flea Market," the oldest and largest flea market in New York. There are various clothes and accessories, and we're especially famous for used instruments and books. We're located at 39th Street and are open on Saturday from 10 a.m. to 6 p.m. Also, visit us online at www.townfm.com. You can see pictures of the market and comments from visitors. If you have things for sale, please call us at 3142-0357.

여: 물건을 저렴한 가격에 사고 싶나요? 뉴욕에서 가장 오래되고 큰 벼룩시장인 'Town Flea Market'으로 오세요. 다양한 옷과 액세서리가 있으며, 특히 중고 악기와 책으로 유명합니다. 39번가에 위치해 있으며 토요일 오전 10시에서 저녁 6시까지 엽니다. 또한 온라인으로 www.townfm.com에 방문해 주세요. 시장 사진과 방문객들의 의견도 볼 수 있습니다. 팔고 싶은 물건이 있으시면 3142-0357로 전화해 주세요.

어휘

flea market 벼룩시장 various[vέ(:)əriəs] 휑 다양한
accessory[əksésəri] 휑 액세서리 especially[ispéʃəli]
(튀) 특히 used[juːzd] 휑 중고의 instrument[ínstrəmənt]
휑 악기 be located at ~에 위치해 있다 comment
[kάment] 휑 논평, 의견 visitor[vízitər] 휑 방문객

문제 해설

Q: 잘못된 정보를 고르시오.
　　Town Flea Market은 39th Street에 위치해 있다고 했다.

mQ3: 온라인 사이트에서 얻을 수 있는 정보를 모두 고르시오.
　　온라인 사이트에서 시장 사진과 방문객들의 의견을 볼 수 있다고 했다.

4

W: Hello. I bought this watch here. Can I exchange it?
M: Okay. When did you buy it?
W: A week ago. Is it possible to exchange it now?
M: Yes. But this watch looks good on you. Why do you want to exchange it?
W: It has a nice design, but I don't like the color. I'd like to get a white one.
M: I'm sorry, but the white ones are sold out.
W: Oh, no! Well, can I get a refund, then?
M: Okay. Did you bring the receipt?
W: Wait. Oh, no! I forgot to bring it. Can I get a refund without it?
M: I'm sorry. You can't.
W: Okay, then I'll come back tomorrow.

여: 안녕하세요. 제가 이 시계를 여기서 샀는데요. 교환할 수 있어요?
남: 네. 언제 사셨어요?
여: 일주일 전에요. 지금 교환하는 게 가능할까요?
남: 네. 하지만 이 시계는 손님에게 잘 어울리는데요. 왜 교환하시려는 거예요?
여: 디자인은 괜찮은데 색깔이 마음에 안 들어요. 흰색으로 하고 싶어요.
남: 죄송합니다만 흰색은 다 팔렸어요.
여: 아, 이런! 저, 그럼 환불받을 수 있어요?
남: 그럼요. 영수증 가져오셨어요?

여: 잠시만요. 아, 이런! 가져오는 걸 깜빡했네요. 영수증이 없어도 환불받을 수 있을까요?
남: 죄송해요. 안 됩니다.
여: 알았어요. 그럼 내일 다시 올게요.

어휘

possible[pάsəbl] 휑 가능한 design[dizáin] 휑 디자인
refund[ríːfʌnd] 휑 환불 receipt[risíːt] 휑 영수증 [문제]
scratch[skrætʃ] 튕 긁다 sale[seil] 휑 판매; 《~s》 판매량;
*세일

문제 해설

Q: 여자가 환불을 받을 수 없었던 이유는?
　　여자는 영수증을 가져오지 않아서 환불받지 못했다.

mQ4: 여자는 시계의 어떤 점이 마음에 들지 않았나?
　　여자는 시계의 색깔이 마음에 들지 않는다고 했다.

5

W: Look at that MP3 player! Isn't it nice?
M: It looks good. Are you going to buy it?
W: I'd like to, but I don't have enough money.
M: Jane, I know how you can get some money. How about selling things we don't need?
W: You mean a garage sale?
M: Yes. Actually, I also need money for my sister's graduation gift.
W: Great! What should we sell?
M: I have some books and CDs that I can sell. How about you?
W: Maybe clothes and sneakers.
M: How about your accessories? You don't wear many of them.
W: That's right. It would be better to sell accessories instead of sneakers.
M: Okay.

여: 저 MP3 플레이어 좀 봐! 괜찮지 않니?
남: 괜찮네. 그거 사려고?
여: 그러고 싶지만 돈이 충분치 않아.
남: Jane, 네가 돈을 좀 구할 수 있는 방법을 알고 있는데. 필요 없는 물건을 파는 게 어때?
여: 차고 세일 말이야?
남: 응. 사실 나도 여동생 졸업 선물 때문에 돈이 필요하거든.
여: 좋아! 뭘 팔아야 하지?
남: 난 팔 수 있는 책이랑 CD가 좀 있어. 넌?
여: 아마 옷이랑 운동화 정도.
남: 액세서리는 어때? 안 하는 것들 많잖아.
여: 맞아. 운동화 대신에 액세서리를 파는 게 낫겠어.
남: 그래.

어휘

garage sale 차고에서 하는 중고품 염가 판매

graduation[ɡræ̀dʒuéiʃən] 몡 졸업　sneakers[sníːkərz]
몡 운동화 한 켤레

어휘 문제 해설

Q: 여자가 팔려고 하는 물건을 두 개 고르시오.

여자는 처음에 옷과 운동화를 팔려고 했으나 결국 운동화 대
신에 액세서리를 팔기로 했다.

mQ5: 남자가 차고 세일을 하려는 이유는?

남자는 여동생 졸업 선물 때문에 돈이 필요하다고 했다.

6

M: When the economy is bad, people don't shop as often. But products like lipstick and scarves sell more. This is because women buy cheaper luxury items instead of expensive ones to cheer themselves up. This is called the "Lipstick Effect." In the 1930s in America, when the economy was bad, lipstick sales went up while other sales went down. That's when people started to call it the "Lipstick Effect." Another famous example was after the 9/11 attacks. At that time, lipstick sales almost doubled.

남: 경제가 안 좋을 때 사람들은 여느 때처럼 쇼핑을 자주 하지
않습니다. 하지만 립스틱과 스카프와 같은 상품들은 더 잘
팔립니다. 왜냐하면 여자들이 기분 전환을 위해 비싼 것 대
신에 보다 저렴한 사치품을 사기 때문입니다. 이것을 '립스
틱 효과'라고 부릅니다. 1930년대 미국의 경제가 안 좋았을
때 다른 상품의 판매량은 감소했는데 립스틱 판매량은 증가
했습니다. 그때부터 사람들은 그것을 '립스틱 효과'라고 불렀
습니다. 또 다른 유명한 예는 9/11 공격 이후였습니다. 그 당
시에 립스틱 판매량이 거의 두 배로 뛰었습니다.

어휘

economy[ikánəmi] 몡 경제　lipstick[lípstik] 몡 립스틱
scarf[skɑːrf] 몡 스카프　luxury[lʌ́kʃəri] 혱 사치품의
effect[ifékt] 몡 효과　example[igzǽmpl] 몡 예　attack
[ətǽk] 몡 공격　double[dʌ́bl] 동 두 배가 되다　[문제]
goods[gudz] 몡 상품　please[pliːz] 동 기쁘게 하다
cosmetic[kɑzmétik] 몡 화장품

문제 해설

Q: '립스틱 효과'를 설명하도록 빈칸을 채우시오.
① 여자들은 립스틱을 사지 않음으로써 돈을 절약하려고 한다
② 립스틱은 더 비싸지만 더 잘 팔린다
③ 여자들은 기분 전환을 위해 보다 저렴한 사치품을 산다
④ 여자들이 외모에 신경을 쓰기 때문에 화장품 판매량이 증
가한다
경제가 안 좋을 때 여자들이 비싼 상품 대신에 값이 싼 사치
품을 사는 현상을 립스틱 효과라고 한다.

mQ6: '립스틱 효과'가 처음 나타난 때는?
1930년대 미국의 경제가 안 좋았을 때 처음 나타났다.

Listening ★ Challenge　p. 18

A 1 ④　2 ②　B 1 ②　2 ③

A [1-2]

W: Do you want to go to the W Mall with me?
M: It's far from here. Why do you want to go there?
W: To buy an MP3 player. I heard they're having a sale now.
M: Why don't you look for one on the Internet? It's much cheaper.
W: I've never bought anything online.
M: It's convenient because you don't need to walk around to shop. And you can compare all the prices at one time.
W: Do you know a good website?
M: You can trust sites like Mega Mall or King Market. I can give you a Mega Mall discount coupon.
W: But I want to look at the items myself.
M: Then, why don't you visit the Cherryville Mall to look at them, and buy one from Mega Mall?
W: Good idea.

여: 나랑 W Mall에 갈래?
남: 여기서 멀잖아. 거기 왜 가려고 하는데?
여: MP3 플레이어 사려고. 지금 세일 중이라고 들었어.
남: 인터넷으로 찾아보는 게 어때? 그게 훨씬 더 싸.
여: 온라인에서 물건을 사 본 적이 없는데.
남: 쇼핑하러 돌아다닐 필요가 없으니까 편해. 그리고 한 번에
모든 가격을 비교해 볼 수도 있고.
여: 좋은 웹사이트 아니?
남: Mega Mall이나 King Market과 같은 사이트는 믿을 만해.
내가 Mega Mall의 할인 쿠폰을 줄 수 있어.
여: 하지만 직접 상품을 보고 싶은데.
남: 그럼 Cherryville Mall에 방문해서 상품들을 보고 Mega
Mall에서 사는 게 어때?
여: 좋은 생각이야.

어휘

mall[mɔːl] 몡 쇼핑몰　look for ~을 찾다　convenient
[kənvíːnjənt] 혱 편리한　compare[kəmpɛ́ər] 동 비교하다
at one time 한 번에　trust[trʌst] 동 믿다　discount
[dískaunt] 몡 할인　[문제] in person 직접, 본인 스스로

문제 해설

Q1: 인터넷 쇼핑의 장점으로 언급되지 <u>않은</u> 것은?

① 매장에서 쇼핑하는 것보다 더 싸다.

② 매장에 직접 갈 필요가 없다.

③ 모든 상품 가격을 비교해 보기 쉽다.

④ 인터넷 사이트에서 종종 할인 판매를 한다.

인터넷에서 구매하면 매장에서 쇼핑하는 것보다 더 싸고, 돌아다닐 필요가 없어서 편하며, 한 번에 모든 가격을 비교해 볼 수 있다고 했다.

Q2: 여자가 MP3 플레이어를 살 곳은?

여자는 Cherryville Mall에서 상품을 직접 보고 Mega Mall에서 구매하기로 했다.

B [1-2]

M: I'm looking for a necklace for my sister. Could you recommend one?

W: How about this cat-shaped one or this heart-shaped one?

M: My sister would like the heart-shaped one. How much is it?

W: It's $54, after a 10% discount.

M: That's good. What colors do you have?

W: There are two colors, silver and pink. But the silver ones are sold out.

M: Can I order a silver one?

W: Yes, but it'll take about two days. Will that be okay?

M: That's fine.

W: Okay. Do you want to pick it up?

M: I don't think I have time. Could you deliver it?

W: Yes, but you'll have to pay $4 for the delivery charge.

M: I see. That's fine.

W: Let's see... today is the 14th. So it'll arrive by the 16th.

M: Thanks. Please wrap it up nicely.

남: 여동생에게 줄 목걸이를 찾고 있는데요. 하나 추천해 주시겠어요?

여: 이 고양이 모양이나 하트 모양 어때요?

남: 제 여동생은 하트 모양을 좋아할 것 같아요. 얼마예요?

여: 10% 할인해서 54달러예요.

남: 괜찮네요. 색깔은 어떤 게 있어요?

여: 은색이랑 분홍색, 두 가지 색깔이 있어요. 하지만 은색은 다 팔렸어요.

남: 은색으로 주문 가능해요?

여: 네, 하지만 이틀 정도 걸릴 거예요. 괜찮으세요?

남: 괜찮아요.

여: 알겠습니다. 찾으러 오실 거예요?

남: 시간이 없을 것 같아요. 배달해주실 수 있어요?

여: 네, 하지만 배송비로 4달러를 지불하셔야 해요.

남: 그렇군요. 괜찮아요.

여: 어디 보자… 오늘이 14일이니까 16일까지는 도착할 거예요.

남: 감사합니다. 예쁘게 포장해 주세요.

어휘

necklace[néklis] 명 목걸이　pick up 찾아가다

delivery[dilívəri] 명 배달　charge[tʃɑːrdʒ] 명 비용

wrap up 포장하다　[문제] arrival[əráivəl] 명 도착

request[rikwést] 명 요청

문제 해설

Q1: 잘못된 정보를 고르시오.

남자는 은색 목걸이를 주문했다.

Q2: 남자는 얼마를 지불해야 하는가?

목걸이 가격 54달러에 배송비를 4달러 더 지불해야 하므로 총 58달러를 지불해야 한다.

Critical ★ Thinking　p. 19

1 ②　2 (1) ⓑ (2) ⓒ

W: Leo, what do you think of this bag?

M: It looks okay. Is it new?

W: Yes. This is a famous designer brand product. Can't you see the difference?

M: Well... I don't know, Judy. You must have spent a lot of money.

W: Let's just say that one month of my salary is gone.

M: That's crazy. Designer products are only expensive because of their names. I don't understand why people waste money on them.

W: But designer products are good quality. I can use them for a long time.

M: Do you think so?

W: Sure. And I don't get tired of them easily because of their neat and simple design. Although they're expensive, they're worth it!

M: Still, I would rather buy several cheaper items than one designer brand product.

여: Leo, 이 가방 어떻게 생각해?

남: 괜찮네. 새 거야?

여: 응. 이거 유명한 디자이너 브랜드 제품이야. 차이 모르겠어?

남: 음… 난 모르겠어, Judy. 돈 많이 썼겠구나.

여: 내 한 달치 봉급이 날라갔다고만 말할게.

남: 말도 안돼. 디자이너 제품은 그 이름 때문에 비싼 것뿐이야. 난 사람들이 왜 거기에 돈을 낭비하는지 이해가 안 돼.

여: 하지만 디자이너 제품이 질이 좋잖아. 오랫동안 사용할 수 있거든.

남: 그렇게 생각해?

여: 물론이지. 그리고 디자인이 깔끔하고 단순해서 쉽게 싫증이 안 나. 비싸긴 하지만 그럴 만한 가치가 있어.

남: 그래도 난 디자이너 브랜드 제품 하나를 사느니 값싼 제품을 여러 개 사겠어.

어휘

designer brand 유명 디자이너 제품 difference[dífərəns] 몡 차이(점) salary[sǽləri] 몡 봉급 waste[weist] 동 낭비하다; 몡 낭비 get tired of ~에 싫증나다 neat[niːt] 톙 깔끔한 simple[símpl] 톙 단순한 worth[wəːrθ] 톙 (~의) 가치가 있는 would rather ~ than … …하느니 오히려 ~하는 편이 낫다 [문제] once[wʌns] 젭 일단 ~하면 keep[kiːp] 동 보유하다, 보존하다 (keep-kept-kept)

문제 해설

Q1: 그들은 주로 무엇에 관해 이야기하고 있는가?
  ① 디자이너 제품이 인기 있는 이유는?
  ② 디자이너 제품이 살 만한 가치가 있는가?
  ③ 디자이너 제품이 비싼 이유는?
  ④ 디자이너 제품이 질이 좋은가?
  두 사람은 디자이너 브랜드 상품을 살 가치가 있는지에 대해 이야기하고 있다.

Q2: 각 인물의 의견을 고르시오.
  ⓐ 디자이너 제품은 사람을 더 돋보이게 해.
  ⓑ 디자이너 제품을 사는 건 돈 낭비야.
  ⓒ 한번 디자이너 제품을 사면 오랫동안 가지고 있을 수 있어.
  (1) Leo는 디자이너 제품은 이름 때문에 비싼 것뿐으로 그것을 사는 사람을 이해할 수 없다고 했다.
  (2) Judy는 디자이너 제품이 질이 좋고 오랫동안 사용할 수 있다고 했다.

UNIT 03 Parties

Getting ★ Ready p. 20

A 1 ⓐ 2 ⓓ 3 ⓕ 4 ⓒ 5 ⓑ 6 ⓔ
B 1 ⓔ 2 ⓕ 3 ⓒ

B 1 남: Wendy의 결혼 피로연은 어땠어?
  여: 너도 왔어야 했어. 아주 재미있었어.
 2 남: 그 파티에 복장 규정이 있어?
  여: 아니. 그냥 최대한 멋지게 차려 입어.

3 남: 파티에 음악 CD 좀 가져갈까?
  여: 그래. 맞춰서 춤 출 게 필요해.

1 (1) ⓒ, ⓔ (2) ⓑ (3) ⓓ / throw a potluck party, What should I cook, make a tuna salad, six bottles of, just in case

2 ① / Can I speak to, What's up, I'll be there, Stop teasing me, as nicely as you can

1

W: Tim, I'm going to throw a potluck party this Saturday. Would you like to come?
M: Sure, Sandra. What should I cook this time?
W: How about making spaghetti? You make really tasty spaghetti.
M: I want to try a different dish. Maybe I can make a tuna salad. What will you cook?
W: I'm going to make some fried chicken. I'll also buy six bottles of soda.
M: Don't you think we'll need more drinks? I'll bring some more soda just in case.
W: Good. And I'll also buy some fruit.

여: Tim, 이번 주 토요일에 포트럭 파티를 열려고 해. 올래?
남: 물론이지, Sandra. 이번엔 무슨 요리를 해야 할까?
여: 스파게티를 만드는 게 어때? 너 스파게티 정말 맛있게 하잖아.
남: 다른 요리를 해보고 싶어. 참치 샐러드를 만들까 봐. 넌 뭘 요리할 건데?
여: 프라이드 치킨을 하려고 해. 탄산음료 6병도 살게.
남: 음료수가 더 많이 필요하지 않을까? 만약을 위해 내가 탄산음료를 좀 더 가지고 가도록 할게.
여: 좋아. 난 과일도 좀 살게.

어휘

throw[θrou] 동 던지다; *개최하다 potluck party 포트럭 파티(각자 음식을 가져오는 파티) tasty[téisti] 톙 맛있는 dish[diʃ] 몡 요리 tuna[tjúːnə] 몡 참치 soda[sóudə] 몡 탄산음료 just in case 만약을 대비해서

문제 해설

Q: 각 범주에 맞는 음식을 고르시오.
  Sandra는 프라이드 치킨과 탄산음료, 과일을, Tim은 참치 샐러드와 탄산음료를 준비하겠다고 했다.

2

(*Telephone rings.*)
W: Hello. Can I speak to Bob?
M: This is he.
W: Hey. This is Mary. What are you doing?

M: I was just cleaning my room. What's up?

W: I'm calling to invite you to my birthday party. It's this Thursday at my house.

M: I'll be there. Um... by the way, did you invite Nora, too?

W: (laughs) Right. You told me you want to date her. I think you love her.

M: Stop teasing me. You know how much I like her.

W: Don't worry. I was about to call her. So dress as nicely as you can.

(전화벨이 울린다.)

여: 여보세요. Bob과 통화할 수 있나요?

남: 전데요.

여: 야. 나 Mary야. 뭐 하니?

남: 방을 청소하는 중이었어. 무슨 일이야?

여: 내 생일 파티에 초대하려고 전화했어. 우리 집에서 이번 목요일에 해.

남: 갈게. 음… 그런데, Nora도 초대했어?

여: [웃으며] 맞다. 너 그 애랑 데이트하고 싶다고 했잖아. 너 그 애를 사랑하는 것 같다.

남: 그만 놀려. 내가 그 앨 얼마나 좋아하는지 알잖아.

여: 걱정하지 마. Nora에게 전화하려던 참이야. 그러니 최대한 멋지게 차려 입기나 해.

어휘

clean[kliːn] ⑧ 청소하다　invite[inváit] ⑧ 초대하다　by the way 그런데　tease[tiːz] ⑧ 놀리다　be about to-v 막 ~하려던 참이다

문제 해설

Q: Mary가 다음에 할 일은?

　Nora에게 생일 파티에 초대하는 전화를 걸던 참이라고 했다.

Listening ★ Practice　p. 22

1 (1) Not Good　(2) Good　(3) Not Good　mQ1 ⓐ
2 ③　mQ2 ⓐ, ⓒ　3 ①, ②　mQ3 ⓑ　4 ③
mQ4 ⓐ　5 (1) ⓒ　(2) ⓑ　(3) ⓐ　mQ5 ⓑ
6 (1) Good　(2) Bad　(3) So-so　mQ6 (1) F　(2) T

1

W: When you're invited to a party, there are some things you should keep in mind. First, arrive at the party on time. If you show up early, it can bother the host. Being more than twenty minutes late is also bad. Second, when you bring new faces to a party, it should be limited to one or two. Bringing too many new people can be rude.

Finally, send a thank-you note to the host after the party. It's polite to send it within 24 hours. It's always nice to express your thanks.

여: 파티에 초대를 받았을 때 유의해야 할 몇 가지 것들이 있습니다. 우선, 파티에 정시에 도착하세요. 일찍 나타나게 되면 주최자에게 방해가 될 수 있습니다. 20분 이상 늦는 것 역시 나쁩니다. 두 번째로, 파티에 새로운 사람들을 데리고 갈 때에는 한두 명으로 제한해야 합니다. 새로운 사람들을 너무 많이 데리고 가는 것은 실례가 될 수 있습니다. 마지막으로, 파티 후에는 주최자에게 감사 편지를 보내세요. 24시간 내에 보내는 것이 예의입니다. 감사를 표하는 것은 항상 좋습니다.

어휘

keep in mind 명심하다, 유의하다　on time 정시에
show up 나타나다　bother[báðər] ⑧ 귀찮게 하다, 성가시게 하다　host[houst] ⑲ 주최자　limit[límit] ⑧ 제한하다
rude[ruːd] ⑱ 무례한　thank-you note 감사 편지
polite[pəláit] ⑱ 예의 바른, 공손한　within[wiðín] ㉖
~ 이내에　express[iksprés] ⑧ 표현하다　[문제] guest
[gest] ⑲ 손님　acceptable[əkséptəbl] ⑱ 받아들일 수 있는

문제 해설

Q: 각 인물이 좋은 손님인지 아닌지 √표 하시오.

　(1) 파티에 20분 일찍 도착했다.

　(2) 파티에 내 친구 한 명을 데리고 갔다.

　(3) 파티가 끝나고 2일 후에 감사 편지를 보냈다.

　파티 시간에 맞춰 도착해야 하고, 한두 명의 친구를 데리고 가는 것은 괜찮으며, 파티가 끝난 뒤 24시간 이내에 감사 편지를 보내라고 했다.

mQ1: 여자는 10분 정도 늦는 것이 어떻다고 했나?

　20분 이상 늦는 것은 예의가 아니라고 했으므로 10분 정도는 괜찮다고 할 수 있다.

2

M: What did you do on the weekend, Kate?

W: I went to Mindy's baby shower.

M: A baby shower? What's that?

W: Oh, it's a party for parents who are expecting a baby. People gather and give gifts to the parents. It's a popular tradition in the U.S.

M: Interesting! So, what did you give as a present? Baby clothes?

W: I was going to buy some baby clothes, but Mindy said she already had enough. So I bought a pair of baby shoes and a hat.

M: Did Mindy like them?

W: Of course! She said they were cute. I can't wait to see Mindy's baby wear them.

남: 주말에 뭐 했니, Kate?

여: Mindy의 베이비 샤워에 갔어.

남: 베이비 샤워? 그게 뭐야?

여: 아, 아기를 낳을 부모를 위한 파티야. 사람들이 모여서 부모
에게 선물을 주는 거야. 미국에서는 인기 있는 전통이야.

남: 흥미로운걸! 그래서 선물로 무엇을 줬어? 아기 옷?

여: 아기 옷을 사려고 했는데 Mindy가 이미 옷이 충분히 있다고
하더라. 그래서 아기 신발 한 켤레와 모자를 샀어.

남: Mindy가 좋아했어?

여: 물론이지! 귀엽다고 하더라. Mindy의 아기가 착용한 걸 어서
보고 싶어.

어휘

baby shower 베이비 샤워(임신 축하 선물을 주는 파티)
be expecting a baby 임신 중이다   gather[ɡǽðər] 동
모이다   tradition[trədíʃən] 명 전통   can't wait to-v 어
서 ~하고 싶다

문제 해설

Q: Kate가 주말에 한 일은?

　출산을 앞둔 친구를 축하하는 파티에 가서 선물을 주었다고
　했다.

mQ2: 여자가 Mindy의 아기를 위해 산 물품을 두 개 고르시오.

　여자는 아기의 신발과 모자를 샀다고 했다.

3

W1: Hi, Lisa. Are you free this Friday?

W2: Yes. What's up, Rachel?

W1: I'm planning to have a pajama party at my
home. Would you like to come?

W2: Of course! What do I need to bring?

W1: Just bring your pajamas.

W2: Okay. And I'll bring some snacks too.

W1: Great. Oh, and you have Beyonce's new
CD, right?

W2: No. Why do you ask?

W1: I want something to dance to at this party.
I'll ask Sarah about it, then.

W2: What about drinks?

W1: I'll buy some. You like Coke, don't you?

W2: Actually, I prefer juice.

W1: Okay. Then I'll buy some juice, too.

여1: 안녕, Lisa. 이번 금요일에 시간 있니?

여2: 응. 무슨 일인데, Rachel?

여1: 우리 집에서 파자마 파티를 하려고 해. 너 올래?

여2: 물론이지! 난 뭘 가져가면 돼?

여1: 파자마만 가져오면 돼.

여2: 알았어. 그리고 간식을 좀 가져갈게.

여1: 좋아. 아, 너 Beyonce의 최신 CD 가지고 있지, 그렇지?

여2: 아니. 그건 왜 물어?

여1: 파티에서 맞춰서 춤을 출 게 필요하거든. 그럼 Sarah에게

물어봐야겠다.

여2: 음료수는 어쩌지?

여1: 내가 살게. 너 콜라 좋아하지?

여2: 실은 주스가 더 좋아.

여1: 좋아. 그럼 주스도 살게.

어휘

pajama party 파자마 파티(10대 소녀들이 친구 집에 모여 밤
새워 노는 모임)   pajamas[pədʒɑ́ːməz] 명 잠옷   snack
[snæk] 명 간식   Coke[kouk] 명 콜라   prefer[prifə́ːr] 동
선호하다

문제 해설

Q: Lisa가 파티에 가지고 갈 것들을 두 개 고르시오.

　Lisa는 파자마와 간식을 가지고 가겠다고 했다.

mQ3: Lisa가 선호하는 음료수 종류는?

　Lisa가 콜라보다 주스를 더 좋아한다고 해서 Rachel은 주스
　도 준비하겠다고 했다.

4

M: Jenny, can I ask you a favor?

W: Sure. What is it, Paul?

M: Sally is coming back from studying abroad.
So, I'm planning a surprise party for her.
Can you give me some advice?

W: Well, first, send invitations explaining that
it's a surprise party.

M: Okay. And?

W: Tell the guests to arrive 30 minutes before
Sally arrives. And prepare her favorite food
and drinks.

M: What else should I do?

W: Why don't you collect some money from
the guests before the party? You can use
it to buy a little present for Sally. She'll be
really happy.

M: Thanks. Jenny! That was a big help.

남: Jenny, 부탁 좀 해도 될까?

여: 물론이지. 뭐야, Paul?

남: Sally가 외국에서 공부하고 돌아와. 그래서 그녀를 위해 깜
짝 파티를 열려고 해. 조언 좀 해 줄 수 있겠니?

여: 음, 우선 깜짝 파티라는 것을 알리는 초대장을 보내.

남: 알았어. 그리고?

여: 손님들에게 Sally가 도착하기 30분 전에 도착해야 한다고 해.
그리고 그 애가 좋아하는 음식과 음료수를 준비하고.

남: 또 무엇을 해야 할까?

여: 파티 전에 손님들에게서 돈을 좀 모으는 게 어떨까? Sally에
게 작은 선물을 사주는 데 쓸 수 있잖아. Sally가 아주 기뻐
할 거야.

남: 고마워, Jenny! 큰 도움이 되었어.

23

study abroad 유학하다　surprise party 깜짝 파티
advice[ədváis] 몡 조언　invitation[invətéiʃən] 몡 초대;
*초대장　explain[ikspléin] 동 설명하다　prepare[pripέər]
동 준비하다　collect[kəlékt] 동 모으다　[문제] celebrate
[séləbrèit] 동 축하하다

문제 해설
Q: Jenny의 조언의 일부가 아닌 것은?
　① 깜짝 파티라고 사람들에게 알려라.
　② 손님들이 Sally가 파티에 오기 전에 도착하도록 해라.
　③ 손님들이 좋아하는 음식을 준비해라.
　④ 파티 전에 돈을 좀 모아라.
　Sally가 좋아하는 음식과 음료수를 준비하라고 했다.

mQ4: 남자가 Sally를 위해 깜짝 파티를 여는 이유는?
　외국에서 공부하던 Sally가 돌아오는 것을 축하하기 위한 파
　티이다.

5

M: I went to a Halloween party yesterday. Everyone was wearing unique costumes. Nick was dressed like Hellboy. He wore a long brown coat with an ugly orange mask. It was so scary. Tim dressed like a pirate. He was wearing black pants with a sword by his side. He also wore a big black hat with bones on the front. It was my favorite costume. Ben was dressed like Dracula. He was wearing a black suit. He even wore white powder and red lipstick. He looked very funny.

남: 전 어제 할로윈 파티에 갔어요. 모두 독특한 의상을 입고 있었어요. Nick은 헬보이처럼 옷을 입었죠. 그는 추한 오렌지색 마스크를 쓰고 긴 갈색 코트를 입었어요. 아주 무서웠답니다. Tim은 해적처럼 입었어요. 그는 검은색 바지를 입고 허리에 칼을 차고 있었죠. 앞쪽에 해골이 그려진 큰 검은색 모자도 썼어요. 제가 제일 좋아하는 의상이었답니다. Ben은 드라큘라처럼 입었어요. 그는 검은 정장을 입고 있었죠. 심지어 흰 파우더와 빨간 립스틱도 발랐어요. 아주 웃겼어요.

Halloween party 할로윈 파티　unique[juːníːk] 혱 독특한　costume[kástjuːm] 몡 복장, 의상　ugly[ʌ́gli] 혱 추한　scary[skέ(ː)ri] 혱 무서운, 두려운　pirate[páiərət] 몡 해적　sword[sɔːrd] 몡 칼　bone[boun] 몡 뼈; *(~s) 해골, 유골　suit[suːt] 몡 정장　powder[páudər] 몡 *(화장)분; 가루

문제 해설
Q: 각 인물에 맞는 의상을 고르시오.
　(1) Nick은 긴 갈색 코트에 오렌지색 마스크를 썼다.
　(2) Tim은 해골이 그려진 검은 모자를 쓰고 칼을 허리에 찼다.

(3) Ben은 검은 정장에 흰 얼굴, 빨간 입술을 하고 있었다.
mQ5: 남자는 누구의 의상을 가장 좋아했나?
　남자는 Tim의 해적 의상이 가장 좋았다고 했다.

6

M: How did Wendy's wedding reception go?
W: It was so much fun. I couldn't stop laughing.
M: What was so funny?
W: The couple did a funny dance together. They prepared it for two weeks.
M: Wow, I wish I had seen it. And how did the wedding hall look?
W: I liked it. It was painted pink, so it looked lovely.
M: Do you think it would be a good place for my wedding reception, too?
W: Not really. The food was a problem. It wasn't very fresh.
M: What about the service?
W: The service wasn't terrible, but it wasn't that great either. If it were my wedding, I'd choose another place.
M: You should get a boyfriend first.

남: Wendy의 결혼 피로연은 어땠어?
여: 아주 재미있었어. 웃음을 멈출 수 없었어.
남: 뭐가 그렇게 재미있었니?
여: 부부가 함께 재미있는 춤을 췄어. 2주 동안 준비했대.
남: 와, 나도 봤으면 좋았을 텐데. 결혼식장은 어땠어?
여: 좋았어. 핑크색으로 칠해져 있어서 예쁘더라.
남: 내 결혼 피로연 장소로도 좋을 거라고 생각해?
여: 그렇지는 않아. 음식이 문제였어. 아주 신선하지가 않더라.
남: 서비스는 어때?
여: 서비스는 나쁘진 않았지만 아주 훌륭하지도 않았어. 내 결혼식이라면 다른 장소를 고를 거야.
남: 넌 우선 남자 친구나 구해.

wedding reception 결혼 피로연　laugh[læf] 동 웃다　wish[wiʃ] 동 ~이기를 바라다　lovely[lʌ́vli] 혱 사랑스런, 아름다운　[문제] so-so[sóusòu] 혱 그저 그런　interior[intí(ː)əriər] 몡 인테리어, 실내 장식

문제 해설
Q: 파티에 대한 여자의 의견에 ✓표 하시오.
　결혼식장은 아름다웠고, 음식은 신선하지 않아 마음에 들지 않았으며, 서비스는 그저 그랬다고 말했다.

mQ6: 사실이면 T, 사실이 아니면 F를 고르시오.
　부부는 이주일 동안 춤을 준비했다고 했고, 남자 친구를 우선 구하라는 남자의 말을 통해 여자에게 남자 친구가 없다는 것을 알 수 있다.

A 1 ② 2 ③   B 1 ③ 2 ①, ③

A [1-2]

W: Dream Party Planner is looking for an assistant party planner. We are one of the largest party planning companies in America. Our office is located at 40 Houston Street, Manhattan. Assistant party planners do the following: First, they meet customers to discuss the details of each party. Then they order food and decorations. Finally, they send invitations. The job's hours are Monday to Friday, from 9 a.m. to 5 p.m. To be an assistant, you must speak fluent English and be good at MS Word, email, and web searching. And we're looking for a friendly person. Send your résumé to Jane@dpt.com by May 4th.

여: Dream Party Planner에서 보조 파티 플래너를 찾습니다. 저희는 미국에서 가장 큰 파티 플래닝 회사들 중 하나입니다. 저희 사무실은 맨해튼 휴스턴가 40번지에 있습니다. 보조 파티 플래너는 다음과 같은 일을 합니다. 우선, 각 파티의 세부 사항을 의논하기 위해 고객들을 만납니다. 그리고 나서 음식과 장식품을 주문합니다. 마지막으로 초대장을 발송합니다. 업무 시간은 월요일부터 금요일, 오전 9시부터 오후 5시까지입니다. 보조가 되기 위해서는 영어를 유창하게 하고 MS 워드와 이메일, 웹 검색에 능해야 합니다. 또한 저희는 친절한 사람을 찾고 있습니다. Jane@dpt.com으로 5월 4일까지 이력서를 보내주세요.

어휘

party planner 파티 기획자, 파티 플래너 assistant [əsístənt] 혱 보조의; 몡 보조 be located at ~에 위치하다 following [fálouiŋ] 몡 다음에 말하는 것 customer [kʌ́stəmər] 몡 고객 discuss [diskʌ́s] 통 상의하다 detail [ditéil] 몡 세부사항 decoration [dèkəréiʃən] 몡 장식; *(~s) 장식품 fluent [flú(ː)ənt] 혱 유창한 friendly [fréndli] 혱 친절한, 친화적인 résumé [rézumèi] 몡 이력서 [문제] job advertisement 구인 광고 announcement [ənáunsmənt] 몡 공지, 발표 pay [pei] 몡 임금, 봉급 requirement [rikwáiərmənt] 몡 필요조건

문제 해설

Q1: 이 담화의 종류는?
   사람을 구하는 구인 광고이다.

Q2: 담화에서 언급되지 <u>않은</u> 것은?
   봉급에 대한 언급은 없었다.

B [1-2]

M: Hello, everyone. I'd like to invite all of you to a special Christmas party. The purpose of this party is to raise money for hungry children. A lot of famous actors and singers, such as Will Smith and Britney Spears, are scheduled to participate. They're going to sell some of their clothes and accessories. The collected money will be used to purchase food for poor children. The party will be held on Christmas at 5 p.m. at the Peace Convention Hall. Formal dress is required for the party. Anyone who wants to support poor children is welcome. I hope you join this special event and spend a great Christmas with us.

남: 안녕하세요, 여러분. 특별한 크리스마스 파티에 여러분 모두를 초대하고 싶습니다. 이 파티의 목적은 배고픈 아이들을 위해 돈을 모금하는 것입니다. Will Smith와 Britney Spears와 같은 많은 유명 배우와 가수들이 참여하기로 예정되어 있습니다. 그들은 자신들의 옷과 액세서리를 팔 것입니다. 모금된 돈은 가난한 아이들을 위한 음식을 사는 데 사용될 것입니다. 파티는 크리스마스 오후 5시 Peace Convention Hall에서 열릴 것입니다. 이 파티에서는 정장을 입으셔야 합니다. 가난한 아이들을 후원하기를 원하시는 분은 누구든 환영합니다. 이 특별한 행사에 참가하셔서 저희와 함께 멋진 크리스마스를 보내시길 바랍니다.

어휘

purpose [pə́ːrpəs] 몡 목적   raise [reiz] 통 (돈을) 모으다 be scheduled to-v ~하기로 예정되어 있다 participate [pɑːrtísəpèit] 통 참가하다   purchase [pə́ːrtʃəs] 통 구매하다   formal dress 정장, 격식을 차린 복장 require [rikwáiər] 통 요구하다   support [səpɔ́ːrt] 후원하다   [문제] dress code 복장 규정

문제 해설

Q1: 이 파티의 목적은?
   유명인사가 참가하기로 예정된 행사이나 가난한 아이들을 위한 모금이 목적인 크리스마스 파티이다.

Q2: 틀린 정보 두 가지를 고르시오.
   파티는 오후 다섯 시에 열릴 것이고 복장 규정은 정장이라고 했다.

1 (1) Against (2) For (3) Against
2 (1) ⓒ (2) ⓐ (3) ⓑ

M1: I'm Paul. I don't understand people who spend a lot of money on their children's birthday parties. Throwing an expensive party is only to show off their money, not to please their children.

W: I'm Ally. If you can afford the money to throw an expensive party, why not? Parents want to offer the best things they can to their children. To some parents, throwing an expensive party can be one way to express their love.

M2: I'm Joe. I don't think that throwing expensive parties for children is a good idea. Many children's parents can't afford expensive parties. When those children see others' luxury birthday parties, they'll feel unhappy.

남1: 난 Paul이야. 난 아이들 생일 파티에 많은 돈을 쓰는 사람들을 이해할 수 없어. 고가의 파티를 여는 것은 아이들을 기쁘게 하기 위해서가 아니라, 단지 그들이 가진 돈을 과시하기 위해서야.

여: 난 Ally야. 고가의 파티를 열 수 있는 형편이 된다면 못 할 이유가 뭐야? 부모들은 자식들에게 가능한 최고의 것을 주고 싶은 거야. 어떤 부모들에겐 고가의 파티를 여는 것이 사랑을 표현하는 한 방식일 수 있어.

남2: 나는 Joe야. 난 아이들을 위해 고가의 파티를 여는 것이 좋은 생각 같지 않아. 많은 아이들의 부모들은 고가의 파티를 열 여유가 없어. 그 아이들이 다른 아이들의 호화로운 생일 파티를 본다면 마음이 안 좋을 거야.

어휘

show off 과시하다 **afford**[əfɔ́ːrd] 통 여유가 있다
offer[ɔ́(ː)fər] 통 주다, 제공하다

문제 해설

Q1: 각 인물이 아이들을 위한 고가의 생일 파티에 대해 찬성하는지 반대하는지 ✓표 하시오.

(1) Paul은 고가의 생일 파티는 돈을 과시하기 위한 것뿐이라고 했으므로 반대하는 입장이다.

(2) Ally는 여유가 된다면 자식에 대한 사랑의 표현이 될 수 있다고 했으므로 찬성하는 입장이다.

(3) Joe는 고가의 생일 파티를 할 수 없는 아이들의 마음을 상하게 할 수 있다고 했으므로 반대하는 입장이다.

Q2: 각 인물의 의견을 고르시오.

ⓐ 일부 부모들은 고가의 파티를 여는 것으로 자식들에 대한 사랑을 보여준다.

ⓑ 고가의 파티를 열 형편이 되지 않는 사람들을 고려해야 한다.

ⓒ 고가의 파티는 돈이 얼마나 많은지 과시하기 위한 것일 뿐이다.

UNIT 04 Health

Getting ★ Ready p. 26

A 1 ① 2 ⓓ 3 ⓒ 4 ⓐ 5 ⓑ 6 ⓔ
B 1 ⓒ 2 ⓑ 3 ⓔ

B 1 남: 네 건강의 비결은 뭐니?
   여: 난 평소에 적게 먹어.

2 남: 요가는 어디에 좋아?
   여: 스트레스를 해소하는 데 좋아.

3 남: 테니스 수업을 얼마 동안 수강하길 원하세요?
   여: 세 달 등록하려고요.

Listening ★ Start p. 27

1 ①, ② / gaining weight, skip breakfast, finish a meal, you're full, used to eat, in calories

2 (1) ⓑ (2) ⓓ (3) ⓐ / Let me introduce you, lots of, have a cold, tastes good, improve your memory

1

M: Doctor, I'm worried that I'm gaining weight.
W: Let's see. Do you eat breakfast?
M: No, I'm never hungry in the morning.
W: It's not a good habit. If you skip breakfast, you may overeat during lunch and dinner.
M: I see.
W: How long does it take for you to finish a meal?
M: Usually ten minutes.
W: When you eat that fast, your body doesn't know you're full. So you may eat more than you need.
M: Wow, I didn't know that.
W: Do you often eat instant food?
M: I used to eat instant food, but now I try not to.
W: Good for you. It is high in calories.

남: 의사 선생님, 제가 체중이 늘고 있어서 걱정이에요.
여: 어디 보죠. 아침을 드시나요?
남: 아니요, 아침에는 전혀 배가 고프지 않아요.
여: 그건 좋은 습관이 아니에요. 아침을 거르면 점심이나 저녁에 과식을 할지도 몰라요.
남: 알겠어요.

여: 식사를 마치는 데 시간이 얼마나 걸리죠?

남: 보통 10분이요.

여: 그렇게 빨리 드시면 몸은 배가 부르다는 걸 알지 못해요. 그래서 필요한 양보다 더 먹게 될지도 몰라요.

남: 와, 그건 몰랐어요.

여: 인스턴트 음식을 자주 먹나요?

남: 전에는 인스턴트 음식을 먹곤 했지만 지금은 안 먹으려고 해요.

여: 잘 하셨어요. 그게 칼로리가 높거든요.

어휘

gain weight 살이 찌다 habit[hǽbit] 몡 습관 skip [skip] 통 거르다, 건너뛰다 overeat[òuvərí:t] 통 과식하다 meal[mi:l] 몡 식사 instant food 인스턴트 식품, 즉석 식품 calorie[kǽləri] 몡 칼로리, 열량

문제 해설

Q: 남자의 두 가지 나쁜 식습관을 고르시오.

아침을 먹지 않는 것과 빨리 먹는 습관이 좋지 않다고 했다.

2

W: Let me introduce you to some healthy foods. First, there's broccoli. You may have heard that broccoli is good for your body. Broccoli prevents cancer and has lots of vitamin C. Secondly, there's garlic. Eat it if you want to have a strong heart or stomach. It's also good when you're tired or have a cold. It has a strong smell, though. And if you're looking for healthy food that tastes good, blueberries are the answer. They're good for your eyes, and improve your memory.

여: 건강에 좋은 몇몇 음식들을 소개하겠습니다. 우선, 브로콜리가 있습니다. 브로콜리가 몸에 좋다는 말을 들어본 적이 있을 것입니다. 브로콜리는 암을 예방하고 많은 양의 비타민 C를 포함하고 있습니다. 두 번째로 마늘이 있습니다. 심장이나 위가 튼튼해지길 원하시면 마늘을 드세요. 피곤할 때나 감기에 걸렸을 때에도 좋습니다. 하지만, 냄새가 강하죠. 그리고 맛이 좋은 건강 음식을 찾으신다면 블루베리가 해답이죠. 눈에도 좋고 기억력을 좋게 해줍니다.

어휘

healthy[hélθi] 혱 건강에 좋은 broccoli[brákəli] 몡 브로콜리 prevent[privént] 통 예방하다 cancer[kǽnsər] 몡 암 vitamin[váitəmin] 몡 비타민 garlic[gάːrlik] 몡 마늘 heart[hɑːrt] 몡 심장 stomach[stʌ́mək] 몡 위 cold[kould] 몡 감기 blueberry[blúːbèri] 몡 블루베리 improve[imprúːv] 통 증진시키다, 개선하다 memory [méməri] 몡 기억력

문제 해설

Q: 각 인물에게 가장 좋은 음식을 고르시오.

(1) Joe: 감기에 걸렸어요.

(2) Amy: 잘 잊어버려요.

(3) Sean: 암에 걸리고 싶지 않아요.

감기에 걸렸을 때는 마늘이 좋고, 기억력을 좋게 해주는 것은 블루베리이고, 암을 예방하는 것은 브로콜리라고 했다.

Listening ★ Practice   p. 28

1 ② mQ1 ⓐ 2 ①, ③ mQ2 ⓑ 3 ③ mQ3 ⓐ
4 ③ mQ4 ⓐ 5 ④ mQ5 ⓒ 6 (1) T (2) F (3) F
mQ6 ⓑ

1

M: Welcome to *The Evening Show*, Sandra.

W: I'm glad to be here again.

M: You received the Grammy for Album of the Year. That's amazing.

W: It's all thanks to the love and support of my fans.

M: You're in your 60s now, but you look so young and energetic. What's your secret?

W: I try to be positive. I always try to have a cheerful view of life.

M: What else?

W: I usually eat lightly.

M: What kind of food do you enjoy?

W: I prefer fish to meat. Fish is low in fat, so it's healthier than meat.

M: I see. Now, we're excited to listen to some of your songs.

W: Okay. The first song I'm going to sing is *Yesterday*.

남: 'The Evening Show'에 오신 걸 환영합니다. Sandra.

여: 다시 나오게 되서 기쁩니다.

남: 그래미 올해의 앨범상을 수상하셨죠. 대단하십니다.

여: 모두 제 팬들의 사랑과 지지 덕분입니다.

남: 이제 60대이신데 매우 젊고 에너지가 넘쳐 보이세요. 비결이 뭐죠?

여: 전 긍정적이려고 노력해요. 항상 삶에 대해 밝은 관점을 가지려고 노력하죠.

남: 또 다른 것은요?

여: 평소에 적게 먹어요.

남: 어떤 종류의 음식을 즐겨 드세요?

여: 육류보다 어류를 선호해요. 어류는 지방 함량이 낮아서 육류보다 더 건강에 좋죠.

남: 알겠습니다. 이제 당신의 노래를 듣게 된다니 흥분이 되네요.

여: 네. 첫 번째로 부를 노래는 'Yesterday'입니다.

어휘

receive[risíːv] 통 받다   support[səpɔ́ːrt] 통 지탱하다;
*명 지지   energetic[ènərdʒétik] 형 에너지가 넘치는
secret[síːkrit] 명 비밀   positive[pázətiv] 형 긍정적인
cheerful[tʃíərfəl] 형 *밝은; 명랑한   view[vjuː] 명 관점, 시
각   lightly[láitli] 부 가볍게; *적게   fat[fæt] 명 지방
[문제] composer[kəmpóuzər] 명 작곡가

문제 해설

Q: 여자의 건강 비결이 아닌 것은?

여자가 운동을 한다는 내용은 언급되지 않았다.

mQ1: 화자 간의 관계는?

쇼 진행자가 가수를 초대해서 대화를 하고 노래를 듣는 상황
이다.

2

M: Ouch! My shoulder hurts.
W: Did you play computer games for a long time again?
M: No. Maybe I slept the wrong way last night.
W: I know a good exercise for shoulder pain.
M: Really? Please show me.
W: First, put both of your hands on your shoulders.
M: Like this?
W: Yes. And turn your arms in a large circle, ten times to the front and ten times to the back.
M: Oh, it's not difficult.
W: There's another position. Lie on your stomach and hold your ankles with your hands.
M: Okay.
W: Raise your upper body and legs, and then slowly put them down.
M: Wow, it's hard.
W: Your shoulder will get better if you do this several times a day.
M: Okay. Thanks.

남: 아야! 어깨가 아파.
여: 또 오랫동안 컴퓨터 게임을 했지?
남: 아니야. 아마 지난밤에 잠을 잘못 잤나 봐.
여: 어깨 통증에 좋은 운동을 알고 있는데.
남: 그래? 보여줘.
여: 우선, 양손을 어깨에 얹어.
남: 이렇게?
여: 응. 그리고 팔로 큰 원을 그리면서 앞으로 열 번, 뒤로 열 번
돌려.
남: 아, 어렵지 않네.
여: 다른 자세도 있어. 엎드려 누워서 손으로 발목을 잡아.

남: 알았어.
여: 상반신과 다리를 들어올려. 그런 다음 천천히 내려놓아.
남: 와, 힘들다.
여: 이렇게 하루에 몇 번씩 하면 어깨가 나아질 거야.
남: 알았어. 고마워.

어휘

Ouch! 아야!   shoulder[ʃóuldər] 명 어깨   hurt[həːrt] 통
아프다   sleep the wrong way 잠을 잘못된 자세로 자다
pain[pein] 명 통증   circle[sə́ːrkl] 명 원   position
[pəzíʃən] 명 자세   ankle[ǽŋkl] 명 발목   raise[reiz] 통 들
어올리다   upper body 상반신   put down 내려놓다

문제 해설

Q: 남자가 시도한 자세 두 가지를 고르시오.

어깨에 손을 얹고 돌리는 자세와 엎드려 누워서 손으로 발목
을 잡고 들어올리는 자세를 취했다.

mQ2: 남자의 어깨가 아픈 이유는?

남자는 잠을 잘못된 자세로 잤기 때문에 아픈 것 같다고 했다.

3

M: Do you think the flu is a cold that has got worse? It's not. Colds and the flu are from totally different viruses. A cold will go away in 3 to 4 days, but if you catch the flu, you could be sick for weeks. When you catch a cold, you might have a slight fever. But when you have the flu, you get a high fever. Also, flu viruses make you very tired and cause muscle pain. Finally, the flu can cause other sicknesses, but colds can't.

남: 독감이 감기가 악화된 것이라고 생각하시나요? 그렇지 않습
니다. 감기와 독감은 완전히 다른 바이러스 때문입니다. 감기
는 3일에서 4일 안에 괜찮아지지만, 독감에 걸리면 몇 주 동
안 아플 수 있습니다. 감기에 걸리면 약간의 열이 날 것입니다.
하지만 독감에 걸리면 고열이 생깁니다. 또한 독감 바이러스
는 사람을 아주 피곤하게 만들고 근육통을 일으킵니다. 마지
막으로 독감은 다른 질병을 야기시킬 수 있지만 감기는 그렇
지 않습니다.

어휘

flu[fluː] 명 독감   get worse 악화되다   totally[tóutəli]
부 완전히, 전적으로   virus[váiərəs] 명 바이러스   go away
사라지다, 낫다   slight[slait] 형 약한   fever[fíːvər] 명 열
cause[kɔːz] 통 일으키다, 야기하다   muscle[mʌ́sl] 명 근육
sickness[síknis] 명 질병   [문제] sneeze[sniːz] 통 재채기
하다

문제 해설

Q: 남자가 주로 이야기하고 있는 것은?

감기와 독감의 차이점에 대해 설명하고 있다.

mQ3: 독감의 증상으로 언급되지 않은 것은?
독감의 증상으로 재채기는 언급되지 않았다.

4

M: What brings you here?

W: I have a headache and a runny nose.

M: Have you been coughing or sneezing?

W: No, but I have a problem digesting my food, too. I think it gets worse when I'm in the office.

M: Is the air conditioner in your office always on?

W: Yes. I usually feel cold in the office.

M: That could be the reason. If there's more than a five-degree difference between outside and inside, that can cause problems.

W: Will I get better by taking medicine?

M: You don't need medicine. Instead, turn up the temperature at work. And air out the office regularly.

W: Okay.

M: Also, drink warm water often. And try to exercise and breathe fresh air.

W: I see. Thank you, doctor.

남: 여기 무슨 일로 오셨나요?

여: 두통이 있고 콧물이 나와요.

남: 기침이나 재채기를 하나요?

여: 아니요, 하지만 먹은 게 소화도 잘 안 돼요. 사무실에 있을 때면 더 심해지는 것 같아요.

남: 사무실에 에어컨이 항상 켜져 있나요?

여: 네. 보통 사무실에 있으면 추워요.

남: 그게 이유일 수 있겠군요. 외부와 실내 사이에 5도 이상 온도 차이가 있으면 그게 문제를 일으킬 수 있어요.

여: 약을 먹으면 나아질까요?

남: 약을 드실 필요는 없어요. 대신, 직장에서 (실내) 온도를 높이세요. 그리고 사무실을 규칙적으로 환기시키세요.

여: 알겠어요.

남: 또, 따뜻한 물을 자주 드세요. 그리고 운동을 하고 맑은 공기를 마시도록 하세요.

여: 알겠어요. 감사합니다. 선생님.

어휘

What brings you here? 무슨 일로 오셨나요?
headache[hédèik] 명 두통   runny nose 콧물   cough [kɔ(ː)f] 동 기침하다   digest[daidʒést] 동 소화하다   air conditioner 에어컨   degree[digríː] 명 (온도계 등의) 도   medicine[médisin] 명 약   turn up 올리다   temperature[témpərətʃər] 명 온도   air out 환기시키다   regularly[régjulərli] 부 규칙적으로   breathe[briːð] 동 숨 쉬다   [문제] spoil[spɔil] 동 상하다

문제 해설
Q: 여자가 아픈 이유는?
의사는 여자의 사무실 온도가 외부에 비해 너무 낮아서 아프게 된 것이라고 했다.

mQ4: 남자가 제안하지 않은 것은?
에어컨의 온도를 높이라고 했지 쓰지 말라는 말은 없었다.

5

W: Are you free this afternoon? Let's go to the movies.

M: I can't. I should go to my yoga class.

W: Yoga? I thought yoga was something women did to lose weight. Why are you doing it?

M: You know I have problems sleeping. But after doing yoga, I sleep well.

W: That's good. What else is good about yoga?

M: It's good for relieving stress. And it makes my skin clear.

W: Really? I'll have to try it for my skin. Which class are you taking?

M: The 6 p.m. class. Let's go together.

W: Oh, I'm not available then. Is there another time?

M: There are classes at 4 p.m. and 8 p.m., too.

W: Eight p.m. sounds good to me.

여: 오늘 오후에 시간되니? 영화 보러 가자.

남: 그럴 수 없어. 요가 수업에 가야 해.

여: 요가? 요가는 여자들이 살을 빼려고 하는 거라고 생각했는데. 넌 왜 하는 거야?

남: 알다시피 내가 잠을 잘 못 자서 문제잖아. 하지만 요가를 하고 나서는 잘 자.

여: 그거 잘됐다. 요가는 또 어떤 점이 좋아?

남: 스트레스를 해소하는 데 좋아. 그리고 피부를 맑게 해 줘.

여: 정말? 나도 피부를 위해 해봐야겠다. 넌 어떤 수업을 들어?

남: 저녁 6시 수업이야. 함께 가자.

여: 아, 그때는 시간이 안 돼. 다른 시간이 있어?

남: 오후 4시와 8시에도 수업이 있어.

여: 오후 8시 수업이 좋을 것 같아.

어휘

yoga[jóugə] 명 요가   lose weight 살을 빼다   relieve [rilíːv] 동 해소하다, 덜다   stress[stres] 명 스트레스   clear[kliər] 형 깨끗한, 맑은   available[əvéiləbl] 형 사용 가능한; *시간이 있는

문제 해설
Q: 여자가 요가를 하고 싶은 이유는?
여자는 피부를 맑게 하고 싶어서 요가를 해봐야겠다고 했다.

mQ5: 여자가 들으려는 수업은 언제인가?
저녁 8시 수업이 알맞겠다고 했다.

6

M: Why do you look so tired?

W: I'm just hot. I get hot easily.

M: Maybe it's because you don't get enough potassium.

W: Potassium? What is that?

M: It's one of the nutrients needed for good health. It's in fruits like bananas and oranges, and vegetables like spinach and tomatoes. So try to eat them a lot.

W: Which has the highest amount of potassium?

M: Tomatoes have the most, followed by spinach, bananas, and oranges.

W: Maybe I should eat tomatoes more often.

M: Also, coffee, alcohol, and sugar can push potassium out of your body. So don't have too much of those.

W: Okay. How about stopping by a supermarket for some tomatoes on the way home?

M: All right.

남: 왜 그렇게 피곤해 보이니?

여: 그냥 더워서. 내가 더위를 많이 타거든.

남: 칼륨을 충분히 섭취하지 않아서 그럴지도 몰라.

여: 칼륨? 그게 뭔데?

남: 건강을 위해 필요한 영양분 중의 하나야. 바나나, 오렌지 같은 과일과 시금치, 토마토 같은 채소에 들어 있어. 그러니 그런 것들을 많이 먹으려고 노력해.

여: 어떤 것에 칼륨이 가장 많이 들어 있는데?

남: 토마토에 가장 많고, 그 다음이 시금치, 바나나, 그리고 오렌지야.

여: 토마토를 좀 더 자주 먹어야 할까 봐.

남: 또, 커피와 술, 설탕은 칼륨을 몸 밖으로 빠져나가게 해. 그러니 그것들을 너무 많이 먹으면 안 돼.

여: 알았어. 집에 가는 길에 토마토 좀 사러 슈퍼마켓에 들르는 게 어때?

남: 좋아.

어휘

potassium[pətǽsiəm] 명 칼륨 nutrient[njúːtriənt] 명 영양분 vegetable[védʒitəbl] 명 채소 spinach[spínitʃ] 명 시금치 amount[əmáunt] 명 양, 분량 alcohol [ǽlkəhɔ̀(ː)l] 명 술 stop by ~에 들르다 on the way home 집으로 가는 길에 [문제] drop by ~에 들르다

문제 해설

Q: 사실이면 T, 사실이 아니면 F를 쓰시오.

(1) 칼륨을 충분히 먹지 않으면 쉽게 더위를 탈 수 있다.

(2) 바나나에는 시금치보다 칼륨이 더 많이 들어 있다.

(3) 칼륨을 설탕과 함께 섭취하는 것이 좋다.

칼륨이 불충분하면 더위를 타며, 칼륨은 바나나보다 시금치

에 더 많이 들어있고, 설탕은 칼륨을 체외로 배출시키므로 먹으면 좋지 않다고 했다.

mQ6: 그들이 다음에 할 일은?

집에 가는 길에 슈퍼마켓에 들러서 토마토를 사기로 했다.

Listening ★ Challenge **p. 30**

A 1 ① 2 ① B 1 ③ 2 ①

A [1-2]

W: Although feet do the important work of supporting our weight, people don't take good care of them. Let me tell you how you should care for your feet. First, it is important to dry in between the toes after washing your feet. To prevent your feet from drying up, use foot cream or lotion. And it's good to wear socks to absorb sweat even in summer. Don't wear the same shoes every day. Bacteria could grow in the shoes. If the bottom of your shoes is too hard, it puts pressure on your ankles and knees, so wear shoes with a cushion.

여: 발은 몸무게를 지탱하는 중요한 일을 하는데도 불구하고 우리는 발을 잘 돌보지 않습니다. 발을 어떻게 돌봐야 하는지 말씀 드릴게요. 우선, 발을 씻은 후에 발가락 사이를 말리는 것이 중요합니다. 발이 건조해지는 것을 예방하기 위해서 발 크림이나 로션을 사용하세요. 그리고 여름에도 땀을 흡수하도록 양말을 신는 것이 좋습니다. 매일 같은 신발을 신지 마세요. 박테리아가 신발에서 자랄 수 있습니다. 신발의 바닥이 너무 딱딱하면 발목과 무릎에 압력을 가할 수 있으니 쿠션이 있는 신발을 신으세요.

어휘

weight[weit] 명 무게; *체중 take good care of ~을 잘 돌보다 toe[tou] 명 발가락 prevent A from v-ing A가 ~하는 것을 막다 lotion[lóuʃən] 명 로션 absorb [æbsɔ́ːrb] 동 흡수하다 sweat[swet] 명 땀 bacteria [bæktí(ː)əriə] 명 박테리아, 세균 bottom[bátəm] 명 바닥 pressure[préʃər] 명 압력 knee[niː] 명 무릎 cushion [kúʃən] 명 쿠션 [문제] treat[triːt] 동 다루다 remove [rimúːv] 동 제거하다

문제 해설

Q1: 여자는 주로 무엇에 대해 이야기하고 있나?

① 발을 제대로 돌보는 방법

② 발이 건조하지 않게 하는 방법

③ 발이 신체를 위해 하는 일

④ 신발에서 박테리아를 없애는 것의 중요성

발을 잘 돌보기 위해 해야 할 일들에 대한 내용이다.

Q2: 잘못하고 있는 사람은?

① Jill: 난 여름에 양말을 신지 않으려고 해.

② Tom: 나는 샤워 후에 바로 발을 말려.

③ Betty: 난 항상 쿠션이 있는 신발을 사.

여름에도 땀 흡수를 위해서 양말을 신는 것이 좋다고 했다.

B [1-2]

W: I want to work out. What kind of programs do you have?

M: Swimming, yoga, tennis, and weight training. What's the purpose of your exercise?

W: I want to lose weight for the summer.

M: Then, how about doing weight training and swimming?

W: I'll just sign up for weight training.

M: Okay. Could you give us your name, please?

W: I'm Cathy Brown.

M: You can choose between a daily class and a three-times-a-week class.

W: Three times a week will be fine for me.

M: Okay. When do you want to start?

W: From May 14th.

M: How long do you want to register for? If you register for over six months, you can get a 10% discount.

W: Well, I'll just sign up for a month. How much will it be?

M: It's $90. Thank you for joining us.

여: 운동을 하고 싶어요. 어떤 종류의 프로그램이 있나요?

남: 수영과 요가, 테니스, 웨이트 트레이닝이 있어요. 운동하는 목적이 뭐죠?

여: 여름을 대비해 살을 빼고 싶어요.

남: 그럼 웨이트 트레이닝과 수영을 하는 게 어떨까요?

여: 웨이트 트레이닝만 등록할게요.

남: 좋습니다. 성함을 좀 알려주시겠어요?

여: 전 Cathy Brown이에요.

남: 매일반과 주 3회 반 중에 선택하실 수 있어요.

여: 주 3회 반이 좋을 것 같아요.

남: 알겠습니다. 언제 시작하시겠어요?

여: 5월 14일부터요.

남: 기간은 얼마나 등록하시겠어요? 6개월 이상 등록하시면, 10% 할인을 받으실 수 있어요.

여: 음, 그냥 한 달만 신청할게요. 얼마죠?

남: 90달러예요. 가입해 주셔서 감사합니다.

어휘

work out 운동하다   weight training 웨이트 트레이닝
purpose [pə́ːrpəs] 명 목적   sign up for 등록하다, 참가하다   daily [déili] 형 매일의   register [rédʒistər] 통 등록하

다   discount [dískaunt] 명 할인   [문제] membership [mémbərʃip] 명 회원임

문제 해설

Q1: 틀린 정보를 고르시오.

여자는 매일반이 아니라 주 3회 반에 등록하기로 했다.

Q2: 여자는 얼마 동안 체육관에 다닐 것인가?

한 달만 등록한다고 했다.

Critical ★ Thinking   p. 31

1 ④   2 (1) ⓒ   (2) ⓑ

M: Jenny, let's have lunch together.

W: Sorry, Steve. I'm on a diet. So I'm just going to have a few tomatoes.

M: What? When did you start dieting?

W: It's been a week. I eat tomatoes for lunch and don't eat dinner.

M: Skipping meals isn't a good way of losing weight.

W: Well... this is the only way to lose a lot of weight in a short time.

M: But you'll probably gain back more weight after the diet. The best way to lose weight is through balanced eating and exercise.

W: But I gain weight easily even though I don't eat that much. So I have no other choice.

M: I'll lend you a book about eating a healthy diet. You'll change your mind after reading it.

W: All right. Thanks for your concern.

남: Jenny, 함께 점심 먹자.

여: 미안해, Steve. 난 다이어트 중이야. 그래서 토마토 몇 개만 먹으려고 해.

남: 뭐? 다이어트를 언제 시작했는데?

여: 일주일 되었어. 점심에는 토마토를 먹고 저녁은 먹지 않아.

남: 식사를 거르는 것은 살을 빼는 좋은 방법이 아니야.

여: 음… 단시간에 체중을 많이 줄이는 유일한 방법이야.

남: 하지만 다이어트 이후에 다시 살이 더 찔지도 몰라. 살을 빼는 최선의 방법은 균형이 잡힌 식사와 운동을 통한 것이야.

여: 하지만 난 그렇게 많이 먹지 않는데도 쉽게 살이 쪄. 그래서 다른 방법이 없어.

남: 건강한 식사하기에 대한 책을 빌려 줄게. 읽고 나면 생각이 바뀔 거야.

여: 그래. 걱정해줘서 고마워.

어휘

be [go] on a diet 다이어트를 하는 중이다   balanced

[bǽlənst] 형 균형이 잡힌   concern[kənsɔ́ːrn] 명 걱정, 관심
[문제] effect[ifékt] 명 영향   proper[prápər] 형 적절한

Q1: 그들은 주로 무엇에 대해 이야기하고 있는가?
　　① 다이어트의 나쁜 영향
　　② 살을 빼는 가장 빠른 방법
　　③ 다이어트에 좋은 음식
　　④ 다이어트를 하는 최선의 방법
　　다이어트를 하는 최선의 방법에 대한 내용이다.

Q2: 각 인물의 의견을 고르시오.
　　ⓐ 다이어트를 하기 전에 의사를 만나라.
　　ⓑ 식사를 거르는 것이 살을 빼는 빠른 방법이다.
　　ⓒ 살을 빼기 위해 적절한 식사와 운동을 해라.
　　(1) Steve는 균형이 잡힌 식사와 운동을 살을 빼는 최선의
　　　　방법으로 생각한다.
　　(2) Jenny는 식사를 거르는 것이 살을 빼는 가장 빠른 방법
　　　　이라고 생각하고 있다.

UNIT 05 Transportation & Location

Getting ★ Ready   p. 32

A 1 ⓔ 2 ⓒ 3 ⓖ 4 ⓗ 5 ⓑ 6 ⓐ
B 1 ⓑ 2 ⓓ 3 ⓐ

B 1 여: 왜 교통이 정체되는 거지?
　　 남: 지금 러시아워잖아.
　2 여: 출발 시각이 언제죠?
　　 남: 뉴욕행 기차는 10시에 출발해요.
　3 여: 네가 지금 어디 있는지 알아?
　　 남: 나는 Main Avenue와 만나는 Charles Street에 있어.

Listening ★ Start   p. 33

1 ③ / Where to, will it take, due to, traffic jam,
  because of roadwork, Why don't you call
2 ③ / Similar to a motorcycle, three wheels,
  Along with a driver, no doors, other vehicles

1

M: Good morning. Where to, ma'am?
W: To Harbor City, please. How long will it take?
M: It usually takes about 15 minutes. But it
   might take longer due to heavy traffic.
W: It's not rush hour, so why is there a traffic

jam? Was there a car accident?
M: I don't think so. It's because of roadwork.
W: Oh, I see. I think I'm going to be late for my
   appointment with my friend.
M: Why don't you call your friend now?
W: I think I should.

남: 좋은 아침입니다. 어디로 모실까요, 손님?
여: Harbor City로요. 얼마나 걸릴까요?
남: 보통 15분 정도 걸려요. 하지만 교통 체증 때문에 더 걸릴지
　　도 몰라요.
여: 러시아워가 아닌데 왜 교통이 혼잡하죠? 교통사고가 있었나
　　요?
남: 그런 것 같지는 않고요. 도로 공사 때문이에요.
여: 아, 알겠어요. 친구와의 약속시간에 늦을 것 같네요.
남: 지금 친구에게 전화를 하시는 게 어떨까요?
여: 그래야 할 것 같군요.

Where to? 어디로 모실까요?   **due to** ~ 때문에
heavy traffic 교통 체증   **rush hour** 러시아워(혼잡한 출
퇴근 시간)   **traffic jam** 교통 정체   **accident**[ǽksidənt]
명 사고   **roadwork**[róudwə̀ːrk] 명 도로 공사
appointment[əpɔ́intmənt] 명 약속

Q: 교통 체증이 심한 이유는?
　　남자의 말에 따르면 교통 체증은 도로 공사 때문이다.

2

W: This kind of transportation is common in
   Thailand. Similar to a motorcycle, it is
   powered by an engine and has handlebars. It has three wheels, one in the front
   and two in the back. The driver sits in the
   front, and the passenger seat is in the back.
   Along with a driver, it can hold two or three
   passengers. It has a roof but no doors. So
   when you use this kind of transportation,
   the pollution from other vehicles may be
   unpleasant.

여: 이 교통수단은 태국에서 흔합니다. 오토바이와 비슷해서 엔
　　진으로 동력을 얻고 핸들이 있습니다. 세 개의 바퀴가 있는데,
　　하나는 앞에 두 개는 뒤에 있습니다. 운전자는 앞에 앉고 승
　　객의 좌석은 뒤에 있습니다. 운전자와 더불어 두세 명의 승
　　객을 수용할 수 있습니다. 지붕은 있지만 문이 없습니다. 그
　　래서 이 교통수단을 이용할 때에는 다른 차들에서 나오는 공
　　해가 불쾌할지도 모릅니다.

transportation[træ̀nspərtéiʃən] 명 교통수단   **common**

[kámən] 형 흔한 similar to ~와 비슷한 motorcycle
[móutərsàikl] 명 오토바이 power[páuər] 동 ~에 동력을
공급하다 engine[énʤin] 명 엔진 handlebar[hǽndlbàːr]
명 (자전거 등의) 핸들 wheel[hwiːl] 명 바퀴 passenger
[pǽsənʤər] 명 승객 along with ~와 더불어 roof[ru(ː)f]
명 지붕 pollution[pəlúːʃən] 명 공해 vehicle[víːikl] 명
차량, 운송수단 unpleasant[ʌnplézənt] 형 불쾌한

문제 해설

Q: 여자가 이야기하고 있는 교통수단의 종류는?

바퀴가 앞에 하나, 뒤에 두 개로 총 세 개이며 엔진으로 움직
이는 태국의 대표적 교통수단인 툭툭(Tuk Tuk)에 대한 내용
이다.

Listening ★ Practice   **p. 34**

1 ③ mQ1 ⓑ 2 ② mQ2 ⓑ 3 ② mQ3 ⓒ
4 ③ mQ4 (1) F (2) T 5 ② mQ5 ⓒ
6 (1) ⓓ (2) ⓐ (3) ⓑ mQ6 ⓑ

1

W: Joe, do you know how to get to Dodger
Stadium?
M: Oh, are you going to watch a baseball
game?
W: Yes, there's a Dodgers game this evening.
How can I get there?
M: The bus is quicker than the subway,
because there is a direct bus.
W: How long does it take?
M: About 20 minutes. The stadium is about a
ten-minute walk from the bus stop.
W: Ten minutes? That's quite far. I don't want
to walk a lot.
M: Take a subway then. The subway station is
just in front of the stadium.
W: That's good. How long does it take?
M: About 40 minutes.
W: That sounds like my best choice.

여: Joe, 다저스타디움으로 가는 방법 알아?
남: 아, 야구 경기 보려고?
여: 응, Dodgers 경기가 오늘 저녁에 있어. 거기 어떻게 갈 수
있지?
남: 직행 버스가 있어서 버스가 지하철보다 더 빨라.
여: 얼마나 걸려?
남: 20분 정도. 경기장은 버스 정류장에서 걸어서 10분 정도 거
리에 있어.
여: 10분? 꽤 멀다. 많이 걷고 싶지 않은데.
남: 그럼 지하철을 타. 지하철역은 경기장 바로 앞에 있어.

여: 그거 잘 됐다. 얼마나 걸려?
남: 40분 정도.
여: 그게 나에겐 최선의 선택인 것 같아.

어휘

stadium [stéidiəm] 명 경기장 direct [dirékt] 형 직통인
quite [kwait] 부 꽤, 아주 choice [tʃɔis] 명 선택 [문제]
advantage [ədvǽntiʤ] 명 이점

문제 해설

Q: 여자가 이용할 교통수단은?

버스 정류장에서 10분이나 더 걸어야 하기 때문에 경기장 바
로 앞까지 가는 지하철을 타겠다고 했다.

mQ1: 버스를 타면 좋은 점은?

지하철은 40분이 걸리지만 직행 버스는 20분이 걸리고 내려
서 10분을 걸어야 하므로 시간이 더 적게 걸린다.

2

(Telephone rings.)
W: Thank you for calling Farmer John's
Restaurant.
M: Hello. I'm on my way to your restaurant,
but I seem to have got lost.
W: Do you know where you are?
M: I'm on Baker Avenue where it meets
Charles Street.
W: I got it. Go straight one block along Baker
Avenue and take a left turn on Oak Street.
M: Take a left turn on Oak Street?
W: Right. Then, you'll see the restaurant on
your right. It'll take about 15 minutes.
M: Fifteen minutes? I have a reservation at six,
so I'm going to be a bit late.
W: Then I'll reschedule it to 6:10. Will that be
okay?
M: Perfect. Thank you.

(전화벨이 울린다.)
여: Farmer John's 레스토랑에 전화 주셔서 감사합니다.
남: 여보세요. 그 식당으로 가는 길인데 길을 잃은 것 같아요.
여: 계신 곳이 어딘지 아세요?
남: Baker Avenue와 Charles Street가 만나는 곳에 있어요.
여: 알겠어요. Baker Avenue를 따라 한 블록을 곧바로 가시고
Oak Street에서 왼쪽으로 도세요.
남: Oak Street에서 왼쪽으로 돌아요?
여: 맞아요. 그러면 오른편으로 식당이 보일 거예요. 15분 정도
걸릴 거예요.
남: 15분이요? 6시로 예약했는데 그럼 조금 늦겠네요.
여: 그럼 6시 10분으로 다시 예약해 드릴게요. 괜찮으시겠어요?
남: 완벽해요. 감사합니다.

어휘

on one's way to ~로 가는 길에　get lost 길을 잃다
go straight 직진하다　take a left[right] turn 왼쪽[오른쪽]으로 돌다　reservation[rèzərvéiʃən] 몡 예약　a bit 약간　reschedule[rì:skédʒu:l] 동 일정을 다시 잡다

문제 해설

Q: Farmer John's 레스토랑을 지도에서 고르시오.
　Baker Avenue와 Charles Street의 교차점에서 Baker Avenue를 따라 한 블록을 가서 Oak Street에서 왼쪽으로 돌면 오른편에 보이는 건물이다.

mQ2: 남자의 예약은 몇 시로 바뀌었나?
　6시 예약이었지만 10분 뒤로 조정했다.

3

M: Have you finished your science report about the ideal transportation of the future?
W: I've almost finished.
M: What did you write about?
W: I chose a car with wings. I hope that someday there's a car that can fly.
M: That would be great. We could easily avoid traffic jams with those cars.
W: Also, they'd have a special sensor that could sense possible danger.
M: Amazing!
W: What do you think the ideal transportation of the future is?
M: I think we should worry more about the environment than design or functions.
W: I think you're right.
M: So I imagined a car which uses the energy from the sun. It's a small car for one person.
W: Great.

남: 미래의 이상적인 교통수단에 대한 과학 보고서 끝냈니?
여: 거의 끝냈어.
남: 무엇에 대해 썼어?
여: 날개가 달린 자동차를 골랐어. 언젠가 날 수 있는 차가 생겼으면 해.
남: 그거 멋지겠다. 그런 차들이 있으면 교통 체증을 쉽게 피할 수 있을 거야.
여: 또, 일어남 직한 위험을 감지하는 특수 센서가 달려 있을 거야.
남: 멋지다!
여: 넌 미래의 이상적인 교통수단이 뭐라고 생각해?
남: 디자인이나 기능보다는 환경에 대해 더 걱정해야 한다고 생각해.
여: 맞는 말인 것 같다.
남: 그래서 태양으로부터 오는 에너지를 사용하는 차를 상상했어. 한 사람이 탈 수 있는 작은 차야.
여: 멋지다.

어휘

ideal[aidí(:)əl] 톙 *이상적인; 상상의　someday[sʌ́mdèi] 児 언젠가, 훗날　avoid[əvɔ́id] 동 피하다　sensor[sénsər] 몡 센서, 감지기　sense[sens] 동 감지하다　possible [pásəbl] 톙 가능한; *있음직한　environment[inváiərənmənt] 몡 환경　function[fʌ́ŋkʃən] 몡 기능　imagine[imǽdʒin] 동 상상하다　energy[énərdʒi] 몡 에너지

문제 해설

Q: 여자가 미래 교통수단으로 생각하는 것은?
　여자는 날개가 달린 자동차를 상상했다.

mQ3: 남자가 미래 교통수단에 대해 중요하게 생각하는 것은?
　남자는 디자인이나 기능보다는 환경과 관련된 사항을 중요하게 생각한다고 말했다.

4

M: Ladies and gentlemen, have you enjoyed your flight? This is Captain Williams speaking. We'll be arriving at Vancouver International Airport in about 15 minutes. All passengers must return to their seats and fasten their seat belts. Also, please put your seats forward, and open the window shades for landing. The local time in Vancouver right now is ten minutes past six. According to the latest weather report, it is rainy in Vancouver, and the temperature is 19 degrees Celsius. Thank you.

남: 신사숙녀 여러분, 즐거운 비행이 되셨나요? 저는 기장 Williams입니다. 우리는 약 15분 후에 밴쿠버 국제 공항에 도착할 것입니다. 모든 승객 여러분께서는 자리로 돌아가서 안전 벨트를 해 주십시오. 또한 의자를 앞으로 세워 주시고 착륙을 위해 창문 덮개를 열어 주십시오. 현재 밴쿠버의 현지 시각은 6시 10분입니다. 가장 최근의 일기예보에 의하면 밴쿠버에는 비가 내리고 있고 기온은 섭씨 19도입니다. 감사합니다.

어휘

flight[flait] 몡 비행　international[intərnǽʃənəl] 톙 국제의　fasten[fǽsən] 동 채우다, 매다　seat belt 안전 벨트　forward[fɔ́:rwərd] 児 앞쪽으로　window shade 창문 덮개　land[lænd] 동 착륙하다　local time 현지 시각　latest[léitist] 톙 최신의　weather report 일기예보　temperature[témpərətʃər] 몡 기온　degree[digrí:] 몡 (온도계의) 도　Celsius[sélsiəs] 톙 섭씨의　[문제] take off 이륙하다

문제 해설

Q: 비행 중에 이 안내방송을 언제 들을 수 있는가?
　착륙하기 전 해야 할 일들에 대한 안내방송이므로 착륙 전임을 알 수 있다.

mQ4: 사실이면 T, 사실이 아니면 F를 쓰시오.

밴쿠버의 현지 시각은 6시 10분이고 밴쿠버에는 비가 오고 있다고 안내했다.

5

M: How can I help you?

W: I'd like to buy a ticket for a ferry to Italy.

M: You can choose from two routes. There is a ferry for Brindisi and one for Bari.

W: When are their departure times?

M: The ferry for Brindisi leaves at 9:30 a.m., and the one for Bari leaves at 1:30 p.m.

W: What's the price?

M: It depends on the type of seat. A cabin seat is 150 euros and a deck seat is 75 euros.

W: So it doesn't depend on my destination, right?

M: Right.

W: I'll buy a ticket for tomorrow to Bari. And I'll take a cabin seat.

M: Okay.

W: Here it is.

남: 무엇을 도와드릴까요?

여: 이탈리아로 가는 페리의 승차권을 사려고 해요.

남: 두 가지 노선 중에 고를 수 있으세요. 브린디시와 바리로 가는 배가 있습니다.

여: 출발 시각이 언제죠?

남: 브린디시로 가는 배는 오전 9시 30분에 떠나고 바리로 가는 배는 오후 1시 30분에 떠납니다.

여: 가격은 얼마죠?

남: 좌석의 종류에 따라 다릅니다. 선실석은 150유로이고 갑판석은 75유로입니다.

여: 그럼 도착지와는 상관없는 것이네요, 그렇죠?

남: 맞습니다.

여: 바리로 가는 내일 승차권을 사겠어요. 그리고 선실석으로 할게요.

남: 알겠습니다.

여: 여기 있습니다.

어휘

ferry[féri] 명 페리, 선박   route[ruːt] 명 노선
departure[dipáːrtʃər] 명 출발   depend on ~에 따라 다르다   cabin[kǽbin] 명 선실   euro[júərou] 명 유로화   deck[dek] 명 갑판   destination[dèstənéiʃən] 명 도착지

문제 해설

Q: 틀린 정보를 고르시오.

바리행 페리의 출발 시각은 오후 1시 30분이다.

mQ5: 페리의 승차권 가격을 결정하는 것은?

선실 좌석인지 갑판 좌석인지에 따라 달라진다.

6

W: This weekend, I'm going to take a trip to Edinburgh. While planning the trip, I couldn't easily decide what transportation to take. At first, I was going to take a plane. But it's the busy season, so the tickets are very expensive. I decided to find another option. I don't like to take trains because they are often delayed. Finally, I decided to take a long-distance bus. It departs London at 11 p.m., and arrives in Edinburgh at 7 a.m. It'll be a long journey, but I'm happy about saving money.

여: 이번 주말에 전 에딘버러로 여행을 갈 거예요. 여행을 계획하면서 어떤 교통수단을 탈지 쉽게 결정할 수 없었죠. 처음엔, 비행기를 타려고 했어요. 하지만 성수기라서 표가 아주 비싸요. 전 다른 선택사항을 찾기로 했죠. 기차는 종종 연착되기 때문에 타고 싶지 않아요. 결국 장거리 버스를 타기로 결정했어요. 런던에서 밤 11시에 출발해서 에딘버러에 오전 7시에 도착해요. 긴 여정이 되겠지만 돈을 아끼니까 좋아요.

어휘

busy season 성수기   option[ápʃən] 명 선택사항
delay[diléi] 동 지연시키다   long-distance[lɔ́ːŋdístəns]
형 장거리의   depart[dipáːrt] 동 출발하다   journey
[dʒə́ːrni] 명 여정, 여행   [문제] run[rʌn] 동 운행하다   fare
[fɛər] 명 요금

문제 해설

Q: 각각의 교통수단에 대한 여자의 의견을 고르시오.

비행기는 성수기 요금이라 너무 비싸고, 기차는 종종 연착되며, 버스는 시간이 오래 걸린다고 생각한다.

mQ6: 여자가 에딘버러에 도착하는 때는?

장거리 버스는 런던에서 밤 11시에 출발해서 에딘버러에 오전 7시에 도착한다.

Listening ★ Challenge   p. 36

A 1 ② 2 ②   B 1 ② 2 ④

A [1-2]

(Telephone rings.)

W: Hello.

M: Hello, this is Alex.

W: Hey, where are you? We've finished preparing for Sally's birthday party.

M: I came out of exit number 4, but I can't find the bakery you mentioned.

W: You should have come out of exit number 3, not number 4.

M: I guess I have to go back into the station, then.

W: Just tell me what you can see around you.

M: There is a church on my left.

W: I got it. Go straight two blocks, and you'll see the bakery. Then turn left at the corner.

M: Okay. And then?

W: Go straight one block and turn left at the corner. We are in the café that is on your right.

M: I see.

W: Don't forget to buy candles for the cake on the way.

M: Okay. Did you buy a birthday card?

W: Yes. Hurry up.

(전화벨이 울린다.)

여: 여보세요.

남: 여보세요, 나 Alex야.

여: 이봐, 어디야? 우린 Sally 생일 파티 준비를 끝냈어.

남: 4번 출구로 나왔는데 네가 말한 빵집을 찾을 수가 없어.

여: 4번이 아니라 3번 출구로 나왔어야지.

남: 그럼 다시 역으로 돌아가야겠다.

여: 그냥 주변에 보이는 걸 얘기해봐.

남: 왼편으로 교회가 있어.

여: 알겠다. 두 블록을 직진하면 빵집이 보일 거야. 그러면 모퉁이에서 왼쪽으로 돌아.

남: 알았어. 그리고 나선?

여: 한 블록을 직진해서 모퉁이에서 왼쪽으로 돌아. 우리는 오른편에 있는 까페에 있어.

남: 알았어.

여: 오는 길에 케이크에 쓸 초 사오는 거 잊지 마.

남: 알았어. 생일 카드는 샀어?

여: 응. 서둘러.

exit[égzit] 명 출구 bakery[béikəri] 명 빵집 mention [ménʃən] 동 언급하다 corner[kɔ́ːrnər] 명 모퉁이 candle[kǽndl] 명 초

문제 해설

Q1: 남자가 가고 있는 카페를 고르시오.

교회가 왼편이 되는 위치에서 시작하여 두 블록 가고 왼쪽으로 돈 뒤 한 블록 더 가서 왼쪽으로 돌면 오른편에 위치한 건물이다.

Q2: 남자가 살 것은?

여자가 생일 케이크에 쓸 양초를 사오라고 했다.

B [1-2]

M: Do you know that each airline has different standards for the temperature on their airplanes? The airlines usually set this standard temperature after studying their passengers. For example, the airlines of Africa and Southeast Asia keep the temperature around 25 degrees. American and European airlines maintain the temperature at around 22 degrees. But there is one interesting fact. The standard temperature is usually colder than most passengers like. This is because if passengers feel cold, they can cover themselves with more blankets. However, if it's too hot, they can only get angry and complain about it.

남: 각 항공사가 자사 비행기의 온도에 대해 각기 다른 표준을 가지고 있다는 것을 아세요? 항공사는 보통 승객을 연구한 다음 이 표준 온도를 정합니다. 예를 들어, 아프리카와 동남아시아의 항공사들은 25도 정도의 온도를 유지합니다. 미국과 유럽 항공사들은 22도 정도의 온도를 유지합니다. 하지만 재미있는 사실이 하나 있습니다. 이 표준 온도는 보통 대부분의 승객이 선호하는 온도보다 더 춥다는 것입니다. 이는 승객들이 춥다고 느끼면 담요를 더 많이 덮으면 되기 때문입니다. 그러나 너무 더운 경우라면 승객들은 화가 나서 불평을 할 수밖에 없습니다.

어휘

airline[ɛ́ərlàin] 명 항공사 standard[stǽndərd] 명 표준; 형 표준의 maintain[meintéin] 동 유지하다, 지속하다 blanket[blǽŋkit] 명 담요 complain[kəmpléin] 동 불평하다 [문제] in-flight[inflàit] 형 기내의, 비행 중의

문제 해설

Q1: 남자는 주로 무엇에 대해 말하고 있나?

① 왜 일부 사람들이 비행기에서 덥다고 느끼는지

② 기내 온도가 어떻게 결정되는지

③ 사람들이 선호하는 기내 온도가 무엇인지

④ 왜 몇몇 항공사들은 다른 곳들보다 더 추운지

기내 표준 온도가 어떻게 정해지는지에 대해 설명하고 있다.

Q2: 아프리카 항공사 비행기의 일반 온도는?

아프리카 항공사들은 25도 정도로 기내 온도를 유지한다고 했다.

Critical ★ Thinking p. 37

1 (1) For (2) For (3) Against

2 (1) ⓐ (2) ⓒ (3) ⓑ

W1: I'm Julia. Cars seriously pollute the air we breathe. Bicycles, however, do not harm the environment. Therefore, we should build more bicycle lanes, and encourage people to use bikes instead of cars.

M: I'm Daniel. According to the law, a bicycle is a kind of vehicle. That means we should ride our bikes on the road. However, doing so is very dangerous for bicycle riders. I think we should build bicycle lanes to protect our citizens.

W2: I'm Sarah. There's just not enough space to build new bicycle lanes in our city. If we build bicycle lanes along the roads, the roads will become narrower. Imagine how bad the traffic jams will be.

여1: 난 Julia야. 자동차는 우리가 숨쉬는 공기를 심각하게 오염시켜. 하지만 자전거는 환경에 해를 끼치지 않아. 그러니까 더 많은 자전거 전용로를 만들어서 사람들이 차 대신에 자전거를 이용하도록 권장해야 해.

남: 난 Daniel이야. 법에 의하면 자전거는 차량의 한 종류야. 그건 자전거를 도로에서 타야 한다는 걸 의미하지. 그렇지만 그렇게 하는 것은 자전거 운전자에겐 아주 위험해. 난 시민들을 보호하기 위해 자전거 전용로를 만들어야 한다고 생각해.

여2: 난 Sarah야. 우리 도시에는 새로운 자전거 전용로를 만들 공간이 충분하지 않아. 도로를 따라 자전거 전용로를 만든다면 도로는 더 좁아질 거야. 교통 체증이 얼마나 심할지 상상해 봐.

어휘

seriously[sí(:)əriəsli] 🖩 심각하게 pollute[pəlú:t] 통 오염시키다 breathe[bri:ð] 통 숨쉬다 harm[ha:rm] 통 훼손하다, 해를 끼치다 therefore[ðɛ́ərfɔ̀ːr] 🖩 그러므로 bicycle lane 자전거 전용로 encourage[inkɔ́:ridʒ] 통 권장하다 law[lɔ:] 명 법 protect[prətékt] 통 보호하다 citizen[sítizən] 명 시민 space[speis] 명 공간 narrow[nǽrou] 형 좁은

문제 해설

Q1: 각 인물이 자전거 전용로 건설에 찬성하는지 반대하는지 ✓표 하시오.

　　Julia는 환경을 위해, Daniel은 자전거 운전자의 안전을 위해 찬성하는 입장이고, Sarah는 교통 체증이 유발될 수 있어 반대하는 입장이다.

Q2: 각 인물과 그들의 의견을 연결하시오.

　　ⓐ 자전거를 타는 것은 환경에 좋은 일이다.

　　ⓑ 더 많은 자전거 전용로를 만드는 것은 교통 체증을 악화시킬 것이다.

　　ⓒ 자전거 전용로는 자전거 운전자의 안전을 위해 필요하다.

UNIT 06 Money

Getting ★ Ready　p. 38

A 1 ⓒ　2 ⓕ　3 ⓔ　4 ⓖ　5 ⓐ　6 ⓑ
B 1 ⓒ　2 ⓐ　3 ⓓ

B 1 여: 환율이 어떻게 돼요?
　　남: 1달러에 1,200원 정도예요.

　2 여: 네가 얼마나 받는지 물어봐도 돼?
　　남: 한 시간에 10달러.

　3 여: 금전 관리 프로그램의 좋은 점이 뭐야?
　　남: 너의 지출 습관을 알 수 있어.

Listening ★ Start　p. 39

1 ③ / working part-time, borrow money, a small amount of money, gets pocket money, how to tell him

2 ① / regular pocket money, how to manage money, different kinds of items, It'll help him, what if, cleaning out the garage

1

M: I'm working part-time after school to earn my own pocket money. After I started working, my friend Gerry started asking to borrow money from me quite often. Each time, he asks for just a small amount of money, like 5 or 10 dollars. The problem is that he never pays me back. Gerry is from a rich family and gets pocket money from his parents. But he spends all that money on stupid computer games. I'm very angry at him, but I don't know how to tell him.

남: 난 용돈을 벌기 위해서 방과 후에 아르바이트를 하고 있어. 내가 일을 시작한 후로 내 친구인 Gerry가 꽤 자주 나에게 돈을 빌려달라고 부탁하기 시작했어. 그 애는 매번 5달러나 10달러와 같이 적은 돈만 요구해. 문제는 그 애가 절대 돈을 갚지 않는다는 거야. Gerry는 집이 부유하고 부모님께 용돈을 받아. 하지만 그 애는 그 모든 돈을 시시한 컴퓨터 게임에 써버려. 난 그 애에게 정말 화가 나지만 그 애한테 어떻게 말을 해야 할지 모르겠어.

어휘

part-time[pá:rttáim] 🖩 파트타임으로 earn[ə:rn] 통 벌다 pocket money 용돈 borrow[bárou] 통 빌리다 pay

back 돌려주다, 갚다   stupid[stjú:pid] 휑 어리석은; *시시한
[문제] jealous[dʒéləs] 휑 질투하는   steal[sti:l] 동 훔치다
(steal-stole-stolen)

문제 해설
Q: 소년의 문제는?
소년은 자신의 친구인 Gerry가 돈을 빌려가기만 하고 갚지
않아 화가 났다.

2

M: Honey, I think it's time to give Paul regular
pocket money. He's 10 years old now.
W: That's a good idea. He should learn how to
manage money.
M: Then let's give him money every Monday.
W: Okay. And how about giving him separate
money for different kinds of items?
M: You mean we should give him one amount
for snacks and another for clothes, like that?
W: That's right. It'll help him, because he has
never managed his own money before.
M: Great. But what if he spends all the money
before Monday?
W: Then we'll make him work to get more
money, by cleaning out the garage.

남: 여보. 이제 Paul에게 정기적으로 용돈을 줘야 할 때인 거 같
아요. 그 애도 이제 10살이잖아요.
여: 좋은 생각이에요. 그 애도 돈을 관리하는 법을 배워야 해요.
남: 그럼 매주 월요일에 돈을 줍시다.
여: 그래요. 그리고 품목별로 돈을 분리해서 주는 게 어때요?
남: 간식용으로 얼마를 주고 옷을 살 용도로 얼마를 주는 식으로
말인가요?
여: 맞아요. 그게 그 애한테 도움이 될 거예요. 그 애는 이전에
자신의 돈을 한 번도 관리해본 적이 없으니까요.
남: 좋아요. 그런데 그 애가 월요일 이전에 돈을 다 써버리면 어
쩌죠?
여: 그럼 돈을 더 받기 위해 차고를 청소한다든지 일을 하도록
해야죠.

어휘
regular[régjulər] 휑 *정기적인; 규칙적인   manage
[mǽnidʒ] 동 관리하다   separate[sépərit] *휑 분리된;
동 분리하다   item[áitəm] 명 항목, 품목   garage[gərá:dʒ]
명 차고

문제 해설
Q: 그들은 주로 무엇에 대해 이야기하고 있는가?
① 용돈을 어떻게 줄 것인가
② 10대들이 돈을 어디에 쓰는가
③ 10대들에게 충분한 용돈은 얼마인가
④ 정기적인 용돈을 주는 것이 왜 중요한가

두 사람은 Paul에게 정기적인 용돈을 언제, 어떤 식으로 줄
것인지에 대해 이야기하고 있다.

1 ②   mQ1 ⓐ   2 ②   mQ2 ⓑ   3 ②   mQ3 ⓐ
4 ①   mQ4 ⓐ   5 ④   mQ5 (1) Short (2) Heavy
6 ①   mQ6 ⓒ

1

M: Hey, are you ready for your trip to Britain?
W: Almost. I've nearly finished doing everything.
M: Did you exchange any money?
W: I don't need to. After my mom went to
France, she gave me 400 euro.
M: But the euro isn't used in Britain. British
people still use the pound.
W: I thought all European countries used the
euro.
M: Most of them do, but some countries like
Sweden and Switzerland have their own
money system.
W: I should go to a bank to exchange money,
then.
M: How much are you going to exchange?
W: Well, what's the exchange rate?
M: 10 US dollars equals about 6 pounds.
W: I think 600 dollars will be enough. That's
about 360 pounds.

남: 얘, 영국에 여행갈 준비는 했니?
여: 거의. 거의 다 됐어.
남: 환전은 했니?
여: 안 해도 돼. 우리 엄마가 프랑스에 다녀오신 후에 나한테
400유로를 주셨거든.
남: 하지만 유로화는 영국에서 사용할 수 없는걸. 영국인들은 아
직도 파운드를 쓰거든.
여: 난 모든 유럽국가에서 유로화를 사용한다고 생각했는데.
남: 거의 그렇긴 한데 스웨덴이나 스위스와 같은 몇몇 국가들은
자신들만의 통화 체계를 갖고 있어.
여: 그럼 은행에 가서 환전을 해야겠다.
남: 얼마나 환전할 거야?
여: 음, 환율이 얼마지?
남: 미화 10달러는 6파운드 정도야.
여: 600달러면 충분할 것 같아. 대략 360파운드 정도 되겠다.

어휘
Britain[brítən] 명 영국   nearly[níərli] 부 거의
exchange[ikstʃéindʒ] 동 교환하다; *환전하다   euro[júərou]
명 유로화   pound[paund] 명 파운드(영국의 화폐 단위)

38

Sweden[swíːdən] 명 스웨덴 Switzerland[swítsərlənd]
명 스위스 exchange rate 환율 equal[íːkwəl] 동 ~와
같다

문제 해설

Q: 유로화를 사용하는 나라는?

영국에서는 파운드를 쓴다고 했고 스웨덴이나 스위스도 유
로화가 아닌 자신들만의 통화 체계가 있다고 했다.

mQ1: 600달러는 파운드로 얼마인가?

600달러를 환전하면 360파운드 정도 된다고 했다.

2

M: I've spent all my pocket money.
W: Already? Didn't you receive it only a few
   days ago?
M: I did. I don't know where all the money has
   gone.
W: Why don't you record your spending? It's
   the best way to manage money.
M: How does that help?
W: Well, you can figure out your spending
   habits. So you can cut down your spending
   and save some money every month.
M: That's what I need.
W: I use an online money managing program.
   It's very easy to use.
M: Can you send me the program?
W: You can download it from the Internet. I'll
   let you know the address.
M: Okay, thanks. I'll check it out.

남: 나 용돈을 다 써 버렸어.
여: 벌써? 불과 며칠 전에 받지 않았니?
남: 그랬지. 돈이 다 어디로 갔는지 모르겠어.
여: 지출 내역을 기록하지 그래? 그게 돈을 관리하는 가장 좋은
   방법이야.
남: 그게 어떻게 도움이 되는 거야?
여: 음, 네 소비 습관을 알 수 있거든. 그래서 매달 지출을 줄이
   고 얼마간의 돈을 절약할 수 있어.
남: 바로 나에게 필요한 거네.
여: 난 온라인상의 금전 관리 프로그램을 이용해. 사용하기 아주
   쉬워.
남: 나한테 그 프로그램 좀 보내줄 수 있어?
여: 인터넷에서 다운로드 받을 수 있어. 내가 주소를 알려 줄게.
남: 알았어, 고마워. 확인해 볼게.

어휘

record[rikɔ́ːrd] 동 기록하다 spending[spéndiŋ] 명 지출
figure out 알아내다 cut down 줄이다 download
[dáunlòud] 동 다운로드 하다 [문제] in advance 미리

keep a record of ~을 기록하다 regularly[régjulərli]
부 규칙적으로, 정기적으로

문제 해설

Q: 여자의 조언은?

남자가 자신의 용돈을 어디에 써 버렸는지 모르겠다고 하자
여자는 지출 내역을 기록해보라고 조언했다.

mQ2: 여자가 다음에 할 일은?

여자는 남자에게 자신이 사용하고 있는 금전 관리 프로그램
을 다운받을 수 있는 인터넷 주소를 알려주겠다고 했다.

3

W: Credit cards are very convenient. You can
   buy products with them even if you don't
   have money at the time. However, it's easy
   to forget how much you've spent. That's
   why you tend to spend more with credit
   cards than with cash. To use your cards
   wisely, it's best to have only one card. Go
   over your credit card bill every month and
   reduce unnecessary purchases. Also, don't
   forget to pay your bill on time. There's a
   charge for late payments. And it's not good
   to use cards overseas because you will be
   charged extra fees.

여: 신용카드는 아주 편리해. 그 당시에 돈이 없어도 물건을 살
   수 있거든. 하지만 돈을 얼마나 썼는지 잊어버리기 쉬워. 그
   래서 현금을 쓸 때보다 신용카드를 쓸 때 더 많이 소비하는
   경향이 있어. 카드를 현명하게 쓰기 위해서는 카드를 한 개만
   쓰는 게 가장 좋아. 매달 신용카드 청구서를 검토해 보고 불
   필요한 구매는 줄여야 해. 그리고 청구 대금을 제때에 납부하
   는 것도 잊지 마. 연체료가 있거든. 그리고 추가 요금이 청구
   되기 때문에 해외에서 카드를 사용하는 건 안 좋아.

어휘

credit card 신용카드 convenient[kənvíːnjənt] 형 편리
한 tend to-v ~하는 경향이 있다 cash[kæʃ] 명 현금
go over 점검하다, 검토하다 bill[bil] 명 *청구서; 계산서
reduce[ridjúːs] 동 줄이다 unnecessary[ʌnnésəsèri] 형
불필요한 purchase[pɔ́ːrtʃəs] 명 구매 charge[tʃɑːrdʒ] 동
청구하다; 명 청구 금액, 요금 payment[péimənt] 명 지불
overseas[òuvərsíːz] 부 해외에서 extra[ékstrə] 형 추가의
fee[fiː] 명 요금 [문제] benefit[bénəfit] 명 이익, 혜택
disadvantage[dìsədvǽntidʒ] 명 불이익, 손해

문제 해설

Q: 신용카드를 현명하게 사용하고 있는 사람은?

① Sam: 난 해외 여행을 할 때 주로 신용카드를 써.

② Angela: 난 나의 지출 습관을 확인하기 위해서 신용카드
   청구서를 검토해.

39

③ Brian: 난 신용카드를 세 개 가지고 있어. 각각 서로 다른 혜택을 제공하니까.

신용카드는 한 개만 쓰는 것이 좋고, 신용카드 청구서를 검토해보아야 하며, 해외여행을 할 때는 신용카드를 쓰지 않는 게 좋다.

mQ3: 신용카드 사용의 단점으로 언급된 것은?

현금을 사용할 때보다 신용카드를 사용할 때 돈을 더 많이 쓰게 된다고 했다.

4

M: Why are you so busy these days? I never see you!

W: I'm working part-time at a hamburger restaurant.

M: A hamburger restaurant? Could I ask how much you get paid?

W: Five dollars and fifty cents per hour.

M: It can't be! According to the law, hourly wages should be more than $7.

W: Really?

M: Yes. I heard employees should get at least $7.25 or something.

W: So should I quit the job? I'm worried because it's not easy to get a new job.

M: Why don't you talk to your boss first? Maybe he simply doesn't know the law.

W: Okay. I think I should.

남: 요즘 왜 그렇게 바빠? 통 볼 수가 없네!

여: 햄버거 가게에서 아르바이트를 하고 있거든.

남: 햄버거 가게? 얼마 받는지 물어봐도 돼?

여: 한 시간당 5달러 50센트.

남: 말도 안돼! 법에 따르면 시간당 임금이 7달러 이상은 돼야 해.

여: 정말?

남: 응. 종업원은 적어도 7달러 25센트 정도는 받아야 한다고 들었어.

여: 그럼 일을 그만둬야 하는 건가? 새로운 일을 구하기가 쉽지 않아서 걱정이야.

남: 너희 사장님에게 먼저 말해보는 게 어때? 그가 단지 법을 모르고 있을지도 모르지.

여: 알았어. 그래야겠다.

hourly[áuərli] 형 한 시간의 wage[weidʒ] 명 임금
employee[implɔ́iːː] 명 고용인, 종업원 at least 적어도
quit[kwit] 동 그만두다 simply[símpli] 부 간단히, 단순히
[문제] poorly[púərli] 부 가난하게; *부족하게 fire[fáiər]
동 해고하다

문제 해설

Q: 여자의 문제는?

법에 따르면 시간당 최저 임금이 7달러 정도인데 여자는 시간당 5달러 50센트를 받고 있다고 했다.

mQ4: 여자가 시간당 받는 금액은?

여자는 시간당 5달러 50센트를 받는다고 했다.

5

W: Billy, what are you reading?

M: It's a very interesting article. It says people who are good-looking earn about 12% more money than those who aren't.

W: Really? Is there any reason for that?

M: Good-looking people are believed to be more helpful.

W: That's interesting. Oh, I read a similar article before. It said taller people earn more money.

M: What about people who weigh a lot like me? Do they earn more money as well?

W: I'm sorry but weight has nothing to do with income.

M: That's too bad. What about people who are short but handsome, like me?

W: Well... I don't know.

여: Billy, 너 뭘 읽고 있니?

남: 아주 흥미로운 기사야. 잘생긴 사람들이 그렇지 않은 사람들보다 돈을 12% 정도 더 많이 번대.

여: 정말? 거기에 무슨 이유라도 있어?

남: 잘생긴 사람들이 더 도움이 된다고 여겨지는 거야.

여: 그거 흥미로운걸. 아, 전에 비슷한 기사를 읽었어. 키 큰 사람이 돈을 더 많이 번다고 하더라.

남: 나처럼 몸무게가 많이 나가는 사람은? 그런 사람도 돈을 더 많이 벌어?

여: 유감이지만 몸무게는 수입이랑 관계가 없어.

남: 유감이네. 나처럼 키는 작지만 잘생긴 사람은?

여: 글쎄… 모르겠어.

어휘

article[áːrtikl] 명 기사 good-looking[gúdlúkiŋ] 형 잘
생긴 helpful[hélpfəl] 형 도움이 되는 similar[símələr]
형 비슷한 weigh[wei] 동 무게가 ~ 나가다 have
nothing to do with ~와 관계가 없다 income[ínkʌm]
명 수입, 소득 [문제] height[hait] 명 키

문제 해설

Q: 돈을 가장 많이 벌 것 같은 사람은?

키가 크고 잘생긴 사람이 돈을 더 많이 번다고 했다.

mQ5: Billy에 관해 사실인 것에 동그라미 하시오.

Billy는 몸무게가 많이 나가고 키가 작다고 했다.

6

M: My hobby is collecting coins. Many people collect coins to earn money by selling their collections. But I started it to learn about other cultures through their money. The basic thing about collecting coins is to know which ones are valuable. People usually think all old money has a high value, but if many people have a particular kind of coin, its value will be low. Also, if the money has a unique design or special history, it goes up in value. Lastly, people will pay more for money which is in good condition.

남: 내 취미는 동전을 모으는 거야. 많은 사람들은 자신의 수집물을 팔아서 돈을 벌려고 동전을 모아. 하지만 나는 화폐를 통해 다른 문화에 대해 배우려고 그것을 시작했어. 동전 모으기에 있어 기본은 어느 것이 가치 있는지 아는 거야. 사람들은 대개 오래된 화폐는 모두 가치가 높다고 생각하지만, 많은 사람들이 특정 종류의 동전을 가지고 있다면 그것의 가치는 낮게 되지. 또한 그 화폐가 특이한 디자인이거나 특별한 역사를 지니고 있다면 가치가 올라가. 마지막으로 사람들은 상태가 좋은 화폐에 돈을 더 많이 지불할 거야.

어휘
collect[kəlékt] 통 모으다 coin[kɔin] 명 동전
collection[kəlékʃən] 명 수집; *수집물 culture[kʌ́ltʃər]
명 문화 basic[béisik] 형 기본적인 valuable[væljuəbl]
형 가치 있는 value[vælju:] 명 가치 particular
[pərtíkjulər] 형 특정한 unique[ju:ní:k] 형 특이한
condition[kəndíʃən] 명 상태; 조건 [문제] rare[rɛər] 형
드문, 희귀한 exhibit[igzíbit] 통 전시하다

문제 해설
Q: 화폐를 가치 있게 만드는 조건이 아닌 것은?
오래된 화폐라도 많은 사람들이 그 화폐를 가지고 있으면 가치는 낮을 것이라고 했다.

mQ6: 남자가 화폐를 모으는 이유는?
남자는 화폐를 통해 다른 문화를 배우려고 화폐를 모으기 시작했다.

Listening ★ Challenge p. 42

A 1 ③ 2 ② B 1 ③ 2 ③

A [1-2]

M: I read a newspaper article about a teenage girl yesterday. She runs an online shopping mall and makes $40,000 a month.
W: That's amazing! What is her key to success?

M: She sells skirts to teenage girls. She understands what they want to wear.
W: She must be a born salesperson. I think I'd like to open a shopping mall for women in their 20s.
M: There are already too many malls like that, so you won't be successful.
W: You have a point. So, would it be better to sell men's wear?
M: I think so. What about selling just one item, like jeans or T-shirts?
W: I agree. I think it would be good to sell jeans.

남: 어제 한 10대 소녀에 관한 신문 기사를 봤어. 그녀는 온라인 쇼핑몰을 운영해서 한 달에 4만 달러를 벌어.
여: 놀랍다! 그 애의 성공 비결이 뭐야?
남: 10대 소녀들에게 치마를 판대. 그 애는 그들이 뭘 입고 싶어 하는지 알잖아.
여: 확실히 타고난 장사꾼이네. 난 20대 여성을 위한 쇼핑몰을 열고 싶어.
남: 그런 쇼핑몰은 이미 너무 많아서 성공할 수 없을 거야.
여: 일리 있는 말이야. 그럼 남성복을 파는 게 나을까?
남: 그럴 것 같아. 청바지나 티셔츠 같은 한 가지 품목만 파는 게 어때?
여: 동감이야. 난 청바지를 파는 게 좋을 것 같아.

어휘
teenage[tí:nèidʒ] 형 10대의 run[rʌn] 통 달리다; *운영하다
key[ki:] 명 열쇠; *(성공의) 비결 success[səksés] 명 성공
born[bɔːrn] 형 타고난 salesperson[séilzpə̀ːrsən] 명 판매원 successful[səksésfəl] 형 성공적인 You have a
point. 일리 있는 말이다.

문제 해설
Q1: 남자가 읽은 기사의 제목으로 가장 알맞은 것은?
① 소녀들이 가장 사고 싶어 하는 것
② 자신의 사업을 시작하는 방법
③ 한 여학생의 성공담
④ 십대들을 위한 온라인 쇼핑몰 상위 3개
남자는 온라인 쇼핑몰을 운영해서 한 달에 많은 돈을 버는 10대 소녀에 관한 신문 기사를 보았다.

Q2: 여자가 온라인에서 팔고자 하는 것은?
여자는 청바지를 파는 게 좋겠다고 했다.

B [1-2]

W: If you were a millionaire, what would you like to do?
M: I'd like to spend my money traveling around the world with my family. I think that would be the best way to spend it.
W: I had the same idea, but I changed my mind.

M: So what would you like to do?

W: I'd like to start an organization for poor people.

M: Oh, really? What made you think of that?

W: I heard about Bill Gates. He donated his money to provide education and health care to people in need.

M: He's a great person, but I don't think I could do that. Making my family happy is more important to me.

W: I understand. But I believe we can make our world a better place by helping others.

여: 네가 백만장자라면 뭘 하고 싶어?

남: 가족들과 세계를 여행하는 데 돈을 쓰고 싶어. 그게 돈을 가장 잘 쓰는 방법인 것 같아.

여: 나도 같은 생각을 갖고 있었는데 생각이 바뀌었어.

남: 그럼 넌 뭘 하고 싶은데?

여: 가난한 사람들을 위한 단체를 설립하고 싶어.

남: 아, 정말? 왜 그런 생각을 하게 됐어?

여: Bill Gates에 대해서 들었거든. 그는 도움이 필요한 사람들에게 교육과 의료를 제공하기 위해서 자신의 돈을 기부했대.

남: 대단한 사람이구나. 하지만 난 그렇게 할 수 있을 것 같지 않아. 우리 가족을 행복하게 해주는 게 나에겐 더 중요해.

여: 이해해. 하지만 난 다른 사람을 도움으로써 세상을 더 좋은 곳으로 만들 수 있을 거라고 믿어.

어휘

millionaire[mìljənέər] 몡 백만장자 mind[maind] 몡 마음 organization[ɔ̀ːrgənizéiʃən] 몡 단체, 조직 donate [dóuneit] 통 기부하다 provide[prəváid] 통 제공하다 education[èdʒukéiʃən] 몡 교육 health care 의료 in need 도움이 필요한 [문제] role[roul] 몡 역할 society[səsáiəti] 몡 사회 share[ʃɛər] 통 나누다

문제 해설

Q1: 그들은 주로 무엇에 대해 이야기하고 있는가?

두 사람은 백만장자가 된다면 돈을 어떻게 쓰는 게 좋을지에 대해 이야기하고 있다.

Q2: 여자와 같은 의견을 가진 인물은?

① Teddy: 난 내 돈을 왜 사회에 기부해야 하는지 모르겠어.

② Stephanie: 가장 중요한 건 내 가족을 행복하게 해주는 거야.

③ Nicole: 우리는 우리가 가진 것을 다른 사람들과 나눠야 해.

여자는 다른 사람을 도와서 세상을 더 좋은 곳으로 만들고 싶어 한다.

Critical ★ Thinking   p. 43

1 (1) Against (2) For (3) For
2 (1) ⓐ (2) ⓑ (3) ⓒ

42

M1: I'm Matt. I don't understand why people waste their money playing the lottery. Yes, it's true that I could win millions of dollars, but I have nearly zero chance of winning. It's better not to have false hope.

W: I'm Janet. I know it's almost impossible to win the lottery. However, I buy one ticket every week so that I can have hope and excitement for a while. I like to have such feelings.

M2: I'm Tom. I don't think it's wasting my money to buy lottery tickets. When we buy lottery tickets, some of the money is spent on helping the poor. So, it's okay even if I don't win the lottery.

남1: 난 Matt야. 난 사람들이 왜 복권을 하는 데 돈을 낭비하는지 이해가 안돼. 그래. 내가 수백만 달러를 딸 수도 있다는 것은 사실이야. 하지만 당첨될 가능성은 거의 없어. 그릇된 희망은 갖지 않는 편이 나아.

여: 난 Janet이야. 복권에 당첨될 가능성이 거의 없다는 건 알아. 하지만 나는 잠시라도 희망과 설렘을 느끼기 위해 매주 한 장씩 사. 그런 기분을 느끼는 게 좋거든.

남2: 난 Tom이야. 난 복권을 사는 게 돈 낭비라고 생각하지 않아. 복권을 사면 그 돈의 일부는 가난한 사람을 돕는 데 쓰여. 그래서 내가 복권에 당첨되지 않는다고 하더라도 괜찮아.

어휘

waste[weist] 통 낭비하다; 몡 낭비 lottery[látəri] 몡 복권 millions of 수백만의 chance[tʃæns] 몡 기회; *가능성 false[fɔːls] 혱 잘못된 impossible[impásəbl] 혱 불가능한 excitement[iksáitmənt] 몡 흥분, 설렘 for a while 당분간 [문제] hopeful[hóupfəl] 혱 희망적인

문제 해설

Q1: 각 인물이 복권을 사는 데 찬성하는지 반대하는지 ✓표 하시오.

Matt는 복권 구입을 돈 낭비라고 생각하여 부정적인 입장이며, Janet과 Tom은 당첨 가능성은 거의 없지만 다른 긍정적인 효과가 있다고 생각하여 찬성하는 입장이다.

Q2: 각 인물과 해당 의견을 연결하시오.

ⓐ 복권을 사는 것은 돈 낭비야.

ⓑ 복권을 산 후에 난 행복감을 느끼고 희망을 갖게 돼.

ⓒ 우리는 복권을 사서 가난한 사람들을 도울 수 있어.

(1) Matt는 당첨 가능성이 거의 없는 복권을 사는 데 돈을 낭비하는 이유를 이해할 수 없다고 했다.

(2) Janet은 잠시라도 희망과 설렘을 느끼기 위해 매주 복권을 산다고 했다.

(3) Tom은 복권을 산 돈의 일부가 가난한 사람을 돕는 데 쓰이므로 복권에 당첨되지 않더라도 괜찮다고 했다.

UNIT 07 Travel

Getting ★ Ready p. 44

A 1 ⓒ 2 ⓐ 3 ⓑ 4 ⓕ 5 ⓓ 6 ⓔ
B 1 ⓔ 2 ⓕ 3 ⓓ

B 1 남: 유럽 여행은 어땠어?
　　여: 문제의 연속이었어.

　2 남: 이 유스호스텔에서 얼마 동안 일했어요?
　　여: 거의 5년이요.

　3 남: 택시 기사에게 팁을 얼마나 줘야 하는지 아니?
　　여: 총 요금의 10%인 것 같아.

Listening ★ Start p. 45

1 (1) Bad (2) Good (3) Good / went to, really crowded, the best place, During the discount season, was able to enjoy, really delicious
2 ③ / get on, woke up, get to the airport, take my eyes off, quickly checked in

1

W1: I'm Becky. I went to Hong Kong once. The streets were narrow and really crowded. It's not a place I want to visit again.
M: I'm Paul. I love shopping and Hong Kong is the best place for it. There are many large and convenient shopping malls. During the discount season, I can purchase good products at low prices.
W2: I'm Cathy. In Hong Kong, I was able to enjoy plenty of delicious Chinese food. I can't forget the mango dessert I had there. I didn't like mango before, but it was really delicious.

여1: 난 Becky야. 난 홍콩에 한 번 갔어. 거리는 좁고 정말 혼잡했어. 다시 가고 싶은 곳은 아니야.
남: 난 Paul이야. 난 쇼핑을 좋아하는데 홍콩은 쇼핑을 위한 최고의 장소야. 크고 편리한 쇼핑몰들이 많이 있지. 할인 기간에는 좋은 상품을 싼 가격에 살 수 있어.
여2: 난 Cathy야. 난 홍콩에서 맛있는 중국 음식을 많이 즐길 수 있었어. 거기서 먹은 망고 디저트를 잊을 수가 없어. 전엔 망고를 좋아하지 않았지만 그건 아주 맛있더라고.

어휘
crowded[kráudid] 휑 붐비는 convenient[kənví:njənt]
휑 편리한 purchase[pə́:rtʃəs] 동 구입하다 be able to-v

~할 수 있다 plenty of 많은 delicious[dilíʃəs] 휑 맛있는 mango[mǽngou] 명 망고 dessert[dizə́:rt] 명 디저트

문제 해설
Q: 각 인물이 홍콩에 대해 어떻게 생각하는지 ✓표 하시오.
　Becky는 다시 가고 싶지 않다고 했고, Paul은 쇼핑하기가 좋다고 했으며, Cathy는 음식이 맛있어서 좋다고 했다.

2

M: Today was the 5th day of my trip. I was going to get on the 11 a.m. flight from Bristol Airport to Copenhagen. But I woke up at 9 a.m. in the morning. I hurried to the train station to get to the airport. On the train, I was so nervous that I couldn't take my eyes off my watch! I arrived ten minutes before the final check-in. I quickly checked in and got on board. It was a miracle that I was on time.

남: 오늘은 여행 다섯째 날이었어요. 저는 브리스틀 공항에서 코펜하겐으로 가는 오전 11시 비행기를 탈 계획이었어요. 그런데 아침 9시에 일어났어요. 공항으로 가기 위해 서둘러 기차역으로 갔죠. 기차에서 너무 긴장이 되어 시계에서 눈을 뗄 수가 없었어요! 최종 탑승 수속 10분 전에 도착했어요. 재빠르게 탑승 수속을 하고 탑승했죠. 제시간에 도착한 건 기적이었어요.

어휘
flight[flait] 명 비행편 hurry[hə́:ri] 동 서둘러 가다
nervous[nə́:rvəs] 휑 긴장한 final[fáinəl] 휑 최종의, 마지막의 check-in[tʃékìn] 명 (비행기의) 탑승 수속 get on board 탑승하다 miracle[mírəkl] 명 기적 [문제]
confused[kənfjú:zd] 휑 혼란스러운 relieved[rilí:vd] 휑 안심한 disappointed[dìsəpɔ́intid] 휑 실망한

문제 해설
Q: 남자의 심정은 어떻게 바뀌었나?
　남자는 비행기를 놓치게 될까 봐 걱정하고 있었는데 다행히 탑승하게 되었으므로 안심했을 것이다.

Listening ★ Practice p. 46

1 ① mQ1 ⓑ 2 ④ mQ2 ⓐ 3 (1) ⓒ (2) ⓑ
(3) ⓐ mQ3 (1) T (2) F 4 ③ mQ4 ⓐ, ⓒ
5 (1) 2 (2) 1 (3) 1 mQ5 ⓐ 6 ①, ③ mQ6 ⓐ

1

(Telephone rings.)
W: Front desk. How may I help you?
M: I'm in room 706. There's a problem with the shower again.
W: Is it the same problem as yesterday, when

43

it wasn't working at all?

M: No. It works, but no hot water is coming out.

W: I'm sorry. I'll call the repairman and send him to fix the problem.

M: But this is the second time. Can't I get another room?

W: I'm sorry, but all rooms are fully booked.

M: I'm so disappointed in this hotel.

W: Why don't I offer you a free traditional Thai massage in our spa during the repair?

M: Well... that sounds nice.

W: I'll reserve the massage right away and then send a repairman to your room.

(전화벨이 울린다.)

여: 프런트 데스크입니다. 무엇을 도와드릴까요?

남: 706호실인데요. 샤워기에 또 문제가 있네요.

여: 어제처럼 전혀 작동이 안 되는 문제인가요?

남: 아니요. 되긴 하는데 온수가 나오지 않아요.

여: 죄송합니다. 수리공에게 전화해서 문제를 해결하도록 보내겠습니다.

남: 하지만 이번이 두 번째잖아요. 다른 방을 얻을 수 없나요?

여: 죄송합니다만, 모든 방이 다 예약이 되었어요.

남: 이 호텔에 아주 실망이네요.

여: 수리하는 동안 저희 스파에서 무료로 전통 태국 마사지를 받도록 해 드리는 건 어떨까요?

남: 음… 그거 좋겠네요.

여: 바로 마사지를 예약하고 수리공을 객실로 보내도록 하겠습니다.

어휘

shower[ʃáuər] 명 샤워기 repairman[ripέərmæ̀n] 명 수리공 fix[fiks] 동 고치다, 수리하다 fully[fúli] 부 완전히 book[buk] 동 예약하다 offer[ɔ́(:)fər] 동 제공하다 traditional[trədíʃənəl] 형 전통적인 massage[məsá:ʤ] 명 마사지 spa[spɑː] 명 스파, 온천 repair[ripέər] 명 수리 reserve[rizə́:rv] 동 예약하다

문제 해설

Q: 여자가 다음에 할 일은?

여자는 남자를 위해 스파를 예약하고 나서 수리공을 객실로 보내겠다고 했으므로 스파에 전화를 할 것이다.

mQ1: 남자의 문제는?

ⓐ 샤워기가 전혀 작동하지 않는다.

ⓑ 샤워기에서 온수가 나오지 않는다.

샤워기에서 온수가 안 나온다고 했다.

2

M: According to the map, the Coffee and Tea Museum should be here.

W: I know. This is Wood Street, right?

M: It says so on that street sign.

W: Could it be that building under construction?

M: It looks too small to be a museum.

W: Look! Read that sign. It says the Coffee and Tea Museum has been moved to a different place.

M: What? I can't believe we wasted half an hour trying to find it.

W: Hmm... what should we do now?

M: Why don't we go to the tourist information center and ask about how to find the museum's new location?

W: That's a good idea.

M: Let's ask about where to eat as well.

W: Okay. Let's hurry.

남: 지도에 따르면 Coffee and Tea Museum은 여기일 텐데.

여: 알아. 여기가 Wood Street 맞지?

남: 저 도로 표지판에 그렇게 쓰여 있어.

여: 저기 공사 중인 건물일 수 있을까?

남: 그건 박물관이라고 하기에는 너무 작아 보여.

여: 봐! 저 표지판을 읽어봐. Coffee and Tea Museum이 다른 곳으로 옮겼다고 쓰여 있어.

남: 뭐라고? 그걸 찾으려고 30분이나 낭비하다니!

여: 음… 이제 뭘 해야 하지?

남: 관광 안내소에 가서 박물관의 새 위치를 찾아가는 방법을 물어보는 게 어때?

여: 좋은 생각이다.

남: 먹을 곳도 함께 물어보자.

여: 알았어. 서두르자.

어휘

museum[mju(:)zí(:)əm] 명 박물관 sign[sain] 명 표지, 간판 construction[kənstrʌ́kʃən] 명 건설 공사 waste[weist] 동 낭비하다 tourist[tú(:)ərist] 명 여행자 location[loukéiʃən] 명 위치

문제 해설

Q: 그들이 박물관에 갈 수 없었던 이유는?

박물관이 다른 곳으로 이전하는 바람에 갈 수 없었다.

mQ2: 그들이 다음에 할 일은?

그들은 관광 안내소로 가서 박물관의 새 위치와 음식점에 대해 물어 보기로 했다.

3

W: Let me recommend to you some places with beautiful night views in Tokyo. The first place is the Mori Tower observatory on the 52nd floor in the city center. You can see Tokyo Tower from here. Secondly, if you visit the Tokyo Government Building in Shinjuku,

44

there's an observatory on the 45th floor. It's in the center of the city, so you can enjoy the city view. Finally, there is Odaiba. Odaiba is a man-made island in the suburbs of Tokyo. The view of the ocean, bridge and ferries looks beautiful at night.

여: 도쿄에서 아름다운 야경을 볼 수 있는 장소들을 여러분께 추천해 드릴게요. 첫 번째 장소는 도시 중심부 52층에 있는 모리 타워 전망대입니다. 이곳에서는 도쿄 타워를 볼 수 있습니다. 두 번째로 신주쿠에 있는 도쿄 정부 청사를 가시면 45층에 전망대가 있습니다. 도시의 중심부에 있기 때문에 도시 경관을 즐길 수 있습니다. 마지막으로 오다이바가 있습니다. 오다이바는 도쿄의 교외에 있는 인공섬입니다. 밤에 보는 바다와 다리, 유람선의 경관이 아름답습니다.

어휘

recommend[rèkəménd] ⑧ 추천하다   observatory [əbzə́ːrvətɔ̀ːri] ⑲ 전망대   floor[flɔːr] ⑲ 층 government[gʌ́vərnmənt] ⑲ 정부   man-made [mǽnméid] ⑲ 인조의, 인공의   island[áilənd] ⑲ 섬 suburb[sʌ́bərb] ⑲ 교외   ocean[óuʃən] ⑲ 바다 bridge[bridʒ] ⑲ 다리   ferry[féri] ⑲ 나룻배, 유람선 [문제] shine[ʃain] ⑧ 빛나다

문제 해설

Q: 각 인물이 갈 장소를 고르시오.
(1) 바다의 야경을 보고 싶어.
(2) 신주쿠에서 도시 경관을 즐기고 싶어.
(3) 밤에 도쿄 타워가 빛나는 모습을 보고 싶어.
바다의 야경을 볼 수 있는 곳은 오다이바이고, 신주쿠에서 도시 야경을 볼 수 있는 곳은 도쿄 정부 청사이며, 도쿄 타워를 볼 수 있는 곳은 모리 타워이다.

mQ3: 사실이면 T, 사실이 아니면 F를 쓰시오.
(1) 모리 타워는 50층이 넘는다.
(2) 오다이바는 도쿄의 중심부에 위치하고 있다.
모리 타워의 52층에 전망대가 있다고 했으므로 모리 타워는 50층 이상이고, 오다이바는 도쿄의 외곽에 있어 바다 경관을 볼 수 있다고 했다.

4

M: I'm planning a trip to India. But I can't choose between New Delhi, Calcutta, and Agra.
W: Don't miss Agra. The Taj Mahal is amazing.
M: Okay. And New Delhi is the capital, so I'll skip Calcutta.
W: Do you want some tips about India?
M: Sure.
W: Always take toilet paper to the restroom. Indians use water instead of toilet paper.

M: Interesting.
W: And you must buy bottled water. I got a stomachache after I drank free water at a restaurant.
M: I'll be careful.
W: And you know what a rickshaw is, right?
M: Is it some kind of transportation pulled by a bicycle?
W: Yes. Always set the price before you get in. If not, the driver might ask for a lot of money later.

남: 인도 여행을 계획하고 있어. 그런데 뉴델리와 캘커타, 아그라 중에서 결정을 할 수가 없네.
여: 아그라를 빼놓지 마. 타지마할이 멋지거든.
남: 알았어. 뉴델리는 수도니까 캘커타를 빼야겠다.
여: 인도에 대한 조언 좀 해 줄까?
남: 그래.
여: 화장실에는 꼭 화장지를 가지고 가. 인도인들은 화장지 대신 물을 쓰거든.
남: 흥미로운걸.
여: 그리고 꼭 생수를 사. 난 음식점에서 무료로 나오는 물을 먹고 나서 배가 아팠어.
남: 조심할게.
여: 그리고 릭샤가 뭔지 알지?
남: 자전거로 끄는 일종의 교통수단이지?
여: 응. 타기 전에 항상 운임을 정해. 그렇지 않으면 기사가 나중에 많은 돈을 달라고 할지도 몰라.

어휘

India[índiə] ⑲ 인도   capital[kǽpitəl] ⑲ 수도   skip [skip] ⑧ 빼다, 건너뛰다   toilet paper 화장지 restroom[réstrùm] ⑲ 화장실   instead of ~대신에 bottled water 생수   stomachache[stʌ́məkèik] ⑲ 복통 free[friː] ⑲ 공짜의, 무료의   rickshaw[ríkʃɔː] ⑲ 릭샤(인력거)   pull[pul] ⑧ 끌다

문제 해설

Q: 여자가 제안하는 조언이 아닌 것은?
① 화장실에 화장지를 가지고 가라.
② 산 생수만 마셔라.
③ 깨끗한 음식점에서 먹어라.
④ 릭샤에 타기 전에 요금을 정해라.
깨끗한 음식점에서 먹으라는 말은 언급되지 않았다.

mQ4: 남자가 갈 도시를 두 개 고르시오.
여자가 추천한 타지마할이 있는 아그라와 수도인 뉴델리에 가겠다고 했다.

5

M: When you travel to America, you should know how much to tip at restaurants, hotels, and so on. Normally, waiters or waitresses give their best service to get more tips, because the tips are their main wage. If you have good service in a restaurant, give 10~15% of the total bill as a tip. But if the service isn't good, leave 5%. In hotels, when a bellboy carries your bag, give him $1 per bag. Also, leave $1 on the bed every morning for the cleaning maid. Tipping 10% to a taxi driver is enough.

남: 미국을 여행할 때 음식점과 호텔 등에서 팁을 얼마나 주어야 하는지 알아야 합니다. 보통, 웨이터나 웨이트리스는 더 많은 팁을 받기 위해 최선의 서비스를 제공하는데, 그 팁이 그들의 주된 임금이기 때문입니다. 음식점에서 좋은 서비스를 받는다면 총 청구액의 10~15%를 팁으로 주세요. 하지만 서비스가 좋지 않다면 5%를 남기면 됩니다. 호텔에서 벨보이가 가방을 들어주면 가방당 1달러를 주세요. 또한 청소해주는 여직원을 위해 매일 아침 1달러를 침대 위에 놓아두세요. 택시 기사에게는 10%의 팁을 주면 충분합니다.

어휘
tip[tip] 통 팁을 주다; 명 팁　and so on 기타 등등
normally[nɔ́ːrməli] 부 보통, 일반적으로　main[mein] 형 주된　wage[weiʤ] 명 임금, 봉급　total[tóutl] 형 총액의
bill[bil] 명 계산서, 청구서　leave[liːv] 통 남기다
bellboy[bélbɔ̀i] 명 (호텔의) 벨보이　per[pər] 전 ~당
maid[meid] 명 하녀, 가정부

문제 해설
Q: 각 상황에서 팁으로 얼마를 줄 것인가?
　벨보이가 가방을 들어줄 때 가방 하나당 1달러라고 했으므로 총 2달러를 주어야 한다. 청소해 주는 여직원에게는 매일 1달러를 준다. 택시요금이 10달러인 경우 그 10%인 1달러를 주면 된다.

mQ5: 남자에 따르면, 음식점 서비스가 마음에 들지 않는다면 얼마를 팁으로 줄 것인가?
　음식점의 서비스가 좋지 않다면 청구서 총액의 5%만 주면 된다고 했다.

6

(Telephone rings.)
M: Hello.
W: Hi, Ted. I'm back.
M: Hey, Marian. How was your trip to Europe?
W: Oh, it was a series of troubles.
M: What happened?
W: In Rome, I had my wallet stolen on the bus.
M: How terrible! Did you lose any money?
W: Yes. But luckily I'd left my passport at the hotel.
M: Good for you.
W: That's not all. Once, I took the wrong train and got off at Valencia instead of Barcelona.
M: Oh, you really had a lot of troubles. By the way, did you buy any souvenirs for me?
W: (laughs) Actually, that's why I called. Do you have any free time tomorrow?
M: Yes. How about meeting at 6 p.m.?
W: Sounds great!

(전화벨이 울린다.)
남: 여보세요.
여: 안녕, Ted. 나 돌아왔어.
남: Marian. 유럽 여행은 어땠어?
여: 아, 문제의 연속이었어.
남: 무슨 일이 있었는데?
여: 로마에서는 버스에서 지갑을 도둑맞았어.
남: 저런! 돈을 잃어버렸어?
여: 응. 그런데 다행스럽게도 여권은 호텔에 두고 나왔지.
남: 다행이네.
여: 그게 다가 아니야. 한번은 기차를 잘못 타서 바르셀로나에 가야 하는데 발렌시아에서 내렸어.
남: 아, 정말 문제가 많았구나. 그건 그렇고, 나한테 줄 기념품은 샀니?
여: [웃으며] 사실은 그래서 전화한 거야. 내일 시간 되니?
남: 응. 저녁 6시에 만나면 어때?
여: 좋지!

어휘
a series of ~의 연속인, 일련의　trouble[trʌ́bl] 명 말썽, 문제　wallet[wálit] 명 지갑　steal[stiːl] 통 훔치다 (steal-stole-stolen)　luckily[lʌ́kili] 부 다행히도　passport[pǽspɔ̀ːrt] 명 여권　souvenir[sùːvəníər] 명 기념품　actually[ǽktʃuəli] 부 사실은

문제 해설
Q: 여자가 겪은 두 가지 문제를 고르시오.
　여자는 버스에서 지갑을 도난당하고, 기차를 잘못 타서 발렌시아에 내렸다.

mQ6: 여자가 남자를 보려고 하는 이유는?
　여자는 남자에게 여행에서 산 기념품을 주기 위해 만나자고 했다.

Listening ★ Challenge　p. 48

A 1 ② 2 ④　B 1 ①, ③ 2 ④

A [1-2]
M: Nice to meet you. I'm Tom.
W: It's good to meet someone from my country. I'm Kelly.

M: How long have you worked in this youth hostel?

W: It's been ten years. I came here as a traveler and fell in love with Greece.

M: I'm going to stay in Athens for three days. Could you recommend some good places?

W: Visit the Temple of Zeus. It is so big that you won't believe your eyes.

M: Oh, I've heard about it.

W: Also, the War Museum and Olympic Stadium are famous. Do you know about Cape Sounion?

M: No, I don't.

W: It takes two hours from Athens by bus. There you can enjoy great coastal views and beautiful sunsets.

M: Thanks for the information. I'll go there today and visit the Temple of Zeus tomorrow.

남: 만나서 반가워요. 난 Tom이에요.

여: 우리나라에서 온 분을 만나니까 좋네요. 난 Kelly예요.

남: 이 유스호스텔에서는 얼마 동안 일했나요?

여: 10년이요. 여행자로 여기에 와서 그리스를 사랑하게 되었죠.

남: 전 3일 동안 아테네에 머무르려고 하는데요. 좋은 곳 좀 추천해 주시겠어요?

여: 제우스 신전에 가세요. 너무 커서 눈으로 봐도 믿기지가 않을 거예요.

남: 아, 들어봤어요.

여: 또 전쟁 박물관과 올림픽 경기장도 유명해요. 수니온 곶은 알아요?

남: 아니요.

여: 아테네에서 버스로 2시간 걸려요. 그곳에서는 멋진 해변 경관과 아름다운 석양을 즐길 수 있답니다.

남: 정보를 줘서 고마워요. 오늘 거기에 가고 내일은 제우스 신전에 가야겠어요.

어휘

youth hostel 유스호스텔 traveler[trǽvələr] 명 여행자
fall in love with ~를 사랑하게 되다 stay[stei] 동 머물다 temple[témpl] 명 사원 Zeus[zuːs] 명 제우스(그리스의 신) cape[keip] 명 곶, 갑 coastal[kóustəl] 형 해변의 sunset[sʌ́nsèt] 명 일몰; *석양 [문제] local[lóukəl] 형 지역의, 현지의

문제 해설

Q1: 화자 간의 관계는?

같은 나라 출신의 유스호스텔 직원과 여행자와의 대화이다.

Q2: 남자가 오늘 갈 곳은?

오늘은 수니온 곶에 가고, 내일은 제우스 신전에 간다고 했다.

B [1-2]

W: Did you call for help, sir?

M: Yes. Do you have any cold medicine on the plane? I feel sick.

W: Yes, we do. What are your symptoms?

M: I have a fever and a sore throat.

W: I see. I'll bring you some medicine and water.

M: I already have water. But could I get one more blanket? I'm cold.

W: Sure. If you feel uncomfortable, let me move you to a seat without neighbors.

M: Is there an available seat?

W: Yes. It's at the back of the plane.

M: I have some luggage in the cabinet above me. Should I bring it?

W: No, just leave it. Next time you travel, tell us you have an illness during check-in. Then we can arrange for you to have a more comfortable seat.

M: Oh, really? That's nice.

W: Now, please follow me.

M: All right.

여: 도움을 요청하셨나요. 손님?

남: 네. 비행기에 감기약이 있나요? 몸이 좋지 않아요.

여: 네, 있습니다. 증상이 어떠신가요?

남: 열이 있고 목이 따끔거려요.

여: 알겠습니다. 약과 물을 가져다 드릴게요.

남: 이미 물은 있어요. 그런데 담요 하나 더 주시겠어요? 추워서요.

여: 물론이죠. 불편하시면 옆 사람이 없는 좌석으로 옮겨 드릴게요.

남: 사용 가능한 좌석이 있어요?

여: 네. 비행기 뒤쪽에 있어요.

남: 위에 있는 캐비닛에 짐이 있어요. 가져가야 하나요?

여: 아니, 그냥 두세요. 다음에 여행하실 때에는, 탑승 수속시에 아프다고 말씀해 주세요. 그러면 더 편안한 좌석에 앉으시도록 준비해드릴 수 있습니다.

남: 아, 정말요? 좋군요.

여: 자, 절 따라오세요.

남: 알겠습니다.

어휘

cold[kould] 명 감기 medicine[médəsin] 명 약
symptom[símptəm] 명 증상 fever[fíːvər] 명 열
sore throat 인후염 blanket[blǽŋkit] 명 담요
uncomfortable[ʌnkʌ́mfərtəbl] 형 불편한 neighbor
[néibər] 명 이웃; *옆자리 사람 available[əvéiləbl] 형 이용
할 수 있는 luggage[lʌ́giʤ] 명 짐, 수하물 cabinet
[kǽbənit] 명 캐비닛 illness[ílnis] 명 질병 arrange
[əréinʤ] 동 마련하다, 준비하다 [문제] request[rikwést]
동 요청하다 baggage[bǽgiʤ] 명 짐, 수하물

문제 해설

Q1: 남자가 부탁한 두 가지를 고르시오.

　남자는 감기약과 담요를 달라고 요청했다.

Q2: 남자가 다음에 할 일은?

　남자는 승무원이 안내하는 좌석으로 자리를 옮길 것이다.

Critical ★ Thinking　p. 49

1 ①　2 ①, ④

W: I heard you're going to Spain. Are you going to stay at Susan's house?

M: No. She's also traveling now. So, I'm thinking of staying at a hotel.

W: Why don't you look for a youth hostel? They're much cheaper.

M: I'm not sure. Hotels are more expensive, but they're cleaner and they have convenient facilities.

W: But you will only sleep there.

M: If I stay at a youth hostel, I'll have to carry things like soap and shampoo myself.

W: That's right. But at a youth hostel, you can exchange travel information with other tourists.

M: But I don't want to sleep in a room with strangers. Plus, what if I get robbed?

W: That doesn't happen very often.

M: Still, I'll choose a hotel for a clean and safe environment.

여: 너 스페인에 간다고 들었어. Susan의 집에서 머물 거니?

남: 아니. 그 애도 지금 여행 중이야. 그래서 호텔에 머물까 생각 중이야.

여: 유스호스텔을 찾아 보는 게 어때? 훨씬 싸.

남: 잘 모르겠어. 호텔은 더 비싸긴 하지만 더 깨끗하고 편리한 시설들이 있잖아.

여: 하지만 거기서 잠만 잘 거잖아.

남: 유스호스텔에 머물면 비누랑 샴푸 같은 것들을 가지고 가야 하잖아.

여: 맞아. 하지만 유스호스텔에서는 다른 여행자들과 여행 정보를 교환할 수 있어.

남: 하지만 낯선 사람들과 한 방에서 자고 싶지 않아. 거기다 도난을 당하기라도 하면 어떻게 해?

여: 그런 일은 자주 있지 않아.

남: 그래도, 난 깨끗하고 안전한 환경 때문에 호텔을 선택할래.

어휘

facility[fəsíləti] 명 시설　**exchange**[ikstʃéindʒ] 동 교환하다　**stranger**[stréindʒər] 명 이방인　**get robbed** 도난

48

당하다　**safe**[seif] 형 안전한　**environment** [inváiərənmənt] 명 환경

문제 해설

Q1: 남자가 스페인에서 머물 곳은?

　남자는 호텔에서 지내겠다고 했다.

Q2: 여자에 따르면 유스호스텔의 두 가지 장점은?

　호텔보다는 가격이 싸고 그곳에 머무는 다른 여행자들과 여행 정보를 교환할 수 있다고 했다.

UNIT 08 Advice

Getting ★ Ready　p. 50

A 1 ⓐ　2 ⓒ　3 ⓕ　4 ⓑ　5 ⓓ　6 ⓖ
B 1 ⓔ　2 ⓒ　3 ⓕ

B 1 여: 너 그가 물건을 훔치는 것을 보고 뭐라고 했니?

　　남: 너무 충격을 받아서 아무 말도 할 수 없었어요.

　2 여: 프레젠테이션을 할 때 가장 중요한 것은 뭐지?

　　남: 학생들이 네 프레젠테이션에 집중하게 만들어야 해.

　3 여: 나 어느 대학에 가야 할까?

　　남: 내가 너라면 스탠포드에서 공부할 기회를 놓치지 않을 거야.

Listening ★ Start　p. 51

1 ③ / used to, going out with, many things to do, listen to me, if I'm late

2 ② / you were accepted by, major in, in that field, it would be better, miss the chance

1

W: My father and I used to be very close. But things changed after I started going out with Mike. Now he tells me to come home by 8 o'clock. It's hard for me. I have many things to do after school besides meeting Mike. I often study in the library and go shopping with my friends. But he doesn't listen to me and keeps making me return home by 8. He even tells me that he'll reduce my pocket money if I'm late. I can't understand him anymore.

여: 아버지와 전 아주 가까운 사이였죠. 하지만 제가 Mike와 사귀기 시작하면서 상황이 변했어요. 요즘 아버지는 저에게 8시

까지 귀가하라고 하세요. 그건 저에겐 힘든 일이에요. Mike 를 만나는 것 말고도 방과 후에 할 일이 많아요. 자주 도서관 에서 공부를 하고 친구들이랑 쇼핑을 가거든요. 하지만 아버지는 제 말을 듣지 않고 계속 8시까지 집에 오라고만 하세요. 제가 늦으면 용돈을 깎겠다고까지 하세요. 전 더 이상 아버지를 이해할 수가 없어요.

문제 해설

Q: 소녀의 아버지는 그녀가 무엇을 하기를 원하나?
아버지가 무조건 8시까지 집에 들어오라고 하셔서 힘들어 하고 있는 내용이다.

2

M: Congratulations. I heard you were accepted by Harvard!

W: Thanks. But I also got accepted by Stanford. I can't decide which university I should go to.

M: What are you going to major in?

W: English literature.

M: Hmm... isn't Stanford more famous in that field?

W: Right. But Professor Cooper teaches at Harvard. She's a great scholar whom I really respect.

M: Really? Then, it would be better to enter that university.

W: The problem is, Harvard is much farther away from my family than Stanford.

M: If I were you, I wouldn't miss the chance to learn from a great scholar.

W: Thanks for your advice.

남: 축하해. 하버드 대학에 합격했다고 들었어!

여: 고마워. 하지만 스탠포드 대학에도 합격했어. 어느 대학을 가야 할지 결정할 수가 없어.

남: 무엇을 전공할 건데?

여: 영문학.

남: 흠… 스탠포드가 그 분야에서 더 유명하지 않나?

여: 맞아. 하지만 Cooper 교수님이 하버드에서 가르치고 계셔. 그분은 내가 아주 존경하는 훌륭한 학자셔.

남: 그래? 그렇다면 그 대학을 가는 게 낫겠네.

여: 문제는 하버드가 스탠포드보다 우리 가족이 사는 곳에서 훨씬 더 멀다는 거야.

남: 내가 너라면 훌륭한 학자의 가르침을 받는 기회를 놓치진 않을 거야.

여: 충고 고마워.

문제 해설

Q: 남자가 여자에게 하버드 대학에 들어가라고 추천한 이유는?
남자는 하버드 대학에 여자가 존경하는 교수가 있다는 것 때문에 그 학교를 추천하고 있다.

Listening ★ Practice p. 52

1 ③ mQ1 ⓐ   2 ③ mQ2 ⓐ   3 ④ mQ3 ⓑ
4 ② mQ4 ⓐ   5 ③ mQ5 ⓐ   6 ④ mQ6 ⓑ

1

M: I couldn't sleep at all last night.

W: Why not?

M: I'm going to a high school reunion this evening. A girl I used to really like will come to the reunion.

W: I see. In that case, you should change your clothes.

M: Okay. What should I wear?

W: What colors of pants do you have?

M: I have black pants and beige pants.

W: What about long-sleeved shirts?

M: I have a white shirt and gray striped shirt.

W: I think beige pants with a white shirt would be the best choice.

M: But I forgot to wash those pants. They're pretty dirty.

W: Okay. Then I recommend the black pants with the gray striped shirt.

M: Thanks. I hope she likes the way I look.

남: 어젯밤에 잠을 한숨도 못 잤어.

여: 왜?

남: 오늘 저녁에 고등학교 동창회에 가기로 했거든. 내가 정말 좋아했던 여자애가 동창회에 올 거야.

여: 그렇구나. 그런 상황이라면, 옷을 갈아입어야겠다.

남: 알았어. 뭘 입어야 할까?

여: 무슨 색깔 바지가 있어?

남: 검정색이랑 베이지색 바지가 있어.

여: 긴소매 셔츠는?

남: 흰색이랑 회색 줄무늬 셔츠가 있어.

여: 흰 셔츠와 베이지색 바지가 최선의 선택인 것 같아.

남: 하지만 그 바지를 세탁하는 걸 잊었어. 꽤 더러운데.

여: 알았어. 그럼, 회색 줄무늬 셔츠에 검정색 바지를 추천할게.
남: 고마워. 그 애가 내 모습을 마음에 들어하면 좋겠다.

reunion[riːjúːnjən] 몡 동창회 beige[beiʒ] 혱 베이지색의
long-sleeved[lɔ́ːŋslíːvd] 혱 긴소매의 gray[grei] 혱 회색
의 striped[straipt] 혱 줄무늬의 pretty[príti] 閉 꽤

문제 해설

Q: 남자가 입을 것은?

베이지색 바지가 세탁되어 있지 않아서 대신 검정색 바지와
회색 줄무늬 긴소매 셔츠를 입기로 했다.

mQ1: 남자의 현재 기분은?

남자는 좋아하는 여자가 동창회에 온다고 해서 들떠 있는 상
태이다.

2

M: How are you doing?
W: I'm pretty busy looking for a job. I applied
   to a couple of companies, but I didn't get
   hired.
M: What companies have you applied to?
W: I applied to ABC and NE Advertising.
M: Those are the most well-known advertising
   companies. It must be hard to get a job in
   such famous companies.
W: I know. Besides, my major is trade.
M: Right. Since you didn't major in advertising,
   it's even harder.
W: I guess so.
M: Why don't you apply to a smaller company
   and try to build your career first? After that,
   you can move to a bigger company.
W: Thanks for your advice.

남: 어떻게 지내?
여: 직장을 구하느라 상당히 바빠. 두 군데 회사에 지원을 했는
   데 취직이 안 됐어.
남: 어떤 회사에 지원했어?
여: ABC와 NE Advertising에 지원했어.
남: 가장 유명한 광고 회사들이잖아. 그런 유명 기업에 취직하기
   는 분명히 어려울 거야.
여: 알아. 게다가 내 전공이 무역이잖아.
남: 맞아. 광고를 전공하지 않았으니 더욱 어렵지.
여: 그런 것 같아.
남: 더 작은 회사에 지원해서 우선 경력을 쌓는 것이 어떨까? 그
   런 후에 더 큰 회사로 옮길 수 있을 거야.
여: 충고 고마워.

apply[əplái] 동 지원하다 get hired 고용이 되다
advertising[ǽdvərtàiziŋ] 몡 광고 well-known[wélnóun]

혱 유명한 major[méidʒər] 몡 전공; 동 전공하다 trade
[treid] 몡 무역 career[kəríər] 몡 *경력; 직업 [문제]
experience[ikspí(ː)əriəns] 몡 경험 intern[íntəːrn] 몡 인
턴, 교육 실습생

문제 해설

Q: 남자의 조언은?

작은 회사에서 경력을 쌓은 후에 큰 회사로 옮길 것을 조언
했다.

mQ2: 여자가 들어가고 싶은 회사의 종류는?

여자는 광고 회사 두 곳에 지원했다고 했다.

3

M: I had a fight with my girlfriend Amy.
W: Were you late for a date again?
M: No. I had a car accident yesterday, but I
   didn't tell Amy about it.
W: Why not?
M: I didn't want to make her worried. But she
   heard about it from another friend.
W: Now I got it. Women want their boyfriends
   to share everything with them, but you didn't.
M: Is that a big problem?
W: Of course. Amy might think you don't trust
   her.
M: Really? Then I should talk to her right now.
   But she's not answering her phone.
W: She must still be at the university because
   of a club meeting. Go meet her instead.
M: Okay, thanks.

남: 나 내 여자 친구 Amy와 싸웠어.
여: 너 또 데이트에 늦었니?
남: 아니. 어제 교통사고가 있었는데 Amy에게 말하지 않았거든.
여: 왜 안 했어?
남: 그 애를 걱정시키고 싶지 않았어. 그런데 그 애가 다른 친구
   에게서 그 얘길 들은 거야.
여: 이제 알겠다. 여자들은 남자 친구가 모든 걸 자신과 공유하
   길 바라는데 넌 그렇게 하지 않았어.
남: 그게 큰 문제야?
여: 물론이지. Amy는 네가 자신을 믿지 않는다고 생각할지도 몰라.
남: 정말? 그럼 당장 그 애와 얘기를 좀 해야겠다. 그런데 전화
   를 안 받아.
여: 클럽 모임 때문에 아직 대학교에 있을 거야. (전화하는) 대신
   가서 만나봐.
남: 알았어. 고마워.

have a fight with ~와 싸우다 accident[ǽksidənt] 몡
사고 trust[trʌst] 동 믿다 answer one's phone 전화
를 받다 [문제] appointment[əpɔ́intmənt] 몡 약속

50

문제 해설

Q: 남자가 여자 친구와 싸운 이유는?

남자가 여자 친구에게 교통사고에 대해 말하지 않아서 싸웠다.

mQ3: 남자가 다음에 할 일은?

여자 친구와 대화를 하기 위해 여자 친구가 있는 학교로 갈 것이다.

4

M: What is your presentation topic for history class?

W: I did some research on Napoleon. But I'm really worried about it.

M: About what? About giving a presentation?

W: Exactly. You know, my last presentation was really bad.

M: Do you mean the presentation about Rome? I liked it. It was a bit boring, though.

W: So how can I make this presentation more interesting?

M: The most important thing is to make the students focus on your presentation.

W: How?

M: Make eye contact and ask questions. It's not good to just stand there and speak.

W: I see.

M: And I often use materials such as video clips or pictures. Those make students interested in the presentation too.

남: 역사 수업에서 네가 할 프레젠테이션 주제가 뭐니?

여: 나폴레옹에 대해 조사를 좀 했어. 하지만 정말 걱정이야.

남: 뭐가? 프레젠테이션을 하는 게?

여: 바로 그거야. 너도 알다시피 지난번 프레젠테이션이 아주 형편없었잖아.

남: 로마에 대한 프레젠테이션 말이야? 난 좋았는데. 좀 지루하긴 했지만.

여: 그럼 어떻게 하면 이번 프레젠테이션을 더 흥미롭게 만들 수 있을까?

남: 가장 중요한 것은 학생들이 네 프레젠테이션에 집중하게 만드는 거야.

여: 어떻게?

남: 눈을 마주치고 질문을 해. 그냥 서서 말만 하는 것은 좋지 않아.

여: 알았어.

남: 그리고 난 동영상 클립이나 사진 같은 자료들을 자주 써. 그런 것들도 학생들이 프레젠테이션에 흥미를 갖게 만들거든.

어휘

presentation [prìːzentéiʃən] 명 프레젠테이션, 발표
research [risə́ːrtʃ] 명 조사, 연구 　focus on ~에 집중하다
contact [kántækt] 명 접촉, 맞닿음 　material [mətí(ː)əriəl]

명 재료; *자료 　video clip 동영상 클립 　[문제]
successful [səksésfəl] 형 성공적인 　feedback [fíːdbæ̀k]
명 감상, 의견

문제 해설

Q: 그들은 주로 무엇에 대해 이야기하고 있는가?

프레젠테이션에 자신이 없는 여자에게 남자가 성공적인 프레젠테이션을 하기 위한 방법을 알려주고 있다.

mQ4: 여자의 프레젠테이션 주제는?

이번 프레젠테이션에는 나폴레옹에 대해 조사했다고 했다.

5

W: Do you have any problems with your family or friends? Do you worry about your future? If so, why don't you get counseling at the Teen Counseling Center? You can get advice about your problems from our professional counselors. This center is for teenagers living in California. You can call, email, or visit our center in person. It is sponsored by the government, so all of our services are offered for free. We're open from 9 a.m. to 6 p.m. on weekdays. On Saturdays, we open at 9 a.m. and close at 1 p.m.

여: 가족이나 친구들과 문제가 있으세요? 미래에 대해 걱정이 되세요? 그렇다면 Teen Counseling Center에서 상담을 받으시는 건 어떨까요? 전문 상담사들로부터 당신의 문제에 대한 조언을 얻을 수 있습니다. 이 센터는 캘리포니아에 살고 있는 십대들을 위한 것입니다. 전화를 하거나 이메일을 보내거나 직접 센터를 방문하시면 됩니다. 정부의 후원을 받으므로 저희의 모든 서비스는 무상으로 제공됩니다. 주중에는 오전 9시부터 오후 6시까지 엽니다. 토요일에는 오전 9시에 열고 오후 1시에 닫습니다.

어휘

counseling [káunsəliŋ] 명 상담 　professional [prəféʃənəl]
형 전문적인 　counselor [káunsələr] 명 상담사 　email
[íːmèil] 동 전자 우편을 보내다 　in person 직접
sponsor [spánsər] 동 후원하다 　government
[gávərnmənt] 명 정부 　for free 무료로 　[문제] support
[səpɔ́ːrt] 명 후원 　volunteer [vàləntíər] 명 자원봉사자

문제 해설

Q: 이 센터에 대해서 틀린 정보를 고르시오.

주중에는 오전 9시부터 오후 6시까지 개방한다.

mQ5: 상담이 무료인 이유는?

센터의 상담이 무료인 이유는 센터가 정부 지원을 받기 때문이라고 했다.

51

6

M: Ms. Taylor, it was such a great honor to be with you on stage.

W: Thank you. It was a nice experience for me, too.

M: How can you act, sing, and dance so well? I wish I were as talented as you.

W: Wasn't it your debut musical performance? You'll get better.

M: But people always tell me I'm not good enough.

W: I heard the same thing when I debuted.

M: I can't believe that!

W: It's true. But I've been practicing every single day for 15 years. That's why I'm here now.

M: I see. I'll keep on trying my best.

남: Taylor 씨, 함께 무대에 설 수 있어서 큰 영광이었어요.

여: 고마워요. 저에게도 멋진 경험이었어요.

남: 어떻게 연기와 노래, 춤을 그렇게 잘 할 수 있으세요? 저도 당신만큼 재능이 있으면 좋겠어요.

여: 이번이 뮤지컬 공연 첫 출연이지 않나요? 점점 좋아질 거예요.

남: 하지만 제가 충분히 잘하는 건 아니라는 얘기를 항상 들어요.

여: 제가 데뷔할 때도 같은 말을 들었어요.

남: 믿을 수가 없어요!

여: 사실이에요. 하지만 전 15년 동안 매일 연습했어요. 그래서 제가 지금 이 자리에 있는 거예요.

남: 알겠습니다. 저도 계속 최선을 다할게요.

어휘

honor [ánər] 몡 영광   stage [steidʒ] 몡 무대   act [ækt]
동 연기하다   talented [tǽləntid] 혱 재능이 있는
debut [déibjuː] 몡 데뷔, 첫 출연; 혱 첫 등장의; 동 데뷔하다
performance [pərfɔ́ːrməns] 몡 공연   every single day
하루도 거르지 않고, 매일   keep on v-ing ~을 계속 하다
try one's best 최선을 다하다   [문제] bitter [bítər] 혱 쓴
loud [laud] 悍 큰 소리로   worm [wəːrm] 몡 벌레
overnight [óuvərnàit] 悍 하룻밤에

문제 해설

Q: 여자의 조언을 가장 잘 묘사한 것은?

① 좋은 약은 입에 쓰다.

② 행동이 말보다 더 중요하다.

③ 일찍 일어나는 새가 벌레를 잡는다.

④ 성공은 하룻밤 사이에 오지 않는다.

처음에는 잘하지 못 했지만 15년 동안 열심히 연습해서 성공할 수 있었다고 했으므로 성공은 시간이 걸린다는 말이 적절하다.

mQ6: 화자 간의 관계는?

둘은 뮤지컬 공연을 함께 했고 데뷔 때의 얘기를 나누는 것으로 보아 뮤지컬 배우이며 선후배 관계이다.

A 1 ② 2 ④ B 1 ② 2 ③

A [1-2]

W: Mr. Jackson, can I talk to you for a second?

M: Sure. Do you have a problem?

W: It's about my friend, Joel. I saw him shoplifting from a store.

M: Oh, boy. Do you know why he would do such a thing?

W: I think he did it for fun. His family isn't poor, so I don't know why else he would steal.

M: Did you say anything to him at that time?

W: No. I was so shocked that I couldn't say anything.

M: He might think you accept that behavior because you kept silent.

W: Then should I tell him that he shouldn't do it again? But what if he hates me?

M: Just think about what's best for him, if you are really worried about him.

W: Okay.

여: Jackson 선생님, 잠시 얘기할 수 있을까요?

남: 물론이지. 무슨 문제가 있니?

여: 친구 Joel에 관한 거예요. 그 애가 상점에서 물건을 훔치는 것을 봤어요.

남: 아, 저런. 그 애가 왜 그런 일을 했는지 아니?

여: 재미로 그런 거 같아요. 집이 가난한 것도 아닌데 절도를 할 다른 이유가 있는지 모르겠어요.

남: 그때 넌 그 애에게 무슨 말을 했니?

여: 아뇨. 너무 충격을 받아서 아무 말도 할 수 없었어요.

남: 네가 입을 다물고 있어서 그 앤 네가 그 행동을 인정한다고 생각할 수도 있겠구나.

여: 그럼 다시는 그러지 말라고 얘기해야 할까요? 그 애가 절 미워하면 어떻게 해요?

남: 네가 그 애를 정말 걱정한다면 무엇이 그에게 최선일지 생각해 봐.

여: 알겠어요.

어휘

shoplift [ʃáplìft] 동 가게 물건을 훔치다   for fun 재미로
steal [stiːl] 동 훔치다, 절도하다 (steal-stole-stolen)
shocked [ʃakt] 혱 충격을 받은   behavior [bihéivjər] 몡
행동   keep silent 침묵을 지키다   [문제] force [fɔːrs] 동
강요하다   attention [əténʃən] 몡 주의, 관심

문제 해설

Q1: 소녀는 Joel이 왜 상점에서 물건을 훔쳤다고 생각하는가?

별다른 이유가 없어 보이고 그냥 재미로 한 것 같다고 했다.

Q2: 소녀가 남자의 조언을 따른다면 어떻게 할 것인가?

소녀는 남자의 조언대로 Joel에게 절도 행위를 하지 말라는 말을 할 것이다.

B [1-2]

M: It's natural that you feel nervous just before taking a test. However, if you become too nervous to focus on your test, you may be experiencing test anxiety. Test anxiety involves symptoms such as stomachaches, headaches, or sweating. Some students even throw up because of strong test anxiety. So, who experiences test anxiety? If you're not prepared for tests, you may experience it. Students who worry about their scores a lot are also likely to get test anxiety. To avoid this nervous feeling, you need to be well-prepared for the test. It's also important not to be afraid of making mistakes.

남: 시험을 치기 직전에 긴장하는 것은 자연스러운 일입니다. 그러나, 너무 긴장해서 시험에 집중할 수 없다면 시험 불안을 겪고 있는 것인지도 모릅니다. 시험 불안은 복통, 두통, 땀을 흘리는 증상을 수반합니다. 어떤 학생들은 심한 시험 불안 때문에 구토하기까지 합니다. 그렇다면, 누가 시험 불안을 경험할까요? 시험에 준비가 되어 있지 않다면 그것을 경험할지도 모릅니다. 자신의 점수에 대해 크게 걱정하는 학생들 역시 시험 불안을 겪을 수 있습니다. 이런 긴장감을 피하기 위해서는 시험을 잘 준비해야 합니다. 실수를 두려워하지 않는 것 또한 중요합니다.

natural[nǽtʃərəl] 형 자연스러운 anxiety[æŋzáiəti] 명 근심, 불안 involve[inválv] 동 포함하다, 수반하다 symptom[símptəm] 명 증상 stomachache[stʌ́məkèik] 명 복통 headache[hédèik] 명 두통 sweat[swet] 동 땀이 나다 throw up 토하다 be likely to-v ~할 것 같다 avoid[əvɔ́id] 동 피하다 be afraid of ~을 두려워하다 make a mistake 실수하다

문제 해설

Q1: 시험 불안에 대해 언급되지 않은 것은?

시험 불안의 정의와 증상, 피하기 위한 방법들이 언급되었다.

Q2: 시험 불안을 느끼지 않을 것 같은 사람은?

① Carol: 시험에서 꼭 만점을 받고 싶어.

② Neil: 공부하는 데 시간을 많이 쓰지 않았어.

③ Bobby: 실수하는 것에 대해 많이 걱정하지 않아.

실수를 두려워하지 않는 사람은 시험 불안을 피할 수 있다고 했다.

1 ④ 2 (1) ⓒ (2) ⓐ

W: I'm Kelly. When I'm worried about something, I ask my friends what to do. My friends and I have a lot in common. We are the same age, study together, and go to the same school. So they can fully understand my problems and give me helpful advice. I've talked with my parents and teachers before, but I noticed they didn't take my problems seriously.

M: I'm Simon. I used to talk to my friends when I needed advice. We felt closer after sharing our secrets. But I couldn't get any useful advice about my problems. Now I ask my parents for advice. They care about me more than anyone else. So they try to find the best solution to my problems.

여: 난 Kelly야. 난 걱정되는 일이 있을 땐 어떻게 해야 할지 친구들에게 물어 봐. 친구들과 나는 공통점이 많거든. 동갑이고, 함께 공부하고, 같은 학교에 다녀. 그래서 그 애들은 내 문제를 전적으로 이해하고 도움이 되는 조언을 해 줄 수 있어. 전에 부모님이나 선생님들과 얘기해 본 적이 있지만 그분들은 내 문제를 심각하게 받아들이지 않는다는 걸 알았어.

남: 난 Simon이야. 난 조언이 필요할 때 친구들에게 얘기를 하곤 했어. 비밀을 나누고 나니 우린 더 친근하게 느껴졌어. 하지만 내 문제에 대해 유용한 조언을 얻을 수는 없었어. 이제 난 부모님의 조언을 구해. 그분들은 다른 누구보다도 나에게 신경을 쓰시거든. 그래서 내 문제에 대해 최선의 해결책을 찾으려고 애쓰시지.

have ~ in common ~한 점에서 같다 fully[fúli] 부 완전히 notice[nóutis] 동 알아차리다 seriously[síəriəsli] 부 심각하게 secret[síːkrit] 명 비밀 care about ~에 대해 마음을 쓰다 solution[səlúːʃən] 명 해결책

문제 해설

Q1: 그들은 주로 무엇에 대해 이야기하고 있는가?

① 자신들이 가장 걱정하는 것이 무엇인지

② 자신들의 문제를 어떻게 해결하는지

③ 왜 학교에 상담자가 필요한지

④ 자신들의 문제에 대해 누구에게 말하는지

자신들의 문제를 누구와 상담하는지에 대한 내용이다.

Q2: 각 인물의 의견을 고르시오.

ⓐ 우리 부모님은 친구들보다 더 나은 해결책을 제안하신다.

ⓑ 친구들이 내 비밀을 다른 애들에게 말할까 봐 걱정이다.

ⓒ 친구들이 다른 누구보다 내 문제를 잘 이해할 수 있다.

Kelly는 친구들이 가장 좋은 조언자라고 했고 Simon은 부모님이 가장 좋은 조언자라고 주장했다.

UNIT 09 Entertainment

Getting ★ Ready p. 56

A 1 ⓒ 2 ⓔ 3 ⓐ 4 ⓓ 5 ⓕ 6 ⓑ
B 1 ⓑ 2 ⓕ 3 ⓐ

B 1 여: 그 영화가 언제 개봉한대?
　　남: 이번 토요일에 개봉해.
　2 여: 그녀는 그 영화에서 무슨 역을 맡니?
　　남: 그녀는 재능 있는 피아니스트 역을 맡았어.
　3 여: 심야 영화 보러 갔니?
　　남: 아니. 무료로 영화 파일을 다운로드했어.

Listening ★ Start p. 57

1 (1) ⓑ (2) ⓓ (3) ⓒ / robots or space, meet aliens someday, watch funny movies, relieve stress, scary and thrilling, what will happen
2 ① / going to the cinema, main character, how the movie ends, you blew it, avoid movie spoilers, important events

1

M1: I'm Peter. I like movies about robots or space. They allow me to see amazing scenes that I could never imagine. I hope I can meet aliens someday, just like in those movies.
W: I'm Jennifer. I like to watch funny movies when I'm depressed. They help me laugh and relieve stress. I rarely watch serious movies that make me sad.
M2: I'm Henry. I enjoy watching movies that are scary and thrilling. When ghosts suddenly come out, I usually scream! But it's fun to try to guess what will happen next.

남1: 난 Peter야. 난 로봇이나 우주에 대한 영화를 좋아해. 상상하지 못했던 놀라운 장면들을 보게 해 주잖아. 그런 영화에서처럼 언젠가 외계인을 만날 수 있다면 좋겠어.
여: 난 Jennifer야. 난 우울할 때 웃긴 영화를 보는 것을 좋아해. 웃게 만들고 스트레스를 풀어주잖아. 날 슬프게 만드는 심각한 영화는 거의 보지 않아.

남2: 난 Henry야. 난 무섭고 스릴이 있는 영화를 보는 걸 좋아해. 유령이 갑자기 나오면 난 보통 비명을 지르지! 하지만 다음에 무슨 일이 일어날지 추측해보는 게 재미있어.

어휘
space[speis] 몡 우주   allow A to-v A를 ~하게 하다
scene[si:n] 몡 장면   imagine[imǽdʒin] 동 상상하다
alien[éiljən] 몡 외계인   depressed[diprést] 혱 우울한
laugh[læf] 동 웃다   relieve[rilí:v] 동 경감하다, 풀게 하다
rarely[réərli] 붸 거의 ~않는   scary[skɛ́(:)əri] 혱 무서운
thrilling[θríliŋ] 혱 스릴이 넘치는   ghost[goust] 몡 유령
suddenly[sʌ́dnli] 붸 갑자기   scream[skri:m] 동 소리지르다 [문제] horror[hɔ́(:)rər] 몡 공포

문제 해설
Q: 각 인물이 제일 좋아하는 영화 장르를 고르시오.
　Peter는 로봇이나 우주에 대한 영화, 즉 공상과학 영화를 좋아하며, Jennifer는 우울할 때 웃기는 영화를 본다고 했으므로 코미디를 좋아하며, Henry는 무섭고 긴장감이 있는 영화, 즉 공포 영화를 좋아한다.

2

M: Where are you going?
W: I'm going to the cinema to watch *Jump*.
M: Oh, I saw that movie yesterday. I was so sad when the main character died in the last scene.
W: No! How could you tell me the ending!
M: Didn't you know that? I thought you knew how the movie ends.
W: No, I didn't. I was so excited about seeing that movie, but you blew it.
M: I didn't mean to. Don't be mad.
W: You know, I didn't read any movie reviews to avoid movie spoilers. But it's useless now.
M: A movie spoiler?
W: It's information about the important events in a movie.
M: I'm sorry.

남: 어디 가는 중이니?
여: 'Jump'를 보러 영화관에 가는 길이야.
남: 아, 어제 그 영화 봤어. 주인공이 마지막 장면에서 죽을 때 너무 슬펐어.
여: 안 돼! 결말을 말해주면 어떻게 해!
남: 너 그거 몰랐어? 영화가 어떻게 끝나는지 네가 아는 줄 알았지.
여: 아니, 몰랐어. 그 영화 본다고 아주 신났었는데 네가 망쳤어.
남: 일부러 그런 건 아냐. 화내지 마.
여: 있잖아, 난 영화 스포일러를 피하려고 어떤 영화 후기도 읽지 않았단 말이야. 그런데 이제 소용이 없어.
남: 영화 스포일러?

여: 영화 속 중요 사건에 대한 정보 말이야.

남: 미안해.

cinema[sínəmə] 몡 영화관   main character 주연
ending[éndiŋ] 몡 결말   blow it 실수하다, 망치다
mean to-v 일부러 ~하다   review[rivjú:] 몡 비평, 후기
spoiler[spɔ́ilər] 몡 망쳐 버리는 사람[물건]   useless[jú:slis]
혱 소용없는   [문제] upset[ʌpsét] 혱 기분이 상한
relieved[rilí:vd] 혱 안심한   pleased[plí:zd] 혱 기쁜

문제 해설

Q: 여자의 현재 심정은?

영화를 보기 전에 영화의 결말을 듣게 되어서 기분이 좋지
않다.

Listening ★ Practice   p. 58

1 ④   mQ1 ⓑ   2 ①   mQ2 ⓐ   3 (1) 0   (2) 2
(3) 3   mQ3 ⓑ   4 (1) ⓑ   (2) ⓒ   (3) ⓐ   mQ4 ⓐ
5 ①   mQ5 ⓑ   6 ②   mQ6 ⓑ

1

W: What movie do you want to see?

M: I want to see *Star Trek*.

W: But the tickets for 2:40 p.m. are all sold out.
We have to wait for hours to see the next
show.

M: Then how about watching *X-men*? There
are several tickets left for the 3:30 show.

W: Sorry, but I've already watched that movie.

M: Never mind. Have you seen *Taken* too?

W: No, not yet. Let's watch it.

M: Great. It's showing on two screens, screen
3 and screen 4.

W: I prefer screen 4. It's a bigger screen with a
better view.

M: Okay. The movie starts at 2:40. Let's go buy
the tickets.

W: Sure. How about buying some popcorn
before entering the theater?

M: Good idea.

여: 어떤 영화를 보고 싶니?

남: 'Star Trek' 보고 싶어.

여: 그런데 오후 2시 40분 표는 전부 매진이야. 다음 편을 보려
면 몇 시간을 기다려야 해.

남: 그럼 'X-men'은 어떨까? 3시 30분 표는 몇 장 남아 있어.

여: 미안하지만 난 그 영화를 벌써 봤어.

남: 그럼 됐어. 'Taken'도 봤어?

여: 아니, 아직. 그걸 보자.

남: 좋아. 두 개 상영관에서 하는데, 3상영관이랑 4상영관이야.

여: 난 4상영관이 더 좋아. 스크린이 더 커서 더 잘 보여.

남: 좋아. 영화는 2시 40분에 시작해. 표를 사러 가자.

여: 그래. 극장에 들어가기 전에 팝콘을 사는 게 어때?

남: 좋은 생각이야.

be sold out 매진되다   show[ʃou] 몡 상영, 상연
Never mind. 괜찮아. 신경 쓰지 마.   view[vju:] 몡 시야

문제 해설

Q: 그들이 보려고 하는 영화는?

'Taken'이라는 영화를 2시 40분에 보기로 결정했다.

mQ1: 그들이 다음에 할 일은?

영화 표를 먼저 사고 극장 안으로 들어가기 전에 팝콘을 사
기로 했다.

2

M: Audrey Hepburn was one of the most loved
actresses in the world. She first appeared
in an European movie in 1948. After she
starred in *Roman Holiday*, she became very
popular. For this movie, she received the
Academy Award for Best Actress. She also
won a Tony Award for her performance in
a play called *Ondine*. Audrey continued to
appear in many movies, including *Breakfast
at Tiffany's*, and *My Fair Lady*. During her
later life, she spent much of her time helping
children in need. She died of cancer in 1993.

남: 오드리 헵번은 세계에서 가장 사랑받는 여배우 중의 한 명
이었다. 그녀는 1948년에 유럽 영화에 처음으로 등장했다.
'Roman Holiday'에 주연으로 출연한 이후로 그녀는 큰 인
기를 얻었다. 그녀는 이 영화로 아카데미 여우주연상을 수상
했다. 또한 'Ondine'이라는 연극에서의 연기로 토니상을 수
상했다. 오드리는 'Breakfast at Tiffany's', 'My Fair Lady'
를 포함한 많은 영화에 계속 출연했다. 노년에는 어려운 처지
에 있는 아이들을 돕는 데 많은 시간을 보냈다. 그녀는 1993
년 암으로 사망했다.

loved[lʌvd] 혱 사랑을 받는   appear[əpíər] 통 나타나다;
*출연하다   star[stɑːr] 통 주연을 하다   receive[risí:v]
통 받다   award[əwɔ́ːrd] 몡 상   win[win] 통 획득하다
performance[pərfɔ́ːrməns] 몡 연기   continue
[kəntínju(ː)] 통 계속하다   in need 어려움에 처한   cancer
[kǽnsər] 몡 암   [문제] effort[éfərt] 몡 노력

문제 해설

Q: 남자가 주로 이야기하고 있는 것은?

① 오드리 헵번의 일생

55

② 오드리 헵번이 주연을 맡은 영화들
③ 아이들을 도우려는 오드리 헵번의 노력
④ 오드리 헵번이 출연한 영화의 성공
배우로서의 성공, 노년의 삶과 죽음까지 언급하고 있으므로
그녀의 일생에 대한 내용이다.

mQ2: 그녀가 아카데미상을 받은 영화를 고르시오.
'Roman Holiday'로 아카데미 여우주연상을 수상했다.

3

W: Thanks for calling Movie House. We are now showing *Terminator* on screen one, *Transformers* on screen two, and *Night at the Museum* on screen three. If you want to know the movie schedule, please press one. If you would like to reserve a ticket, press two. If you want to make a change to your reservation, press three. If you want to cancel your reservation, press four. Please press zero to speak to an operator. Thank you.

여: Movie House에 전화 주셔서 감사합니다. 지금 'Terminator'가 1상영관에서, 'Transformers'가 2상영관에서, 그리고 'Night at the Museum'이 3상영관에서 상영 중입니다. 영화 상영 시간표를 알고 싶으시면 1번을 누르세요. 표를 예매하고 싶으시면 2번을 누르세요. 예매를 변경하고 싶으시면 3번을 누르세요. 예매를 취소하고 싶으시면 4번을 누르세요. 안내원과 통화하고 싶으시면 0번을 누르세요. 감사합니다.

어휘
press[pres] 통 누르다 reserve[rizɔ́ːrv] 통 예약하다
reservation[rèzərvéiʃən] 명 예약 cancel[kǽnsəl] 통 취소하다 operator[ápərèitər] 명 교환원 [문제] staff[stæf] 명 스태프, 직원

문제 해설
Q: 각 인물이 누를 번호는?
안내원과 통화하려면 0번을 눌러야 하고, 표를 예매하려면 2번, 예매를 변경하려면 3번을 눌러야 한다.

mQ3: 'Transformers'는 어디에서 볼 수 있나?
'Transformers'는 2상영관에서 상영 중이라고 했다.

4

M: Do you know what movie was the most successful at the box office?
W: Let me guess. It was *E.T.*, wasn't it? I remember it was a big hit.
M: No. That's ranked fifth.
W: Really? What is the top ranking movie, then?
M: It's *Titanic*. I haven't seen it, but I should take time to watch it.
W: So what movie is ranked in second place?

M: *The Dark Knight*. And *Star Wars* follows along after *The Dark Knight*.
W: Which episode of *Star Wars*?
M: The one released in 1977, the first one. It's an old movie, but I've seen it on DVD.
W: Me too. What about fourth place?
M: *Shrek 2*.

남: 흥행에서 가장 성공적인 영화가 무엇이었는지 알아?
여: 맞춰 볼게. 'E.T.'였지, 아니야? 엄청난 흥행작이었던 걸로 기억하는데.
남: 아니. 그건 5위에 랭크되었어.
여: 정말? 그럼 1위에 랭크된 영화는 뭐야?
남: 'Titanic'이야. 난 못 봤는데 시간 내서 봐야겠어.
여: 그럼 2위에 랭크된 영화는 뭐야?
남: 'The Dark Knight'야. 그리고 'The Dark Knight'의 다음이 'Star Wars'야.
여: 'Star Wars'의 어떤 에피소드인데?
남: 1977년에 개봉된 첫 번째 에피소드야. 오래된 영화이지만 난 DVD로 봤어.
여: 나도. 4위는 뭐야?
남: 'Shrek 2'야.

어휘
successful[səksésfəl] 형 성공적인 box office 매표소; *흥행 성적 hit[hit] 명 히트 작품 rank[ræŋk] 통 등급을 매기다 follow[fálou] 통 따르다; *~의 다음에 오다
episode[épəsòud] 명 에피소드, (연속 영화의) 1회분 이야기
release[rilíːs] 통 개봉하다

문제 해설
Q: 각 빈칸에 알맞은 영화를 고르시오.
2위는 'The Dark Knight'이고 3위는 'Star Wars', 5위는 'E.T.'이다.

mQ4: 남자가 보지 않은 영화를 고르시오.
남자는 'Titanic'을 못 봤다고 했다.

5

W: Look at this. *In Spain* doesn't seem very interesting. It only gets one star.
M: Yes. Someone said the storyline is really boring.
W: Let's see what other people think about *The Man* starring Jim Smith.
M: Okay. Somebody mentioned that the ending is a bit disappointing.
W: Umm... what else is on the list?
M: Look. This movie gets four stars. Many people are recommending it.
W: *The Last Weekend*? Do you know what this movie is about?

M: It's a horror movie starring Sally Taylor.

W: Sorry. You know I can't watch scary scenes.

M: Then why don't we just watch *The Man* tonight? You like Jim Smith.

W: All right.

여: 이것 좀 봐. 'In Spain'이 아주 재미있지는 않은 것 같아. 별점이 하나 뿐이야.

남: 그래. 줄거리가 정말 지루하다고 했네.

여: Jim Smith가 나오는 'The Man'에 대해서는 다른 사람들이 어떻게 생각하는지 보자.

남: 좋아. 누군가 결말이 좀 실망스럽다고 말했네.

여: 흠… 목록에 또 다른 거 뭐 있어?

남: 여기 봐. 이 영화는 별 4개를 받았어. 많은 사람들이 추천하고 있어.

여: 'The Last Weekend'? 무엇에 대한 영화인지 알아?

남: Sally Taylor가 나오는 공포 영화야.

여: 미안해. 나 무서운 장면 못 보는 거 잘 알잖아.

남: 그럼 오늘 밤에는 그냥 'The Man'을 보는 게 어때? 너 Jim Smith 좋아하잖아.

여: 좋아.

어휘

storyline[stɔ́:rilàin] 몡 줄거리   mention[ménʃən] 동 언급하다   disappointing[dìsəpɔ́intiŋ] 혱 실망스러운 [문제] ceremony[sérəmòuni] 몡 식, 의식   refuse[rifjúːz] 동 거절하다

문제 해설

Q: 그들이 하고 있는 것은?
두 사람은 영화평을 읽으면서 볼 영화를 의논하는 중이다.

mQ5: 여자가 'The Last Weekend'를 보기를 거절한 이유는?
여자는 무서운 장면을 볼 수 없다고 했다.

6

M: (excited) Thank you! I feel like I'm dreaming right now. Umm... just after reading the storyline, I knew it would be a great movie. But it wasn't an easy job, because I've never directed such a large-scale movie. I'd like to thank all of my staff, who helped me so much. Hey, Joe! You are the most talented music director in the world! And thank you, Sam. You created such fantastic special effects. Well, all my actors and actresses, I really appreciate your hard work. Oh, today is the best day of my life!

남: [흥분하여] 고맙습니다! 저는 지금 꿈을 꾸고 있는 것 같습니다. 음… 줄거리를 읽자마자 훌륭한 영화가 될 거라는 걸 알았습니다. 하지만 쉬운 일은 아니었는데요, 그런 대규모

의 영화는 감독해 본 적이 없었기 때문입니다. 저에게 많은 도움을 준 모든 스태프들에게 감사드리고 싶습니다. 이봐, Joe! 자넨 세계에서 가장 능력 있는 음악 감독이야. 그리고 Sam, 고마워요. 당신은 아주 환상적인 특수 효과를 연출했어요. 음, 배우 여러분 모두, 노고에 정말 감사드려요. 아, 오늘은 제 인생 최고의 날입니다!

어휘

direct[dirékt] 동 감독하다, 지휘하다   large-scale [láːrdʒskéil] 혱 대규모의   talented[tǽləntid] 혱 재능이 있는 create[kriéit] 동 창작하다   special effects 특수 효과 appreciate[əprí:ʃièit] 동 감사하다

문제 해설

Q: 상황을 가장 잘 묘사한 그림은?
영화 시상식에서 수상 소감을 말하고 있는 상황이다.

mQ6: 남자의 직업은?
이런 대규모의 영화를 처음 감독해 보았다는 말을 통해 영화 감독임을 알 수 있다.

Listening ★ Challenge   **p. 60**

A 1 ② 2 ③   B 1 ③ 2 ③

A [1-2]

W: Last night, *Hollywood Report* showed an interview with Emma Winslet.

M: I didn't watch the show. What was the interview about?

W: About her new movie, *Drummer*.

M: What role does she play in it?

W: She plays a smart cop.

M: I can't wait to see it. When she played a basketball player in her last movie, she looked beautiful even in a uniform.

W: Oh, please stop! You've told me that at least 100 times.

M: Have I? Anyway, when is the movie released?

W: Next Friday. But there will be a red carpet event on Saturday at Mega Theater.

M: No! I have an appointment that day. I'll have to watch it on Sunday instead.

W: Sorry to hear that.

M: But... I can't miss a chance to see Emma. I'll cancel the appointment!

여: 어젯밤에 'Hollywood Report'에서 Emma Winslet과의 인터뷰를 보여줬어.

남: 그 쇼 못 봤어. 뭐에 대한 인터뷰였어?

여: 새 영화 'Drummer'에 대한 거야.

남: 거기서 그녀는 무슨 역을 맡았어?

여: 뛰어난 경찰 역할이야.

남: 어서 보고 싶다. 지난 영화에서 농구 선수로 나왔을 때는 운동복을 입었는데도 아름다워 보였어.

여: 아, 제발 그만! 너 그 얘기 최소한 100번은 했어.

남: 그랬나? 어쨌든 영화는 언제 개봉한대?

여: 다음 주 금요일이야. 하지만 토요일에 Mega Theater에서 레드 카펫 행사가 있을 거야.

남: 이런! 그 날 약속이 있어. 대신 일요일에 봐야겠다.

여: 안됐다.

남: 하지만… Emma를 볼 기회를 놓칠 수는 없지. 약속을 취소해야겠다!

어휘

role[roul] 명 역할   cop[kɑp] 명 경찰   uniform [júːnəfɔ̀ːrm] 명 (운동 선수의) 유니폼, 운동복   at least 최소한   event[ivént] 명 행사   appointment[əpɔ́intmənt] 명 약속   miss[mis] 동 놓치다

문제 해설

Q1: 새 영화에서 Emma Winslet이 맡은 역할은?
새 영화에서는 경찰 역을 맡았다고 했다.

Q2: 남자는 언제 영화를 보러 갈 것인가?
레드 카펫 행사를 보기 위해 토요일 약속을 취소하겠다고 결심했으므로 토요일에 볼 것이다.

B [1-2]

W: Can I use your computer for a short while? I want to know who won the Razzies.

M: What are the Razzies?

W: It means the Golden Raspberry Awards. You know the Academy Awards, right?

M: Of course. They're given to the best movies and actors of the year.

W: Well, the Golden Raspberry Awards are given to the worst ones.

M: That's interesting!

W: Right. And the Razzies are held at the Roosevelt Hotel the night before the Academy Awards.

M: But the winners must be embarrassed. Do they show up to the ceremony?

W: Only a few people have ever showed up to the ceremony since the Razzies started in 1981.

M: They were very brave. Now I want to know the winners of this year.

W: Okay. Let's search the Internet.

여: 잠깐 네 컴퓨터를 쓸 수 있을까? 누가 래지상을 탔는지 알고

싶어.

남: 래지상이 뭐야?

여: 골든 라즈베리 시상식을 의미해. 아카데미 시상식은 알지?

남: 물론이야. 그 해 최고의 영화와 배우에게 수여되는 거잖아.

여: 음, 골든 라즈베리 시상식은 최악인 것에 수여되는 거야.

남: 그거 흥미로운데!

여: 맞아. 래지 시상식은 아카데미 시상식 전날 밤에 Roosevelt 호텔에서 열려.

남: 그런데 수상자들은 당황스럽겠다. 그들이 시상식에 나타나긴 해?

여: 1981년에 래지상이 시작된 이후로 소수의 사람들만이 시상식에 출연했지.

남: 아주 용감했네. 이제 올해의 수상자를 알고 싶어.

여: 알았어. 인터넷을 검색해보자.

어휘

winner[wínər] 명 승리자; *수상자   embarrassed [imbǽrəst] 형 당황한, 난처한   show up 나타나다   brave [breiv] 형 용감한   search[səːrtʃ] 동 검색하다   [문제] vote [vout] 동 투표하다

문제 해설

Q1: 골든 라즈베리 시상식에 대해 사실이 아닌 것은?
① 최악의 영화와 배우를 선정한다.
② 아카데미 시상식 전날 밤에 열린다.
③ 수상자는 한 명도 참석한 적이 없다.
④ 1980년대 초반에 시작되었다.
몇몇의 수상자가 참석한 적이 있다고 했다.

Q2: 그들이 다음에 할 일은?
래지상 수상자를 인터넷으로 검색해서 알아보기로 했다.

Critical ★ Thinking   p. 61

1 ①, ④   2 ③

M: I stayed up late at night watching the movie *Ice Age 3*. I'm so tired.

W: Did you go see a late-night movie?

M: No. I downloaded the movie file for free.

W: What? You shouldn't do that!

M: Why not? I don't want to be bothered with going to the theater.

W: Don't you know you're violating copyright? It's like stealing someone else's things.

M: But everybody does it.

W: That's not important.

M: Come on. It's not a big deal. I can't watch several movies a month with my pocket money.

W: But you should know that it costs a lot of

money to make a movie.

M: Haven't you ever downloaded a movie file for free?

W: No. If we keep downloading, nobody will want to make movies. I don't want to let that happen.

남: 영화 'Ice Age 3'를 보느라고 어젯밤에 늦게 잤어. 아주 피곤하다.

여: 심야 영화를 보러 갔어?

남: 아니. 영화 파일을 무료로 다운로드했어.

여: 뭐? 그러면 안 돼!

남: 왜? 귀찮게 영화관에 가고 싶지 않아.

여: 저작권을 위반하고 있다는 거 몰라? 그건 다른 누군가의 물건을 훔치는 것과 같아.

남: 하지만 모두가 그러잖아.

여: 그건 중요한 게 아냐.

남: 왜 이래. 큰 일 아니잖아. 내 용돈으로는 한 달에 몇 편씩 영화를 볼 수가 없어.

여: 하지만 영화를 만드는 데 많은 돈이 든다는 걸 알아야 해.

남: 넌 영화 파일을 무료로 다운로드한 적 없어?

여: 없어. 우리가 계속 다운로드를 한다면 아무도 영화를 만들고 싶지 않을 거야. 난 그런 일이 생기게 하고 싶지 않아.

어휘

stay up late 늦게까지 깨어 있다 late-night[léitnáit] 형 심야의 download[dáunlòud] 동 다운로드하다 bother[báðər] 동 ~을 귀찮게 하다 violate[váiəlèit] 동 위반하다 copyright[kápiràit] 명 저작권 big deal 큰 일 pocket money 용돈 [문제] jail[dʒeil] 명 교도소 affect[əfékt] 동 영향을 주다 discourage[diskə́:ridʒ] 동 낙담시키다 gain[gein] 동 얻다 popularity[pàpjulǽrəti] 명 인기

문제 해설

Q1: 남자가 영화를 다운로드하는 두 가지 이유를 고르시오.
① 돈을 아낄 수 있다.
② 밤 늦게 영화를 볼 수 있다.
③ 같은 영화를 여러 번 볼 수 있다.
④ 극장에 가지 않고 영화를 즐길 수 있다.
영화를 여러 편 볼 돈이 없다고 했고, 극장에 가는 것이 귀찮다고 했다.

Q2: 영화를 다운로드하는 것에 대한 여자의 의견은?
① 다운로드하는 사람들은 감옥에 가야 한다.
② 영화의 가격에 영향을 줄 수 있다.
③ 영화 제작자들을 낙담시킬 수 있다.
④ 영화가 짧은 시간에 인기를 얻을 수 있게 해 준다.
사람들이 계속 다운로드를 하면 아무도 영화를 만들고 싶지 않을 거라고 했다.

UNIT 10 Jobs

Getting ☆ Ready p. 62

A 1 ⓓ 2 ⓑ 3 ⓒ 4 ⓐ 5 ⓔ 6 ⓕ

B 1 ⓐ 2 ⓑ 3 ⓒ

B 1 여: 무엇 때문에 직장을 그만두게 되었니?
남: 해야 할 일이 너무 많았어.

2 여: 어떤 종류의 직장을 얻길 원하니?
남: 활동적인 걸 하고 싶어.

3 여: 놀이 공원에서 하는 일은 어때?
남: 일에 아주 만족해.

Listening ☆ Start p. 63

1 ③ / deal with, raise the pet, On average, sound great, graduate from

2 (1) ⓓ (2) ⓒ (3) ⓕ / work with, study music carefully, what's going on, get pain, find out, what kinds of games

1

M: Do you know what pet lawyers do? Pet lawyers deal with legal problems to do with pets. For example, when a pet owner dies, they help decide who will raise the pet. Also, when a dog bites someone, they defend the pet owner. Are you curious about their income? On average, they earn $90,000 a year. It may sound great, but it's difficult to become a pet lawyer. They must graduate from law school and pass a special exam.

남: 애완동물 변호사들이 무슨 일을 하는지 아십니까? 애완동물 변호사는 애완동물과 관련된 법률 문제를 다룹니다. 예를 들어, 애완동물의 주인이 사망했을 때 누가 애완동물을 키울지를 결정하는 데 도움을 줍니다. 또한, 개가 사람을 물었을 때 애완동물의 주인을 변호합니다. 수입에 대해 궁금하세요? 그들은 평균적으로 일년에 90,000달러를 법니다. 좋아 보일지 모르지만 애완동물 변호사가 되기는 어렵습니다. 법과대학원을 졸업해야 하고 특별 시험을 통과해야 합니다.

어휘

pet lawyer 애완동물 변호사 deal with ~을 다루다, 처리하다 legal[líːɡəl] 형 법률적인 to do with ~와 관계가 있는 owner[óunər] 명 주인, 소유주 raise[reiz] 동 기르다, 키우다 bite[bait] 동 물다 defend[difénd] 동 변호하

다 curious[kjú(:)əriəs] 형 궁금해하는 income[ínkʌm]
명 수입 on average 평균적으로 graduate from ~을
졸업하다 law school 법과대학원

Q: 애완동물 변호사에 대해 언급된 것이 <u>아닌</u> 것은?

① 애완동물 변호사가 하는 일

② 애완동물 변호사가 되는 방법

③ 애완동물 변호사가 되는 것이 매우 인기 있는 이유

④ 애완동물 변호사가 버는 돈의 액수

이 직업이 인기가 있다는 내용은 언급되지 않았다.

2

W1: I'm Maria. I work with an orchestra of over 40 people. I don't play a musical instrument, though. Instead, I study music carefully and lead the musicians so that they give a beautiful performance.

M: I'm Eddy. My job is filming videos for TV news. I can show people what's going on through my camera. I sometimes get pain in my shoulders because of the camera, but I'm happy with my job.

W2: I'm Cindy. As I play computer games, I try to find out what is good or bad about them. I also research what kinds of games people want to play. After that, I create new games.

여1: 난 Maria야. 난 40명 이상의 단원을 가진 오케스트라와 일해. 하지만 악기를 연주하는 것은 아니야. 대신 음악을 신중하게 연구하고 연주자들이 아름다운 공연을 할 수 있도록 이끌지.

남: 난 Eddy야. 나의 일은 TV 뉴스를 위해 동영상을 촬영하는 일이야. 내 카메라를 통해 어떤 일이 일어나고 있는지를 사람들에게 보여줄 수 있어. 카메라 때문에 때때로 어깨에 통증이 있지만 내 일이 좋아.

여2: 난 Cindy야. 난 컴퓨터 게임을 하면서 그것들의 좋은 점과 나쁜 점을 찾아내려고 해. 또 사람들이 어떤 종류의 게임을 하고 싶어 하는지 조사하기도 해. 그 후에 새로운 게임을 만들지.

orchestra[ɔ́ːrkəstrə] 명 오케스트라 musical
instrument 악기 lead[liːd] 동 이끌다 (lead-led-led)
musician[mjuːzíʃən] 명 음악가, 연주자 film[film] 동 촬영
하다 pain[pein] 명 통증 research[risə́ːrtʃ] 동 조사하다
create[kriéit] 동 창작하다 [문제] composer[kəmpóuzər]
명 작곡가 cameraperson[kǽmərəpə́ːrsən] 명 카메라맨,
촬영 기사 conductor[kəndʌ́ktər] 명 지휘자

Q: 각 인물의 직업을 고르시오.

(1) 오케스트라에서 악기는 연주하지 않고 연주자들을 이끈다고 했으므로 지휘자이다.

(2) 카메라로 TV 뉴스를 위한 동영상을 찍는 직업은 카메라맨이다.

(3) 컴퓨터 게임의 장단점을 찾아내고 연구해서 새로운 게임을 만들어낸다고 했으므로 게임 프로그래머이다.

Listening ★ Practice   p. 64

1 ②   mQ1 ⓒ   2 ④   mQ2 ⓑ   3 ③   mQ3 ⓐ
4 ③   mQ4 ⓒ   5 ①   mQ5 (1) F (2) T   6 ②
mQ6 ⓑ

1

M: Let's go see the movie, *First Kiss*.

W: I heard that movie is really boring.

M: But I have to watch it. My sister prepared all the food that appears in the movie.

W: Is your sister a cook?

M: Not really. Her job is making food look delicious in pictures and movies.

W: How does she do that?

M: The easiest way is to choose the right tableware, such as plates and spoons.

W: I see. I guess even a plate could make a meal look different.

M: And sometimes she uses lipstick to make a strawberry look redder.

W: That's funny. Does she only work in film making?

M: No. She works for TV shows and writes books as well.

남: 영화 'First Kiss'를 보러 가자.

여: 그 영화는 아주 지루하다고 들었는데.

남: 하지만 난 꼭 봐야해. 내 여동생이 그 영화에 나오는 음식을 다 준비했거든.

여: 여동생이 요리사야?

남: 그건 아니야. 사진과 영화에서 음식이 맛있게 보이도록 만드는 일을 해.

여: 어떻게 그렇게 하는데?

남: 가장 쉬운 방법은 접시나 숟가락과 같은 적절한 식기류를 고르는 거야.

여: 그렇구나. 접시 하나만으로도 음식이 달라 보일 수 있다는 거겠지.

남: 그리고 때론 딸기를 더 붉게 보이도록 립스틱을 쓰기도 해.

여: 재미있다. 그녀는 영화 제작 일만 해?

남: 아니. TV 프로그램 일도 하고 책도 써.

★ ★

delicious[dilíʃəs] 형 맛있는 tableware[téiblwὲər] 명 식탁용 식기류 plate[pleit] 명 접시 meal[miːl] 명 식사, 요리 strawberry[strɔ́ːbèri] 명 딸기 film making 영화 제작

문제 해설

Q: 남자의 여동생의 직업은?

카메라로 찍었을 때 음식이 맛있어 보이도록 만든다고 했으므로 푸드 스타일리스트임을 알 수 있다.

mQ1: 남자가 'First Kiss'를 보고 싶어 하는 이유는?

남자의 여동생이 영화 작업에 참여했기 때문에 봐야 한다고 했다.

2

W: I'd like to work part-time, but I don't know what to do.
M: What about working at a summer camp?
W: I've done it before, so I'd like to do something new.
M: Then, you could write reviews after playing new video games. That would be fun.
W: Well... I'm not good at games.
M: That's too bad. How about working at a fitness center?
W: As a personal trainer?
M: Right. I heard that job isn't so difficult.
W: That sounds interesting. I'll think about it.
M: Why don't you ask Bill about the job in detail? He already does that.
W: Really? I should call Bill, then.
M: Wait! I'm going to meet him for lunch now. Join us.
W: Thanks!

여: 아르바이트를 하고 싶은데 무엇을 해야 할지 모르겠어.
남: 여름 캠프에서 일하는 건 어때?
여: 전에 해 본 적이 있어서 새로운 일을 하고 싶어.
남: 그렇다면 새로 나온 비디오 게임을 해 보고 후기를 쓰는 일을 할 수도 있어. 재미있을 거야.
여: 음… 난 게임을 잘 못해.
남: 그거 안됐다. 피트니스 센터에서 일하는 건 어때?
여: 개인 트레이너로?
남: 그렇지. 그 일이 아주 어렵진 않다고 들었어.
여: 재미있을 거 같아. 그걸 생각해 봐야겠다.
남: Bill에게 그 일에 대해 자세히 물어 보는 게 어때? 그 애가 이미 그 일을 하고 있어.
여: 정말? 그럼 Bill에게 전화해야지.
남: 잠깐! 지금 그 애랑 만나 점심 먹을 거야. 함께 가자.
여: 고마워!

review[rivjúː] 명 평, 후기 be good at ~을 잘하다 fitness center 피트니스 센터, 헬스 클럽 personal[pə́ːrsənəl] 형 개인의 trainer[tréinər] 명 트레이너, 훈련자 in detail 자세하게

문제 해설

Q: 여자가 관심이 있는 아르바이트는?

여자는 피트니스 센터에서 개인 트레이너 일을 하려고 한다.

mQ2: 그들이 다음에 할 일은?

Bill을 함께 만나 점심을 먹기로 했다.

3

(*Telephone rings.*)
M: Hello.
W: Hello, Stanley. It's Jennifer.
M: Hey, what's up?
W: I heard you work at an amusement park these days. How's your work?
M: I'm very satisfied with the work. It pays well, and I'm having a lot of fun.
W: Isn't it hard because of the hot weather?
M: Actually, it doesn't matter because I work indoors. But I do find it difficult to smile to customers all day long.
W: Oh, I can imagine.
M: Anyway, why don't you visit me at work?
W: Actually, that's why I'm calling. Can you give me a discount? I'm planning to go there next weekend.
M: Sure. I can give you 50% off.
W: Thanks!

(전화벨이 울린다.)

남: 여보세요.
여: 여보세요, Stanley. 나 Jennifer야.
남: 그래, 무슨 일이야?
여: 요즘 너 놀이 공원에서 일한다고 들었어. 일은 어때?
남: 일이 아주 만족스러워. 월급이 많고 아주 재미있어.
여: 날씨가 더워서 힘들지 않아?
남: 사실, 실내에서 일하니까 상관없어. 하지만 하루 종일 고객들에게 미소를 지어야 하는 건 정말 힘들어.
여: 아, 상상이 된다.
남: 어쨌든, 나 일하는 곳에 오는 건 어때?
여: 사실, 그래서 전화한 거야. 할인 좀 해줄 수 있니? 다음 주말에 거기 가려고 하는데.
남: 물론이지. 50% 할인해 줄 수 있어.
여: 고마워!

amusement park 놀이 공원 be satisfied with ~에

만족하나 indoors[indɔ́ːrz] ® 실내에서 customer
[kʌ́stəmər] ® 고객, 손님 all day long 하루 내내
imagine[imǽdʒin] ® 상상하다 [문제] repeat[ripíːt] ®
반복하다

관심이 있다 essay[ései] ® 수필, 에세이 well-organized
[wèlɔ́ːrgənaizd] ® 잘 조직된 personality[pə̀rsənǽləti] ®
성격 be full of ~으로 가득하다 [문제] talent[tǽlənt] ®
재능 salary[sǽləri] ® 봉급

문제 해설

Q: 남자의 일에서 힘든 점은?

남자가 힘들어 하는 점은 고객들에게 하루 종일 미소를 지어
야 한다는 점이다.

mQ3: 여자가 남자에게 전화를 건 이유는?

할인을 받기 위해 전화했다.

문제 해설

Q: 그들이 여자의 장래 직업에 대해 고려하지 <u>않은</u> 점은?

봉급에 대한 언급은 없었다.

mQ4: 여자에게 좋을 직업은?

흥미와 재능을 모두 고려해, 여행을 하면서 글을 쓸 수 있는
여행 작가가 적절하다.

4

W: What do you want to be, Tim?

M: I want to be a math teacher. What about you?

W: Well, I have no idea, so I'm very worried.

M: You should consider several things when deciding your future job. First, think about what you're interested in.

W: Well, I like to travel and take pictures.

M: And then consider what you're good at.

W: I'm good at writing. People say my essays are easy to read and well-organized.

M: I agree. Finally, you must consider your personality.

W: I'm full of energy, so I want to do something active.

M: Then how about becoming a travel writer? You can write while traveling around the world.

W: Great!

5

M: Bella Department Store is looking for personal shoppers. The job includes recommending proper clothes to our customers according to their job, age, and lifestyle. We only want graduates with a degree in fashion design. We also prefer experienced workers. If you are friendly, active and humorous, you'll be welcomed. Any women aged 26 to 35 can apply. Please send your resume to our website www.bellastore.com by July 21st. We'll let you know the result by email a week later.

여: 넌 뭐가 되고 싶어, Tim?

남: 수학 교사가 되고 싶어. 넌 어때?

여: 음, 아무 생각이 없어서 아주 걱정이야.

남: 장래의 직업을 결정할 때 몇 가지를 고려해야 해. 우선, 네가
흥미가 있는 게 뭔지 생각해봐.

여: 음, 여행하는 거랑 사진 찍는 걸 좋아해.

남: 그런 다음 네가 잘하는 걸 고려해 봐.

여: 난 글을 잘 써. 남들이 내 에세이가 읽기 쉽고 짜임새가 있다
고들 해.

남: 동의해. 마지막으로 너의 성격을 고려해야 해.

여: 난 에너지가 넘치니까 뭔가 활동적인 걸 하고 싶어.

남: 그럼 여행 작가가 되는 게 어때? 세계를 여행하면서 글을 쓸
수 있잖아.

여: 좋아!

어휘

consider[kənsídər] ® 고려하다 be interested in ~에

남: Bella 백화점에서 물품 구매 상담원을 찾고 있습니다. 고객들
에게 그들의 직업과 나이, 생활 방식에 맞는 적절한 옷을 추
천해 주는 일이 포함됩니다. 패션 디자인 학위가 있는 분만
원합니다. 또한 경력이 있는 직원을 선호합니다. 친절하고 활
동적이면서 유머가 있다면 환영입니다. 26세에서 35세 사이
의 여성이라면 지원할 수 있습니다. 저희 웹사이트인 www.
bellastore.com로 7월 21일까지 이력서를 보내주시기 바랍
니다. 일주일 후에 이메일로 결과를 알려드립니다.

어휘

personal shopper 물품 구매 상담원 include[inklúːd]
® 포함하다 proper[prápər] ® 적절한 lifestyle[láifstàil]
® 생활 방식 graduate[grǽdʒuət] ® 졸업생 degree
[digríː] ® 학위 apply[əplái] ® 지원하다 resume
[rézumèi] ® 이력서 result[rizʌ́lt] ® 결과

문제 해설

Q: 이 직업에 적절한 사람을 고르시오.

26세에서 35세 사이의 여성으로, 패션 디자인 학위를 가지고
있고 되도록 업무 경력이 있는 사람을 원한다고 했다.

mQ5: 사실이면 T, 사실이 아니면 F를 쓰시오.

(1) 온라인으로 7월 21일부터 지원할 수 있다.

(2) 결과는 이메일로 전달될 것이다.

웹사이트로 7월 21일까지 이력서를 보내고 결과는 일주일 후
에 이메일로 알려주겠다고 했다.

6

W: You look busy, Michael.

M: I need to make a video resume to apply for a job at Tiger Advertising Company.

W: I heard many companies require video resumes these days.

M: Right. But I don't know how to make my video unique. I don't want to just stand and introduce myself.

W: Yes, that would be boring. I think you must advertise yourself in a new, interesting way.

M: Do you have any idea?

W: What about making a resume like a TV advertisement for yourself?

M: That's a good idea!

W: Last month, there was a video resume contest held by Next Game Company. You could get some ideas from it.

M: Thanks a lot.

여: 바쁜 것 같네, Michael.

남: Tiger 광고 회사에 입사 지원하기 위해서 동영상 이력서를 만들어야 해.

여: 요즘 많은 회사들이 동영상 이력서를 요구한다고 들었어.

남: 맞아. 하지만 어떻게 내 동영상을 특이하게 만들지를 모르겠어. 그냥 서서 내 소개만 하고 싶진 않아.

여: 그래, 그건 지루할 거야. 새롭고 흥미로운 방식으로 널 광고해야 할 거 같은데.

남: 무슨 아이디어 있니?

여: 너에 대한 TV 광고처럼 이력서를 만드는 게 어때?

남: 좋은 생각이다!

여: 지난 달에 Next 게임 회사가 주최한 동영상 이력서 경연 대회가 열렸어. 거기서 아이디어를 얻을 수 있을지 몰라.

남: 정말 고마워.

어휘

require[rikwáiər] 동 요구하다 unique[juːníːk] 형 독특한 introduce[intrədjúːs] 동 소개하다 advertise[ǽdvərtàiz] 동 광고하다 advertisement[ædvərtáizmənt] 명 광고 hold[hould] 동 개최하다 (hold-held-held) [문제] impression[impréʃən] 명 인상

문제 해설

Q: 그들은 주로 무엇에 대해 이야기하고 있는가?

동영상 이력서를 어떻게 만들 것인가에 대한 내용이다.

mQ6: 남자가 지원하려는 회사의 종류는?

남자는 광고 회사에 지원한다고 했다.

A 1② 2① B1④ 2④

A [1-2]

W: When I started working at this company, I was really happy. This company is very famous and pays employees well. But soon I found it's not what I wanted. I work in a marketing department and meet new people every single day. But I'm a shy person, so I feel uncomfortable doing my job. I'm sure it would be best for me to change jobs. Now I'm thinking of learning to cook in Italy. It was my old dream. But I'm worried it's too late to start a new life. Also, I don't speak Italian. I really can't decide what to do.

여: 이 회사에서 일하기 시작했을 때 전 매우 기뻤어요. 이 회사는 아주 유명하고 직원의 임금이 높습니다. 하지만 곧 이것이 제가 원하는 것이 아니라는 걸 알게 되었어요. 저는 마케팅 부서에서 일하면서 매일 새로운 사람들을 만납니다. 그런데 전 수줍음을 타는 사람이라서 이 일을 하는 것이 불편하게 느껴집니다. 직업을 바꾸는 것이 제겐 최선일 거라고 확신합니다. 그래서 전 이탈리아에서 요리를 공부할까 생각 중입니다. 그건 제 오랜 꿈이에요. 하지만 새로운 인생을 시작하기엔 너무 늦은 것이 아닌지 걱정됩니다. 전 이탈리아어도 모릅니다. 어떻게 해야 할지 정말 결정할 수가 없어요.

어휘

employee[implɔ́iiː] 명 직원 marketing[máːrkitiŋ] 명 마케팅 department[dipáːrtmənt] 명 부서 uncomfortable[ʌnkʌ́mfərtəbl] 형 불편한 [문제] suit [suːt] 동 ～에 잘 맞다

문제 해설

Q1: 여자가 자신의 직업에 불만족스러워 하는 이유는?

① 봉급이 너무 적다.

② 자신의 성격에 맞지 않는다.

③ 회사의 미래가 밝지 않다.

④ 너무 바빠 개인 시간을 가질 수 없다.

수줍은 성격이라 새로운 사람들을 매일 만나야 하는 일이 맞지 않는다고 했다.

Q2: 여자가 배우길 원하는 것은?

여자는 이탈리아에 가서 요리를 배우고 싶다고 했다.

B [1-2]

W: Mr. Archer, you didn't major in interior design, did you?

M: No. My major is fashion design, but I worked for Sam's Interiors for three years.

63

W: How was your job at Sam's?

M: I was often very busy, but I enjoyed working with good co-workers.

W: What projects did you participate in?

M: I designed the interiors of the W Mall and Best Stores.

W: What made you quit the job?

M: My dream is to be a hotel interior designer. But Sam's usually does mall interiors.

W: I see. Could you tell me about your personality?

M: I'm a creative person and I always try to look on the bright side. And when a task is given to me, I do my best to complete it.

W: What are your weaknesses?

M: Well, I'm not really humorous enough to make people laugh.

여: Archer 씨, 인테리어 디자인을 전공하지 않으셨죠?

남: 네. 제 전공은 패션 디자인입니다만, Sam's Interiors에서 3년 동안 일했습니다.

여: Sam's에서의 일은 어땠나요?

남: 많이 바빴지만 좋은 동료들과 일하는 게 즐거웠어요.

여: 어떤 프로젝트에 참여했었죠?

남: W Mall과 Best Stores의 인테리어를 디자인했습니다.

여: 왜 그 일을 그만두었죠?

남: 제 꿈은 호텔 인테리어 디자이너가 되는 것입니다. 하지만 Sam's는 주로 쇼핑몰의 인테리어 디자인을 하거든요.

여: 알겠습니다. 자신의 성격에 대해 말씀해 주시겠어요?

남: 전 창의적인 사람이고 항상 밝은 면을 보려고 합니다. 그리고 과제가 주어졌을 때 완수하기 위해 최선을 다합니다.

여: 약점은 어떤 것들이 있죠?

남: 음, 사람들을 웃길 정도로 유머러스하지는 않아요.

어휘

interior[intí(:)əriər] 명 인테리어, 실내 장식
co-worker[kóuwə̀:rkər] 명 동료   project[prádʒekt] 명
프로젝트   participate in ~에 참여하다   quit[kwit] 동
그만두다 (quit-quit-quit)   creative[kriéitiv] 형 창의적인
task[tæsk] 명 과제, 업무   complete[kəmplí:t] 동 완수하다
weakness[wí:knis] 명 약점   [문제] previous[prí:viəs]
형 이전의   get along with ~와 잘 지내다   exactly
[igzǽktli] 부 정확히, 엄밀히   positive[pázitiv] 형 긍정적인
responsible[rispánsəbl] 형 책임감 있는

문제 해설

Q1: 남자가 이전 직장을 그만둔 이유는?

① 할 일이 너무 많았다.

② 더 큰 회사에서 일하고 싶었다.

③ 동료 직원들과 잘 어울리지 못했다.

④ 자신이 하고 싶은 일이 아니었다.

64

그는 호텔 인테리어 디자인을 하고 싶었는데 이전 직장은 쇼핑몰 인테리어 디자인을 주로 하기 때문이라고 했다.

Q2: 남자의 성격을 묘사하는 말이 아닌 것은?

밝은 면을 본다는 것은 긍정적인 성격이고, 맡은 일을 완수한다는 것은 책임감이 있다는 것이다.

Critical ★ Thinking   p. 67

1 ②   2 (1) ⓑ (2) ⓐ

W: What do you want to be in the future, Jack?

M: I wanted to be a pilot at first, but now I want to be a surgeon.

W: Oh, you want to help patients, right?

M: Honestly, that's not the reason. I just want to earn huge amount of money.

W: What? Have you considered your interest or personality?

M: Not really. I believe that having a lot of money will make me happy.

W: Perhaps, but I don't think it's the most important thing.

M: Then, what do you think is the most important thing when choosing a job, Amy?

W: I think people should choose a job they can do well. So I want to be a teacher.

M: That sounds like the perfect job for you.

여: 장래에 뭐가 되고 싶니, Jack?

남: 처음엔 조종사가 되고 싶었는데 지금은 외과 의사가 되고 싶어.

여: 아, 환자들을 돕고 싶구나, 그렇지?

남: 솔직히, 그게 이유는 아냐. 난 그저 많은 돈을 벌고 싶을 뿐이야.

여: 뭐? 네 관심사나 성격에 대해 고려해 보긴 한거야?

남: 꼭 그렇진 않아. 많은 돈이 있으면 행복해질 거라고 믿어.

여: 그럴지도 모르지만 그게 가장 중요한 거라고 생각하진 않아.

남: 그럼 넌 직업을 선택할 때 가장 중요한 게 뭐라고 생각하니, Amy?

여: 자신이 잘할 수 있는 일을 선택해야 한다고 생각해. 그래서 난 교사가 되고 싶어.

남: 너에겐 완벽한 직업인 것 같구나.

어휘

pilot[páilət] 명 조종사   surgeon[sə́:rdʒən] 명 외과 의사
patient[péiʃənt] 명 환자   honestly[ánistli] 부 솔직히
reason[rí:zən] 명 이유

문제 해설

Q1: 남자가 되고 싶어 하는 것은?

남자는 돈을 많이 벌기 위해 외과 의사가 되고 싶다고 했다.

Q2: 각 인물에게 장래 직업을 선택하는 데 중요한 것은?

　　ⓐ 일을 잘할 수 있는 것

　　ⓑ 돈을 많이 버는 것

　　ⓒ 자유 시간을 충분히 갖는 것

　　ⓓ 남을 도울 수 있는 것

　　Jack은 돈을 많이 버는 것을 중요하게 생각하고 Amy는 잘
　　하는 일을 하는 것이 중요하다고 했다.

UNIT 11 Culture

Getting ★ Ready　p. 68

A 1 ⓔ　2 ⓐ　3 ⓑ　4 ⓓ　5 ⓕ　6 ⓒ

B 1 ⓔ　2 ⓒ　3 ⓕ

B 1 남: 이 제스처가 나쁜 걸 의미하니?

　　여: 응. 네가 화났다는 의미야.

　2 남: 저 탑은 왜 문화유산 유적지로 선정되었지?

　　여: 세계 역사의 중요한 사건들과 연관이 있거든.

　3 남: 너희 나라에는 특별한 식사 예절이 있니?

　　여: 응. 웃어른이 식사를 시작하기 전에 먹지 않아.

Listening ★ Start　p. 69

1 ④ / English tradition, in the 19th century, hungry after lunch, consisted of, their busy schedules

2 ④ / what's wrong with you, gestured okay, index finger, mean something bad, It's interesting, got upset

1

M: It's an English tradition to have "afternoon tea" at around 4 or 5 p.m. It was started by Anna Russell in the 19th century. At that time, the English ate a heavy breakfast, light lunch, and late dinner. Anna was always hungry after lunch, so she had afternoon tea with her friends. Her afternoon tea consisted of black milky tea with sandwiches, scones, cakes and biscuits. Now the English rarely have afternoon tea because of their busy schedules. But when they do, they simply have black milky tea with biscuits.

남: 오후 4시나 5시쯤에 '애프터눈 티(오후의 차)'를 즐기는 것은 영국의 전통입니다. 그것은 19세기에 Anna Russell에 의해 시작되었습니다. 그 당시 영국인들은 든든한 아침과 가벼운 점심, 늦은 저녁을 먹었습니다. Anna는 점심 식사 후에 항상 배가 고파서 친구들과 애프터눈 티를 즐겼습니다. 애프터눈 티는 샌드위치와 스콘, 케이크, 비스킷을 곁들인 밀크홍차로 이루어져 있었습니다. 이제 영국인들은 바쁜 일상 때문에 애프터눈 티를 거의 즐기지 않습니다. 그러나 즐길 때에는 간단히 비스킷과 밀크홍차를 마십니다.

어휘

tradition[trədíʃən] 몡 전통　century[séntʃəri] 몡 세기
consist of ～로 이루어지다　black milky tea 밀크홍차
scone[skoun] 몡 스콘(핫케이크의 일종)　biscuit[bískit]
몡 비스킷　rarely[rέərli] 뷔 좀처럼 ～하지 않는, 드물게

문제 해설

Q: 애프터눈 티에 관해서 언급되지 않은 것은?

　어떻게 인기를 얻게 되었는지는 언급되지 않았다.

2

M: Kate, what's wrong with you?

W: You asked me to go to the library after school, so I gestured okay. What's wrong?

M: That gesture doesn't mean okay.

W: What do you mean?

M: You made a ring with your thumb and index finger, right?

W: Yes. That's the sign for okay here. Didn't you know that?

M: Really? I had no idea.

W: Does it mean something bad in Brazil?

M: Yes. It has a very insulting meaning.

W: Oh, now I understand. It's interesting that gestures have different meanings in different countries.

M: Yes, it is. I'm sorry that I got upset.

W: No problem.

남: Kate, 너 왜 그래?

여: 네가 나보고 방과 후에 도서관에 가자고 해서 좋다는 제스처를 했는데. 뭐가 잘못됐어?

남: 그 제스처는 좋다는 의미가 아니잖아.

여: 무슨 말이야?

남: 엄지와 검지손가락으로 원을 만들었잖아, 그렇지?

여: 응. 그게 여기선 좋다는 표시잖아. 그거 몰랐니?

남: 정말이야? 몰랐어.

여: 브라질에서는 그게 나쁜 걸 의미하니?

남: 응. 아주 모욕적인 의미야.

여: 아, 이제 이해가 돼. 제스처가 나라마다 다른 의미를 가진다

65

는 게 재미있다.

남: 그래. 화를 내서 미안해.

여: 괜찮아.

어휘

gesture[ʤéstʃər] ⑧ 몸짓(제스처)으로 나타내다; ⑲ 몸짓
thumb[θʌm] ⑲ 엄지손가락 index finger 검지손가락
insulting[insʌ́ltiŋ] ⑱ 모욕적인 get upset 화내다
[문제] misunderstand[mìsʌndərstǽnd] ⑧ 오해하다
body language 신체 언어

문제 해설

Q: 남자가 화난 이유는?

① Kate가 그에게 욕을 했다.

② Kate가 말하는 방식이 마음에 들지 않았다.

③ Kate가 함께 도서관에 가지 않으려고 했다.

④ Kate의 제스처를 오해했다.

Kate의 '좋다'는 의미의 제스처를 자신의 나라에서 쓰이는 안 좋은 의미로 오해했다.

Listening ★ Practice p. 70

1 (1) ⓒ (2) ⓐ (3) ⓑ mQ1 ⓒ 2 ④ mQ2 ⓑ
3 (1) ⓒ (2) ⓐ mQ3 ⓑ 4 (1) ⓐ (2) ⓓ mQ4 ⓐ
5 ② mQ5 ⓒ 6 (1) Good (2) Good (3) Bad
mQ6 (1) T (2) F

1

M: I saw a great documentary yesterday.

W: What was it about?

M: It showed traditional wedding customs in different countries.

W: Like what?

M: In America, for example, guests throw rice at the married couple. It's to wish them to have many children and be rich.

W: Interesting.

M: And in Sweden, a bride's parents put gold and silver coins in the bride's shoes.

W: I see.

M: There's more. In Belgium, the bride holds a handkerchief during the ceremony. After, she hangs the handkerchief on the wall of her house until someone in her family gets married.

W: Sounds interesting. I'd like to watch that documentary now. Which channel was it on?

M: K-channel.

W: Great. I'll download the show from the website.

남: 어제 재밌는 다큐멘터리를 봤어.

여: 뭐에 관한 거였는데?

남: 여러 나라들의 전통적인 결혼 관습을 보여주는 거였어.

여: 예를 들어?

남: 예를 들면, 미국에서 하객들은 결혼한 부부에게 쌀을 던져. 아이를 많이 갖고 부자가 되라고 빌어 주기 위해서야.

여: 재미있네.

남: 그리고 스웨덴에서는 신부의 부모가 신부의 신발에 금화와 은화를 넣어.

여: 그렇구나.

남: 더 있어. 벨기에에서는 신부가 예식 중에 손수건을 들고 있어. 식이 끝나면 신부는 가족 중의 누군가가 결혼할 때까지 자기 집 벽에 그 손수건을 걸어 둬.

여: 흥미롭다. 지금 그 다큐멘터리 보고 싶어. 어떤 채널에서 했어?

남: K 채널이야.

여: 좋아. 웹사이트에서 그 프로그램을 다운로드해야겠다.

어휘

documentary[dàkjuméntəri] ⑲ 다큐멘터리, 기록 영화
traditional[trədíʃənəl] ⑱ 전통적인 custom[kʌ́stəm]
⑲ 관습 rice[rais] ⑲ 쌀 married[mǽrid] ⑱ 결혼한
bride[braid] ⑲ 신부 coin[kɔin] ⑲ 동전 Belgium
[béldʒəm] ⑲ 벨기에 handkerchief[hǽŋkərtʃi(ː)f] ⑲ 손수건 ceremony[sérəmòuni] ⑲ 의식, 식 get married 결혼하다

문제 해설

Q: 각 나라의 결혼 관습을 고르시오.

미국에서는 결혼한 부부에게 하객들이 다산과 부를 기원하며 쌀을 던지고, 스웨덴에서는 신부의 부모가 신부의 신발에 금화와 은화를 넣어두며, 벨기에에서는 예식 중 신부가 손수건을 들고 있다고 했다.

mQ1: 여자가 다음에 할 일은?

여자는 다큐멘터리가 흥미롭다면서 웹사이트에서 다운로드하겠다고 했다.

2

M: Happy Travel would like to introduce a new tour package. This special package allows you to experience the traditional culture of the Aborigines, the native people of Australia. First, there's a traditional dance show. You can join the performers and dance on the stage. Next, native people will teach you how to throw boomerangs and play a traditional musical instrument called the didgeridoo. It sounds like things from nature, such as animals or wind. This tour departs on Thursdays and returns on Tuesdays. The price is $3,000 for adults and $2,000 for children.

남: Happy Travel이 새로운 패키지여행 상품을 소개해드립니다. 이 특별 패키지는 호주 원주민들인 Aborigine의 전통 문화를 경험할 수 있게 해 줍니다. 첫 번째로 전통 댄스 쇼가 있습니다. 무대에서 공연자들과 함께 춤을 출 수 있습니다. 다음으로 원주민들이 부메랑 던지는 법과 didgeridoo라고 불리는 전통 악기를 연주하는 법을 가르쳐 드립니다. 이 악기는 동물이나 바람 같은 자연의 소리를 냅니다. 이 투어는 목요일에 출발하여 화요일에 돌아옵니다. 가격은 성인은 3,000달러이고 어린이는 2,000달러입니다.

어휘

tour package 투어 패키지, 패키지 여행   experience
[ikspí(:)əriəns] 동 경험하다   Aborigine[æ̀bərídʒəniː]
명 호주 원주민   native[néitiv] 형 토착의, 원주민의
performer[pərfɔ́ːrmər] 명 공연자   boomerang
[búːməræ̀ŋ] 명 부메랑   musical instrument 악기
depart[dipáːrt] 동 출발하다   adult[ədʌ́lt] 명 어른, 성인

문제 해설

Q: 투어 프로그램에 포함되어 있지 않은 것은?
호주의 동물을 관람하는 일정은 언급되지 않았다.

mQ2: 사실인 것은?
투어는 매주 목요일에 출발하여 화요일에 돌아오는 일정이라고 했다.

남: 음식을 조금 남기는 게 먹을 걸 충분히 접대받았다는 뜻이거든.
여: 일본에선 접시에 밥을 남기면 더 먹길 원한다는 뜻이야.
남: 흥미로운걸. 일본에 또 다른 특별한 식사 예절이 있니?
여: 저녁 식사에 초대받으면 최소한 밥 두 공기를 먹어야 해.
남: 적게 먹는 사람은 어떻게 해?
여: 그릇이 누구든 두 공기를 먹을 수 있을 만큼 작아.
남: 그렇구나.
여: 그리고 국물을 먹을 때 그릇에 입을 대고 마셔. 국물에 든 건더기는 젓가락으로 먹어.

어휘

table manners 식사 예절   invite[inváit] 동 초대하다
plate[pleit] 명 접시   leave[liːv] 동 남기다   at least 최소한   bowl[boul] 명 공기, 그릇   lightly[láitli] 부 가볍게, 적게   solid[sálid] 형 고체의, 딱딱한   chopstick[tʃápstìk]
명 젓가락

문제 해설

Q: 접시에 음식이나 밥을 남기는 것의 의미는?
중국에서 음식을 남기는 것은 충분히 먹었다는 의미이고, 일본에서는 반대로 더 먹고 싶다는 의미이다.

mQ3: 일본에서 초대를 받았을 때 좋은 식사 예절로 여겨지는 것은?
밥을 두 공기는 먹어야 좋은 예절이라고 했다.

67

3

W: Are there any special table manners in your country?
M: Yes. In China, when invited to dinner, you should not eat all of the food on your plate.
W: Why is that?
M: Leaving some food means you were given enough to eat.
W: In Japan, leaving rice on the plate means you want to eat more.
M: Interesting. Are there any other special table manners in Japan?
W: When invited to dinner, you should eat at least two bowls of rice.
M: How about someone who eats lightly?
W: The bowl is small enough that anyone can eat two.
M: I understand.
W: And when we have soup, we drink it out of the bowl. We eat solid food from the soup with chopsticks.

여: 너희 나라에는 특별한 식사 예절이 있니?
남: 응. 중국에선 저녁 식사에 초대를 받았을 때, 자기 접시에 있는 음식을 다 먹으면 안 돼.
여: 왜 그래?

4

W: Tim, I'm going to travel India to see the Taj Mahal.
M: Do you mean the beautiful white castle, Cindy?
W: It's not a castle. It's a tomb built by a king for his dead wife.
M: I didn't know that.
W: It was chosen as one of the World Cultural Heritage sites by UNESCO.
M: World Cultural Heritage sites? How are they selected?
W: They are sites which are old, unique or related to important events in world history. Like Angkor Wat or the Tower of London.
M: I want to visit one of the World Cultural Heritage sites.
W: Your aunt lives in Beijing. Why don't you visit the Great Wall? It's also a World Cultural Heritage site.
M: Maybe I should go there this summer.

여: Tim, 나 타지마할을 보러 인도로 여행갈 거야.
남: 아름다운 하얀 성 말하는 거지, Cindy?
여: 그건 성이 아니야. 왕이 죽은 부인을 위해 지은 무덤이야.
남: 그건 몰랐어.

여: 유네스코에 의해 세계 문화 유산 유적지 중의 하나로 선정되
었어.

남: 세계 문화 유산 유적지? 그건 어떻게 선정되는 거지?

여: 오래되거나, 독특하거나, 세계 역사의 중요한 사건과 관련된
유적지들이야. 앙코르 와트나 런던 타워 같은 거지.

남: 세계 문화 유산 유적지 중의 한 곳을 가보고 싶다.

여: 너네 고모가 베이징에 사시잖아. 만리장성에 가보는 건 어때?
그것도 세계 문화 유산 유적지야.

남: 이번 여름에 거기 가도록 해야겠다.

어휘

Taj Mahal 타지마할(인도 아그라에 있는 대리석 묘) castle
[kǽsl] 명 성, 궁궐 tomb[tuːm] 명 무덤 heritage
[héritidʒ] 명 유산 site[sait] 명 장소; *유적 UNESCO 유
네스코(유엔 교육 과학 문화 기구) select[silékt] 동 선택하다
related to ~와 관련된 the Great Wall 만리장성

문제 해설

Q: 각 인물이 갈 곳을 고르시오.

　　Cindy는 타지마할을 보러 인도에 가겠다고 했고 Tim은
Cindy의 조언에 따라 중국의 만리장성을 보러 가기로 했다.

mQ4: 타지마할은 무엇인가?

　　왕이 죽은 아내를 위해 지은 무덤이라고 했다.

5

W: I'm going to tell you how Mexicans get
ready for New Year. The day before New
Year's Day, people sweep all the dust out of
their houses. They do this to get rid of bad
luck from the old year and make room for
good luck in the coming year. Also, they put
coins in their shoes to wish for wealth. For
women, wearing red underwear on New
Year's Day will bring love. Yellow will bring
money and white will bring marriage.

여: 멕시코 사람들이 어떻게 새해를 준비하는지 얘기해 드리려
고 합니다. 새해 첫날이 되기 전날에는 집 밖으로 먼지를 모
두 쓸어냅니다. 이것은 지난해의 나쁜 운을 없애 버리고 새해
의 좋은 운을 위한 공간을 만들기 위한 것입니다. 또한, 부를
기원하기 위해 신발에 동전을 넣습니다. 여자가 새해 첫날에
빨간 속옷을 입으면 사랑이 옵니다. 노란색은 돈을, 흰색은
결혼을 가져올 것입니다.

어휘

Mexican[méksikən] 명 멕시코 사람 New Year's Day
새해 첫날 sweep[swiːp] 동 쓸어버리다 dust[dʌst] 명 먼
지 get rid of ~을 없애다 make room 공간을 만들다.
비우다 wealth[welθ] 명 부 underwear[ʌ́ndərwɛ̀ər]
속옷 marriage[mǽridʒ] 명 결혼

문제 해설

Q: 여자는 주로 무엇에 대해 이야기하고 있는가?

① 멕시코 사람들이 나쁜 운을 피하기 위해 무엇을 하는지
② 멕시코 사람들이 새해를 어떻게 준비하는지
③ 멕시코 사람들이 새해를 위해 무엇을 사는지
④ 멕시코 사람들이 좋은 운을 불러오기 위해 무엇을 입는지
멕시코 사람들이 새해를 맞이하는 모습에 대한 내용이다.

mQ5: 멕시코 여성들이 결혼을 하기 위해서 입을 속옷의 색깔은?

　　빨간색 속옷은 사랑, 노란색은 돈, 흰색은 결혼을 불러온다고
했다.

6

M: Do you know that the shape of Thailand
looks like an elephant's head? That might be
one of the reasons why elephants are Thai
people's favorite animals. Up until 1917, the
elephant was on the national flag. Because
of the great love for elephants, there are
many superstitions about them in Thailand.
Thai people believe that passing under the
belly of an elephant makes wishes come
true. To dream of holding an elephant in
one's arms means that good things will
happen. But dreaming of getting an
elephant as a present means something
unlucky will happen.

남: 태국의 모양이 코끼리 머리 같다는 것을 아세요? 그것이 태
국 사람들이 가장 좋아하는 동물이 코끼리인 이유 중의 하나
일지도 모릅니다. 코끼리는 1917년까지 국기에 등장했습니다.
태국에는 코끼리에 대한 대단한 사랑 때문에 그것에 대한 미
신이 많이 있습니다. 태국 사람들은 코끼리의 배 밑으로 지나
가면 소원이 이루어진다고 믿습니다. 코끼리를 품에 안는 꿈
은 좋은 일이 일어날 것을 의미합니다. 그러나 코끼리를 선물
로 받는 꿈은 불행한 일이 일어날 것을 의미합니다.

어휘

shape[ʃeip] 명 모양 Thailand[táilænd] 명 태국 Thai
[tai] 형 태국의 national flag 국기 superstition
[sùːpərstíʃən] 명 미신 belly[béli] 명 배 come true 이루
어지다, 실현되다 hold ~ in one's arms ~을 안다
unlucky[ʌnlʌ́ki] 형 불행한

문제 해설

Q: 행운을 가져올지 불행을 가져올지 동그라미 하시오.

　　코끼리를 안는 꿈과 코끼리의 배 아래로 지나가는 것은 좋은
일이 일어날 것을 의미하지만, 코끼리를 선물로 받는 꿈은
불행한 일이 일어날 것을 의미한다.

mQ6: 사실이면 T, 사실이 아니면 F를 쓰시오.

　　(1) 태국은 지도에서 볼 때 코끼리의 머리처럼 보인다.

　　(2) 지금도 태국의 국기에는 코끼리가 있다.

　　태국의 모양이 코끼리 머리 같다고 했고, 1917년까지 국기에
코끼리가 있었다고 했다.

★ ★

Listening ★ Challenge   **p. 72**

A 1 ② 2 ① B 1 ④ 2 (1) F (2) F (3) T

A [1-2]

W: Jack, here's an interesting article about greetings in various countries.

M: What's so interesting?

W: Well, Tibetans greet by pulling their ears and sticking out their tongues.

M: That sounds funny.

W: Yes! And the Maoris of New Zealand greet by pressing their noses together.

M: Wow, that's friendly.

W: But the most interesting one is the Eskimo greeting. They slap the other person's cheek.

M: If that happened to me without knowing why, I would be really angry.

W: So would I!

M: So are you going to borrow that magazine today?

W: Yes, I am. Why?

M: I want to read it, too. It seems to contain very interesting articles.

W: Oh, there are more on the shelf. So you can borrow one, too.

M: Really? Do you know which section it's in?

W: Yes. It's right there in the culture section.

M: Thanks.

여: Jack, 여기 여러 나라의 인사법에 대한 흥미로운 기사가 있어.

남: 뭐가 그렇게 재미있어?

여: 음, 티베트 사람들은 귀를 잡아당기고 혀를 내밀어서 인사한대.

남: 재미있는데.

여: 그래! 그리고 뉴질랜드의 마오리족은 코를 서로 눌러서 인사한대.

남: 와, 그거 친근하다.

여: 하지만 가장 흥미로운 것은 에스키모 인사법이야. 그들은 서로의 뺨을 때린대.

남: 이유도 모르고 그런 일이 나에게 일어나면 아주 화가 나겠다.

여: 나도 그럴 거야!

남: 너 오늘 그 잡지 빌려 갈 거야?

여: 응. 왜?

남: 나도 읽고 싶어서. 아주 흥미로운 기사들이 있는 것 같아.

여: 아, 선반에 더 있어. 그러니 너도 빌릴 수 있을 거야.

남: 그래? 그게 어느 구역에 있는지 알아?

여: 응. 문화 구역에 바로 있어.

남: 고마워.

어휘

article[áːrtikl] 몡 기사   greeting[gríːtiŋ] 몡 인사
Tibetan[tibétən] 몡 티베트 사람   greet[griːt] 동 인사하다
pull[pul] 동 당기다   stick out 내밀다   tongue[tʌŋ]
몡 혀   Maori[máuri] 몡 마오리 사람   press[pres] 동 누르다   Eskimo[éskəmòu] 혱 에스키모의; 몡 에스키모 사람
slap[slæp] 동 찰싹 때리다   cheek[tʃiːk] 몡 뺨   borrow
[bárou] 동 빌리다   contain[kəntéin] 동 포함하다   shelf
[ʃelf] 몡 선반   section[sékʃən] 몡 구역

문제 해설

Q1: 잘못 인사하고 있는 사람은?
    뉴질랜드의 마오리족 사람들은 서로의 코를 누르는 인사를 한다고 했다.

Q2: 이 대화가 이루어지고 있는 장소는?
    잡지에 난 기사에 대해 이야기하다가 그 잡지를 대출하기 위해 책을 찾으러 가는 내용으로 보아 도서관임을 알 수 있다.

B [1-2]

M: My Finnish friend suggested that we go to the sauna together. Isn't that strange?

W: Not really. Finns often invite others to the sauna to get to know them better.

M: Really?

W: Oh, yes. Finns love saunas. They visit them at least once a week.

M: Why are saunas so popular here?

W: Well, Finland is a cold country. I guess saunas are the best way to feel warm in a short time.

M: Have you visited a sauna here in Finland?

W: Yes. Steam is made by pouring cold water over hot stones.

M: Interesting.

W: Also, saunas are usually near a cold lake. So, when Finns get too hot in the sauna, they go and bathe in the lake.

M: I see.

W: And one more thing – don't miss out on sausages with beer while taking a break at the sauna.

남: 내 핀란드 친구가 사우나에 같이 가자고 제안했어. 이상하지 않아?

여: 그런 것 같지 않은데. 핀란드 사람들은 종종 다른 사람들과 더 친해지려고 그들에게 사우나에 같이 가자고 해.

남: 정말?

여: 어. 핀란드 사람들은 사우나를 좋아해. 일주일에 적어도 한 번은 가.

남: 사우나가 여기서 왜 그렇게 인기가 있는 거야?

여: 음, 핀란드는 추운 나라잖아. 사우나가 짧은 시간 내에 몸을 데우는 최선의 방법이 아닐까 싶어.

남: 여기 핀란드에서 사우나에 가본 적 있니?

여: 응. 차가운 물을 뜨거운 돌에 부어서 증기를 만들어.

남: 흥미로운걸.

여: 또, 사우나는 보통 차가운 호수 옆에 있어. 그래서 핀란드 사람들은 사우나에서 너무 더우면 호수에 가서 몸을 담그지.

남: 그렇구나.

여: 그리고 한 가지 더. 사우나에서 휴식을 취할 때 맥주와 소시지를 잊지 마.

Finnish[fíniʃ] 형 핀란드의, 핀란드 사람의 suggest [səgdʒést] 동 제안하다 sauna[sɔ́:nə] 명 사우나 Finn[fin] 명 핀란드 사람 Finland[fínlənd] 명 핀란드 steam[sti:m] 명 증기 pour[pɔːr] 동 붓다 lake[leik] 명 호수 bathe [beið] 동 목욕을 하다 sausage[sɔ́(ː)sidʒ] 명 소시지 beer[biər] 명 맥주 take a break 휴식을 취하다 [문제] relaxed[rilǽkst] 형 긴장을 푼 nearby[níərbài] 형 가까운, 옆의

문제 해설

Q1: 여자에 따르면 사우나가 핀란드에서 인기가 있는 이유는?
① 아픈 사람들에게 좋다.
② 긴장을 푸는 데 도움이 된다.
③ 친구를 사귀는 좋은 방법이다.
④ 몸을 빨리 따뜻하게 만들어 준다.
추운 나라인 핀란드에서 빨리 따뜻함을 느낄 수 있는 최선의 방법이라고 했다.

Q2: 핀란드의 사우나에 관해 사실이면 T, 사실이 아니면 F를 쓰시오.
(1) 핀란드 사람들은 친한 친구만 사우나에 초대한다.
(2) 증기는 뜨거운 물을 차가운 돌에 부어 만들어진다.
(3) 핀란드 사람들은 사우나에서 너무 뜨겁다고 느끼면 가까운 호수에 몸을 담글 것이다.
친해지기 위해 사우나에 초대한다고 했으므로 친한 친구와만 가는 것은 아니며, 증기는 찬물을 뜨거운 돌에 부어서 만든다고 했고, 사우나에서 더워지면 바로 옆의 호수에 몸을 담근다고 했다.

Critical ★ Thinking p. 73

1 (1) For (2) Against (3) For
2 (1) ⓓ (2) ⓒ (3) ⓑ

M1: I'm Nick. Recently, a movement has begun to stop bullfighting. But bullfighting was started in the 17th century. Many Spanish people consider it a kind of art, as well as a national cultural heritage. As it's a long Spanish tradition, it should not be banned.

W: I'm Kate. Thousands of bulls are killed every year because of bullfighting. Killing animals for people's pleasure isn't the right thing to do. Keeping a country's tradition and cultural heritage cannot be an excuse for killing animals.

M2: I'm Jason. Many tourists expect to watch bullfighting in Spain. Bullfighting is a big part of the Spanish tourism industry. It really helps our country's economic growth.

남1: 난 Nick이야. 최근에 투우를 중지하자는 운동이 시작되었어. 하지만 투우는 17세기에 시작되었어. 많은 스페인 사람들은 그것을 국가의 문화유산일 뿐 아니라 일종의 예술이라고 생각하지. 그것은 스페인의 오랜 전통이기 때문에 금지되어선 안 돼.

여: 난 Kate야. 해마다 수천 마리의 소가 투우 때문에 죽게 돼. 사람들의 즐거움을 위해 동물을 죽이는 건 옳은 일이 아니야. 나라의 전통과 문화유산을 지킨다는 것이 동물을 죽이는 핑계가 될 수는 없어.

남2: 난 Jason이야. 많은 관광객들이 스페인에서 투우를 보고 싶어해. 투우는 스페인 관광 산업에서 큰 비중을 차지해. 우리나라의 경제 성장에 정말 도움이 된다구.

recently[rí:səntli] 부 최근에 movement[mú:vmənt] 명 운동, 움직임 bullfighting[búlfàitiŋ] 명 투우 Spanish [spǽniʃ] 형 스페인의 consider[kənsídər] 동 여기다 ban [bæn] 동 금지하다 pleasure[pléʒər] 명 즐거움 excuse [ikskjú:s] 명 핑계, 이유 tourism industry 관광 산업 economic[ì:kənámik] 형 경제적인 growth[grouθ] 명 성장 [문제] play a big role in ~에 큰 역할을 하다 right[rait] 명 권리 enjoyment[indʒɔ́imənt] 명 즐거움

문제 해설

Q1: 각 인물이 투우에 찬성하는지 반대하는지 ✓표 하시오.
Nick은 투우가 오랜 전통이며 국가 문화유산이기 때문에, Jason은 스페인 관광 산업의 중요한 부분이기 때문에 투우에 찬성하고 있다. Kate는 인간의 즐거움을 위해 동물을 죽이는 것은 옳지 않기 때문에 투우에 반대하는 입장이다.

Q2: 각 인물의 의견을 고르시오.
ⓐ 투우를 중지하는 법을 만들어야 한다.
ⓑ 투우는 스페인 경제에서 큰 역할을 한다.
ⓒ 동물의 권리가 인간의 즐거움보다 더 중요하다.
ⓓ 투우는 오랜 역사를 가진 훌륭한 문화유산이다.
Nick은 투우를 문화유산으로 생각하고, Kate는 인간의 즐거움보다 동물의 권리를 귀하게 여기며, Jason은 투우가 국가 경제에서 중요한 역할을 한다고 생각한다.

★ ★

UNIT 12 IT

Getting ★ Ready p. 74

A 1 ⓗ 2 ⓒ 3 ⓕ 4 ⓖ 5 ⓐ 6 ⓔ
B 1 ⓕ 2 ⓑ 3 ⓓ

B 1 남: 컴퓨터를 주로 무엇을 하는 데 쓸 거니?
　　여: 숙제를 하는 데 쓸 거야.
　2 남: 인터넷을 검색하는 중이니?
　　여: 아니, 내 블로그에 미디어 파일을 업로드하는 중이야.
　3 남: 그 웹사이트는 무슨 용도야?
　　여: 사람들이 사진을 공유하고 무료로 다운로드해.

Listening ★ Start p. 75

1 ③ / laptop computer, making presentations, care about the price, it shouldn't be noisy, after-sales service, national brand computers
2 ② / Internet addiction, among teenagers, a fixed amount of time, special software, place your computer, find hobbies

1

M: I'm going to buy a laptop computer for the first time. What should I consider?
W: What will you mainly use the computer for?
M: I need it for making presentations during my business trips.
W: I see. How much are you willing to pay?
M: I don't care about the price. All I'm considering is quality.
W: If you're traveling with it, it should be light.
M: You're right. Also, it shouldn't be noisy.
W: Right. You should also consider whether you can get good after-sales service.
M: Oh, I hadn't thought about that.
W: For good after-sales service, national brand computers are better than foreign ones.
M: Okay. Thanks for the advice.

남: 처음으로 노트북 컴퓨터를 사려고 해. 무엇을 고려해야 할까?
여: 컴퓨터를 주로 무엇을 하는 데 쓸 거니?
남: 출장 중에 프레젠테이션을 하는 데 필요해.
여: 그렇구나. 가격은 얼마나 생각하고 있니?
남: 가격은 상관 없어. 내가 고려하는 것은 품질뿐이야.
여: 여행에 가지고 다닐 거라면 가벼워야 해.

남: 맞아. 소음이 나서도 안 돼.
여: 그래. 애프터서비스를 잘 받을 수 있는지도 고려해봐야겠지.
남: 아, 그건 생각하지 못했네.
여: 애프터서비스를 잘 받으려면 외국 브랜드보다는 국내 브랜드 컴퓨터가 더 나아.
남: 알았어. 조언 고마워.

어휘

laptop computer 노트북 컴퓨터 for the first time 처음으로 mainly[méinli] ⓟ 주로 make a presentation 프레젠테이션을 하다, 발표하다 business trip 출장 be willing to-v 기꺼이 ~하다 quality[kwáləti] ⓜ 질, 품질 noisy[nɔ́izi] ⓗ 시끄러운 after-sales service 판매 후의 서비스, 애프터서비스 national[nǽʃənəl] ⓗ 국내의 foreign[fɔ́:rən] ⓗ 외국의 [문제] local[lóukəl] ⓗ 지역의

문제 해설

Q: 남자가 고를 컴퓨터는?
　가볍고, 소음이 없고, 애프터서비스가 편리한 국내 브랜드로 선택할 것이다.

2

M: Lately, Internet addiction has become a serious social problem. It's especially serious among teenagers. Here are some tips to prevent Internet addiction. First, always set a fixed amount of time for using the Internet. If you can't control yourself, you can get help from special software which sets a time limit on your Internet use. Also, place your computer in the living room. If you spend time on the computer alone in your bedroom, it's harder to control yourself. Lastly, find hobbies you can enjoy with family or friends.

남: 요즘 인터넷 중독은 심각한 사회 문제가 되었습니다. 이는 특히 십대들 사이에서 심각합니다. 여기 인터넷 중독을 예방하는 몇 가지 방법들이 있습니다. 우선, 항상 인터넷을 사용하는 일정한 시간을 정해 두세요. 스스로 통제가 되지 않으면, 인터넷 사용 시간을 제한하는 특수한 소프트웨어가 도움이 될 것입니다. 또한, 컴퓨터를 거실에 두세요. 혼자 침실에서 컴퓨터를 하는 데 시간을 보내다 보면 자제하기가 더 힘들 것입니다. 마지막으로, 가족이나 친구들과 즐길 수 있는 취미를 찾으세요.

어휘

lately[léitli] ⓟ 최근에 addiction[ədíkʃən] ⓜ 중독 serious[sí(:)əriəs] ⓗ 심각한 social problem 사회문제 prevent[privént] ⓥ 예방하다 set[set] ⓥ 정하다 fixed[fikst] ⓗ 고정된, 일정한 control[kəntróul] ⓥ 제어하다, 통제하다 software[sɔ́(:)ftwɛ̀ər] ⓜ 소프트웨어 limit

71

[límit] 몡 제한   place[pleis] 동 놓다, 두다   [문제]
certain[sə́ːrtən] 형 확실한; *일정한   block[blɑk] 동 막다
besides[bisáidz] 전 ~ 이외에

문제 해설
Q: 남자가 알려준 조언이 <u>아닌</u> 것은?

① 인터넷 사용에 일정 시간만을 쓰라.

② 인터넷을 차단하는 소프트웨어를 사라.

③ 컴퓨터를 거실에 설치하라.

④ 인터넷 사용 외에 다른 관심거리를 가져라.

인터넷 차단이 아니라 일정 시간 동안만 인터넷을 쓸 수 있게 해 주는 소프트웨어를 쓰라고 했다.

Listening ★ Practice   p. 76

1 ④ mQ1 ⓐ 2 ③ mQ2 ⓐ 3 ① mQ3 ⓒ
4 ① mQ4 ⓑ 5 ① mQ5 ⓐ 6 ④ mQ6 ⓑ

1

(*Telephone rings.*)

M: Hello?

W: Daniel, this is Sandy. Are you on messenger?

M: No, I'm watching TV right now.

W: So you're not talking with me on messenger, right?

M: No. My computer isn't even on.

W: Someone just asked me for money using your ID.

M: What? So did you send the money?

W: Of course not. The way he talked was a little different from you. So I called to check.

M: I heard that people have been asking for money on messenger services using other people's ID and password these days.

W: So what should I do?

M: Save that message and call the police.

W: Okay. Don't forget to change your messenger password quickly.

(전화벨이 울린다.)

남: 여보세요?

여: Daniel, 나 Sandy야. 메신저에 접속해 있니?

남: 아니, 난 지금 TV를 보고 있어.

여: 그럼 메신저에서 나랑 얘기하고 있지 않은 거지, 그렇지?

남: 아니야. 컴퓨터를 켜지도 않았어.

여: 누군가 네 ID로 나에게 돈을 요구했어.

남: 뭐? 그래서 돈을 보냈니?

여: 물론 아니지. 말하는 방식이 너랑 좀 다르더라고. 그래서 확인하려고 전화한 거야.

남: 요즘 사람들이 다른 사람의 ID와 비밀번호를 사용해서 메신

저에서 돈을 요구하고 있다고 들었어.

여: 이제 어떻게 하지?

남: 그 메시지를 저장하고 경찰에 전화해.

여: 알았어. 잊지 말고 네 메신저 비밀번호를 어서 바꿔.

어휘
messenger[mésəndʒər] 몡 인터넷 메신저   ID[àidíː] 몡 아이디   password[pǽswə̀ːrd] 몡 비밀번호   save[seiv] 동 저장하다   [문제] chat[tʃæt] 동 이야기하다, 채팅하다

문제 해설
Q: 여자가 남자에게 전화한 이유는?

여자는 자신에게 메신저로 돈을 요구한 사람이 친구가 맞는지 확인하기 위해 전화했다.

mQ1: 여자가 다음에 할 일은?

여자는 메시지를 저장한 다음에 경찰에 신고할 것이다.

2

M: What are you watching?

W: I'm watching an online Chinese lecture.

M: Is it good? I'm interested in taking online Chinese classes.

W: I'm quite satisfied with it. I think online classes are better than offline classes.

M: What makes you think so?

W: You can only attend a lecture once at an academy. But online, you can watch it over and over again.

M: That's good. What else?

W: It's so much cheaper.

M: How much is it for a month?

W: Advanced and intermediate classes are $60. And beginner's classes are $50.

M: Wow, they're really cheap.

W: I'll send you a link to the site. You can preview a class for free.

M: That's great.

남: 뭘 보고 있니?

여: 난 온라인 중국어 강좌를 보고 있어.

남: 좋아? 온라인 중국어 수업에 나도 관심이 있는데.

여: 상당히 만족스러워. 난 오프라인 수업보다 온라인 수업이 더 나은 것 같아.

남: 왜 그렇게 생각해?

여: 학원에서는 강의에 한 번만 참석할 수 있잖아. 그런데 온라인은 계속 다시 볼 수 있어.

남: 그거 좋다. 또 뭐가 있지?

여: 가격이 훨씬 싸.

남: 한 달에 얼마인데?

여: 고급과 중급 수업은 60달러야. 그리고 초급 수업은 50달러야.

남: 와, 정말 싸구나.

★ ★

여: 사이트 링크를 보내 줄게. 무료로 수업을 미리 볼 수 있어.

남: 그거 좋네.

어휘

lecture[léktʃər] 명 강좌 be satisfied with ~에 만족하다 offline[ɔ́ːflàin] 형 오프라인의 attend[əténd] 동 참석하다 academy[əkǽdəmi] 명 학원 over and over again 계속해서 advanced[ədvǽnst] 형 고급의, 고등의 intermediate[intərmíːdiət] 형 중급의 beginner[bigínər] 명 초급자 link[liŋk] 명 링크, 연결 preview[príːvjùː] 동 미리보다 [문제] advantage[ədvǽntidʒ] 명 이점 well-known[wélnóun] 형 잘 알려진

문제 해설

Q: 그들은 주로 무엇에 관해 이야기하고 있는가?

계속 다시 볼 수 있고 값이 싼 온라인 중국어 수업의 좋은 점에 대해 이야기하고 있다.

mQ2: 초급자를 위한 온라인 중국어 수업은 얼마인가?

초급 수업은 한 달에 50달러라고 했다.

3

M: Is this your photo album? Can I look at it?

W: Sure.

M: Wow, you had your picture taken with Johnny Depp. Where did you meet him?

W: Actually, I've never met him.

M: What are you talking about?

W: I edited the photo using the Photoshop program.

M: I can't believe it! And you look so much prettier in the photo.

W: It's also the power of technology. I cleaned up my skin and made my hair shiny.

M: No wonder! Did you learn how to use the program in school?

W: No, I studied on my own.

M: How?

W: There are many free Internet sites teaching how to use Photoshop.

M: Great. Maybe I should learn how to use it.

남: 이게 네 사진 앨범이니? 좀 봐도 돼?

여: 물론이지.

남: 와, Johnny Depp과 사진을 찍었구나. 어디서 그를 만났어?

여: 사실, 만난 적은 없어.

남: 무슨 얘기야?

여: 포토샵 프로그램을 이용해서 사진을 편집한 거야.

남: 믿을 수가 없어! 그리고 너 사진이 훨씬 더 예쁘게 나왔어.

여: 그거 역시 기술의 힘이지. 피부를 깨끗하게 하고 머리칼을 빛나게 했거든.

남: 어쩐지! 학교에서 그 프로그램 쓰는 법을 배웠니?

여: 아니, 독학했어.

남: 어떻게?

여: 포토샵 사용법을 가르쳐주는 무료 인터넷 사이트가 많아.

남: 좋아. 나도 사용하는 법을 배워야 할까 봐.

어휘

have one's picture taken 사진을 찍다 actually [ǽktʃuəli] 부 사실 edit[édit] 동 수정하다, 편집하다 technology[teknálədʒi] 명 기술 skin[skin] 명 피부 shiny[ʃáini] 형 빛나는 No wonder! 어쩐지! on my own 스스로

문제 해설

Q: 그들이 보고 있는 화면을 고르시오.

여자가 영화배우인 Johnny Depp과 함께 찍은 사진을 컴퓨터 화면에서 보고 있다.

mQ3: 여자는 어떻게 포토샵 사용법을 배웠나?

인터넷 무료 사이트에서 사용법을 독학했다.

4

W: Twitter is a kind of a blogging service. It allows users to upload messages from cell phones or messenger services as well as by visiting the site. On Twitter, the message must be less than 140 letters. You just simply write short comments on the board whenever you want. That's why Twitter is called a mini blog. If you want to check out another person's messages, you should become his or her "follower." You don't need a person's permission to be their follower. If you become someone's follower, messages that person writes are updated on your Twitter page, too.

여: 트위터(Twitter)는 블로그 서비스의 일종입니다. 이것은 사용자들이 사이트를 방문했을 때뿐 아니라 핸드폰이나 메신저 서비스로도 메시지를 올릴 수 있게 해 줍니다. 트위터에서는 메시지가 140자 이하이어야 합니다. 원할 때는 언제든지 게시판에 짧은 말을 쓰기만 하면 됩니다. 트위터가 미니 블로그라고 불리는 이유가 그것입니다. 다른 사람의 메시지를 확인하고 싶으면 그 사람의 '팔로워(follower)'가 되어야 합니다. 팔로워가 되기 위해 그 사람의 승인이 필요하지는 않습니다. 누군가의 팔로워가 되면 그 사람이 쓰는 메시지가 당신의 트위터 페이지에도 업데이트됩니다.

어휘

Twitter[twítər] 명 트위터(블로그, 미니홈피, 메신저 기능을 혼합한 소셜 네트워크 서비스) blogging service 블로그를 제공하는 서비스 upload[ʌ́plòud] 동 업로드하다 as well as ~뿐만 아니라 letter[létər] 명 글자 comment [kɑ́ment] 명 의견, 평 board[bɔːrd] 명 게시판

73

follower[fálouər] 명 추종자, 지지자 permission
[pərmíʃən] 명 허가, 승인 update[ʌ̀pdéit] 동 업데이트하다,
갱신하다

문제 해설
Q: 트위터에 대해 잘못 말하고 있는 사람은?
　① 사이트를 방문해야만 메시지를 업로드할 수 있어.
　② 140자가 넘는 메시지를 쓸 수 없어.
　③ Joe의 트위터 페이지에 가지 않고도 그가 업데이트한 메
　　시지를 볼 수 있어.
　핸드폰이나 메신저 서비스로도 메시지를 올릴 수 있다고 했다.

mQ4: 트위터가 미니 블로그라고 불리는 이유는?
　블로그처럼 메시지를 쓸 수 있지만 140자 이하의 짧은 메시
지만 가능하므로 미니 블로그라 불린다고 했다.

어휘
suddenly[sʌ́dnli] 부 갑자기 slow down 느려지다
memory[méməri] 명 (컴퓨터의) 메모리, 기억 장치 space
[speis] 명 공간 unknown[ʌ̀nnóun] 형 모르는, 미상의
run[rʌn] 동 실행시키다 virus[váiərəs] 명 바이러스
vaccine[væksíːn] 명 백신, 치료제 address bar 주소창
[문제] out-of-date[àutəvdéit] 형 구식의, 낡은
connection[kənékʃən] 명 연결

문제 해설
Q: 남자의 컴퓨터가 느려진 이유는?
　친구의 CD에서 바이러스가 옮아서 느려진 것 같다고 했다.

mQ5: 그들이 다음에 할 일은?
　바이러스를 없애기 위해 온라인 사이트에서 백신 프로그램
을 살 것이다.

5

M: My computer suddenly slowed down.
　Maybe it's because it's too old.
W: Are you sure it isn't because there's not
　enough memory?
M: I've checked it. It has enough space.
W: Did you open an unknown email?
M: No. Oh, I think it slowed down after I ran a
　CD from a friend.
W: That CD must've had a computer virus.
M: Should I go to the service center?
W: I'll teach you what to do. Buy a vaccine
　program online and run it on your computer.
M: Do you know any good sites that sell
　vaccine programs? Let's find one now.
W: Okay. Type in www.vaccine11.com in the
　address bar. I'll let you know which vaccine
　program to buy.
M: Thanks.

6

M: What are you doing?
W: I'm surfing the Internet.
M: Are you updating your blog again?
W: No. I'm looking for photos for my science
　report. But they're hard to find.
M: Why don't you try the NEclick site?
W: I've never heard about it. Is it a site that
　sells photos?
M: No. It's where people upload pictures they
　took. They share photos and download
　them for free.
W: What about copyrights?
M: If you don't use it for business, it's okay.
W: For business?
M: Yes. For example, you can't use the photos
　for books or advertisements.
W: Is there any way to use them for business?
M: Yes. You need to contact the owner of the
　picture and get their permission.
W: I see.

남: 내 컴퓨터가 갑자기 느려졌어. 아마 너무 오래되어서 그런가 봐.
여: 메모리가 충분하지 않아서 그런 건 아닌지 확실해?
남: 확인했어. 공간은 충분해.
여: 모르는 이메일을 열었니?
남: 아니. 아, 친구의 CD를 실행시킨 후에 느려졌던 것 같아.
여: 그 CD에 컴퓨터 바이러스가 있었던 게 틀림없어.
남: 서비스 센터에 가야 할까?
여: 내가 무엇을 해야 하는지 알려 줄게. 온라인에서 백신 프로
　그램을 사서 네 컴퓨터에서 실행시켜.
남: 백신 프로그램을 파는 괜찮은 사이트 알아? 지금 하나 찾아
　보자.
여: 좋아. www.vaccine11.com을 주소창에 쳐봐. 어떤 백신을
　사야 할지 알려 줄게.
남: 고마워.

남: 뭐 하고 있어?
여: 인터넷 검색하고 있어.
남: 네 블로그를 또 업데이트하는 중이야?
여: 아니. 과학 보고서에 쓸 사진을 찾는 중이야. 그런데 찾기가
　힘들어.
남: NEclick 사이트를 사용해 보는 게 어때?
여: 그거 들어본 적 없는데. 사진을 파는 사이트니?
남: 아니. 사람들이 자신이 찍은 사진을 업로드하는 곳이야. 사
　진을 공유하고 무료로 다운로드해.
여: 저작권은 어떻게 하고?
남: 상업적으로 쓰지 않으면 괜찮아.
여: 상업적으로?

남: 응. 예를 들어, 책이나 광고에 그 사진들을 쓸 수 없어.
여: 상업적으로 쓸 수 있는 방법이 있기는 해?
남: 응. 그 사진의 소유자와 연락해서 허가를 받아야지.
여: 그렇구나.

어휘
surf the Internet 인터넷을 검색하다 share[ʃɛər] 동 공
유하다 copyright[kápiràit] 명 저작권 for business
상업적으로 advertisement[ædvərtáizmənt] 명 광고
contact[kántækt] 동 연락하다 owner[óunər] 명 소유자
[문제] fee[fiː] 명 요금 exchange[ikstʃéindʒ] 동 교환하다

문제 해설

Q: NEclick의 사진을 상업적으로 쓰기 위해서 해야 할 일은?

　① 소유자에게 약간의 요금을 지불한다.

　② 사진의 저작권을 산다.

　③ 소유자와 사진을 교환한다.

　④ 소유자에게 허가를 받는다.

　상업적으로 쓰기 위해서는 소유자의 허가를 받아야 한다고
　했다.

mQ6: 여자가 사진을 찾으려고 하는 이유는?

　과제물인 과학 보고서에 쓸 사진을 찾는 중이다.

Listening ★ Challenge   p. 78

A 1 (1) ⓐ (2) ⓒ (3) ⓑ 2 ②　B 1 ③　2 ②

A [1-2]

M: Recently, an American company researched what is most important to people when choosing a new cell phone. This research focused on two groups, people aged 18 to 24 and those aged 25 to 44. Both groups chose price as the most important thing and brand as the next. The older group chose ease of use as the third most important factor, while the younger group chose battery life. Design was chosen as the fourth most important thing by the older group, while ease of use was chosen by the younger group. The older group chose battery life as least important, while the younger group chose design.

남: 최근에 한 미국 회사가 사람들이 새로운 핸드폰을 고를 때 가
장 중요시 여기는 것이 무엇인지 조사했습니다. 이 조사는 18
세에서 24세까지의 사람들과 25세에서 44세까지의 사람들로
구성된 두 집단에 초점을 두었습니다. 두 집단 모두 가격을
가장 중요한 것으로, 그리고 상표를 그 다음으로 선택했습니
다. 나이가 많은 집단은 사용의 용이함을 세 번째 중요한 요
건으로 선택했는데, 나이가 적은 집단은 배터리의 수명을 선

택했습니다. 나이가 많은 집단은 디자인을 네 번째 중요한 것
으로 선택한 반면, 어린 집단은 사용의 용이함을 선택했습니
다. 나이가 많은 집단은 배터리 수명을 가장 덜 중요한 것으로,
어린 집단은 디자인을 선택했습니다.

어휘
research[risə́ːrtʃ] 동 조사하다, 연구하다 ease[iːz] 명 쉬
움, 용이함 factor[fǽktər] 명 요건, 요인 while[hwail]
접 ~할 동안, *그런데, 한편으로는 battery life 배터리 수명
least[liːst] 부 가장 적게

문제 해설

Q1: 나이가 더 많은 집단의 결과에 따라 빈칸을 채우시오.

　공통적으로 가격을 가장 중요한 요건으로, 상표를 그 다음으
　로 골랐다고 했고, 나이가 더 많은 집단은 사용의 용이함, 디
　자인, 배터리 수명 순으로 선택했다.

Q2: 나이가 더 어린 집단에 따르면 가장 덜 중요한 것은?

　가장 중요하지 않은 요건으로 디자인을 선택했다.

B [1-2]

M: What are you doing?

W: I'm uploading pictures and recipes of food
　I made onto my blog.

M: Wow, almost 1,000 people visited your
　blog today.

W: It's no big deal. It happens everyday.

M: Wow, I also have a blog, but not many
　people visit it. How can I make my blog
　more popular?

W: What's your blog about?

M: I post movie reviews.

W: Visit other blogs with similar topics and
　exchange information. For example, visit
　blogs about movie stars or entertainment.

M: Why should I do that?

W: Then they'll visit your blog, too.

M: Oh, that's a good idea.

W: Also, you need to update your information
　often and upload some photographs or
　media files.

M: But I'm not good at editing them.

W: It's easy. I'll teach you how.

M: Thanks a lot.

남: 뭐 하고 있니?

여: 내 블로그에 내가 만들었던 음식의 사진과 조리법을 업로드
　하고 있어.

남: 와, 오늘 거의 1,000명이나 되는 사람들이 네 블로그에 왔네.

여: 별 거 아냐. 일상적인 일인 걸.

남: 와, 나도 블로그가 있는데 사람들이 많이 안 와. 어떻게 내

블로그를 더 인기 있게 만들 수 있을까?

여: 네 블로그는 뭐에 관한 건데?

남: 영화 후기를 게시해.

여: 비슷한 주제를 가진 다른 블로그에 가 보고 정보를 교환해.
예를 들어, 영화 배우나 연예와 관련된 블로그에 가봐.

남: 왜 그래야 하는데?

여: 그러면 그 사람들도 네 블로그를 찾아올 거야.

남: 아, 그거 좋은 생각이다.

여: 또, 정보를 자주 업데이트하고 사진이나 미디어 파일을 올릴
필요가 있어.

남: 하지만 난 편집을 잘 못해.

여: 쉬워. 내가 방법을 알려 줄게.

남: 정말 고마워.

어휘

recipe[résəpì] 명 조리법   almost[ɔ́ːlmoust] 부 거의
big deal 대단한 것, 큰 일   post[poust] 동 게시하다
review[rivjúː] 명 후기, 관람평   similar[símələr] 형 비
슷한   entertainment[èntərtéinmənt] 명 연예   media
file 멀티미디어 파일(사운드 및 비디오 프로그램 파일) [문제]
decorate[dékərèit] 동 장식하다   blogger[blɔ́gər] 명 블
로거, 블로그하는 사람   cover[kʌ́vər] 동 다루다, 포함하다
video clip 동영상 클립

문제 해설

Q1: 그들은 주로 무엇에 관해 이야기하고 있는가?
인기가 많은 블로그를 가지고 있는 여자가 남자에게 블로그를
인기 있게 만드는 방법을 알려주는 내용이다.

Q2: 여자의 조언을 따르는 사람은?
① Ted: 내 블로그에서는 여러 가지 종류의 주제를 다뤄.
② Billy: 난 자주 블로그를 업데이트하고 동영상 클립을 게
시해.
③ John: 난 다른 블로거들과 오프라인에서 정보를 교환해.
업데이트를 자주 하고 미디어 파일을 올리라고 했다. 여러
종류의 주제를 다루라는 조언이나 오프라인에서 다른 블로
거들을 만나라는 언급은 없었다.

Critical ★ Thinking   p. 79

1 ③ 2 ④

M: Look! My game money is all gone. I haven't
logged in recently.

W: Someone might be playing online games
with your ID. Did you lend it to someone?

M: Never. How in the world could someone
find out my ID and password?

W: Have you saved them on a public computer
before?

M: I think I have in a school library. What
should I do?

W: Change your ID and password right away.

M: Okay.

W: And visit a site where you can report illegal
ID use. Illegal use of another person's ID is
common nowadays.

M: I didn't know it could happen to me.

W: To prevent it, make sure to log out so that
your personal information won't be saved
on public computers.

M: I wish I had known about this sooner. Then
I wouldn't have lost my game money.

남: 이것 봐! 내 게임머니가 다 사라졌어. 최근에 접속하지도 않았
는데.

여: 누군가 네 아이디로 온라인 게임을 하고 있는 건지 몰라. 누
군가에게 아이디를 빌려 줬니?

남: 절대 아냐. 도대체 어떻게 내 아이디와 비밀번호를 알아낼 수
있는 거지?

여: 전에 공용 컴퓨터에서 그것들을 저장한 적 있니?

남: 학교 도서관에서 했던 것 같아. 어떻게 하지?

여: 아이디와 비밀번호를 당장 바꿔.

남: 알았어.

여: 그리고 불법 아이디 사용을 고발하는 사이트에 가봐. 불법적
으로 다른 사람 아이디를 쓰는 게 요즘 흔하대.

남: 나에게 그런 일이 생길 줄 몰랐어.

여: 예방을 위해선 반드시 로그아웃을 해서 네 개인 정보가 공용
컴퓨터에 저장되지 않도록 해.

남: 더 일찍 이걸 알았더라면 좋았을 걸. 그럼 게임머니를 잃지
않았을 텐데.

어휘

game money 게임머니(온라인 게임 내에서 통용되는 화폐)
log in ~에 접속하다   in the world 도대체   public
computer 공용 컴퓨터, 여러 사람이 같이 쓰는 컴퓨터
report[ripɔ́ːrt] 동 보고하다, 신고하다   illegal[ilíːgəl] 형 불
법의   common[kámən] 형 흔한   nowadays[náuədèiz]
부 요즘에   make sure 확실히 ~하다   log out 로그아웃하다
personal information 개인(신상) 정보 [문제] theft
[θeft] 명 훔침, 도용

문제 해설

Q1: 남자에게 일어난 일은?
① 누군가 그의 온라인 비밀번호를 바꿨다.
② 누군가 그의 개인 정보를 팔았다.
③ 누군가 그의 아이디로 온라인 게임을 했다.
④ 누군가 그의 아이디로 메신저에 접속했다.
온라인 게임머니가 사라진 것을 보고 누군가 자신의 아이디
로 게임을 했다는 것을 알았다.

Q2: 여자에 따르면, 아이디 도용을 예방하는 방법은?
여자는 공용 컴퓨터를 사용한 후 반드시 로그아웃을 하여 개
인 정보를 남기지 않도록 해야 한다고 조언했다.

JUNIOR
LISTENING EXPERT

Level 3